W9-AEF-113

Editing D. H. Lawrence

Editing D. H. Lawrence
New Versions of a Modern Author

*Edited by Charles L. Ross and
Dennis Jackson*

Ann Arbor

THE UNIVERSITY OF MICHIGAN PRESS

Copyright © by the University of Michigan 1995
All rights reserved
Published in the United States of America by
The University of Michigan Press
Manufactured in the United States of America
⊗Printed on acid-free paper

1998   1997   1996   1995   4   3   2   1

Library of Congress Cataloging-in-Publication Data

Editing D. H. Lawrence : new versions of a modern author / edited by
  Charles L. Ross and Dennis Jackson.
      p.   cm. — (Editorial theory and literary criticism)
  Includes index.
  ISBN 0-472-10612-0 (alk. paper)
    1. Lawrence, D. H. (David Herbert), 1885–1930—Criticism, Textual.
  2. Literature publishing—Great Britain—History—20th century.
  3. Lawrence. D. H. (David Herbert), 1885–1930—Publishers.
  4. Lawrence, D. H. (David Herbert), 1885–1930—Editors.   5. English
  fiction—20th century—Criticism, Textual.   6. Fiction—Editing—
  History—20th century.   7. Modernism (Literature)—Great Britain.
  8. Transmission of texts.   I. Ross, Charles L., 1945–
  II. Jackson, Dennis, 1945–   .   III. Series.
  PR6023.A93Z6255   1995
  823'.912—dc20   95-10370
                                                                 CIP

Contents

Citations and Abbreviations

All references to D. H. Lawrence's works are—unless otherwise indicated—to Cambridge University Press texts cited in the bibliography on pages 239–49 in this volume.

The following abbreviations are used in the text:

CUP	Cambridge University Press
A1	first American edition
E1	first English edition
G	galley
MS, MSS	manuscript, manuscripts
TS, TSS	typescript, typescripts
TSR	typescript revised

Introduction

Charles L. Ross

In *A Critique of Modern Textual Criticism* (1983), Jerome McGann predicted that "textual criticism is in the process of reconceiving its discipline"
(2). Textual critics and editors, who traditionally consider themselves con-
servers or restorers of texts, responded belatedly to the challenges of struc-
turalist and poststructuralist theory that had reshaped literary studies in
the 1960s and 1970s. In the decade since McGann's *Critique,* however,
books and articles dedicated to the interplay of textual criticism and literary theory have proliferated. Surveying the field for the Modern Language
Association, D. C. Greetham lists dozens of recently published or forthcoming studies that link textual criticism and editing to theory, with such
titles as *The Textual Condition, Theories of the Text, The Matter of Text,* and
The Language of Editing.

More important, the import of this linkage has changed radically in
the past decade. In *Textual and Literary Criticism* (1959), for example,
Fredson Bowers gave professional pride of place to textual critics, whose
work is neglected by literary critics to the detriment of literary studies:
"We should be seriously disturbed by the lack of contact between literary
critics and textual critics," Bowers cautioned. "Every practising critic, for
the humility of his soul, ought to study the transmission of some appropriate text" (4). Such an exercise might inoculate critics against both "sleazy
editing" and exegetical excesses based on faulty texts. Literary critics,
Bowers implied, had more to learn from textual critics and editors than
vice versa.

This conception of textual editing as the ground of literary study does
not mean that the Anglo-American tradition has ignored theory over the
past quarter century. Fredson Bowers and G. Thomas Tanselle joined in

critical and philosophical debates over authorial "intention," which, as Karl Kroeber summed up, have been "one of [the American academy's] principal argumentative foci since the 1890s" (329). Nevertheless, it is an irony of literary history that as Derrida, Barthes, and Foucault arrived on these shores in the 1960s, declaring the demotion or death of the author and the indeterminacy of meaning, editors embarked on authoritative editions of classic American writers that assume the determinacy of an author's "final intentions" (Tanselle, "Final"). By granting professional seals of approval to these editions, moreover, the Modern Language Association of America implies that editors belong to a guild with fixed procedures and standards.

Despite recent calls for a rapprochement between editors and theorists, then, a chasm still yawns between their domains. Nor does responsibility for this gap lie solely with textual critics. Avant garde theory has largely ignored editorial practice, turning a blind eye to the theoretical implications of evidence unearthed by textual archaeology during the preparation of scholarly editions. Few literary theorists, even those who promote rhetoric or reception-history, consult the evidence of variability in the textual apparatuses of critical editions. Stanley Fish's "Interpreting the Variorum" is a qualified exception that proves the rule. In analyzing the "semantic or syntactic slide" in the reading experience of Milton's sonnet "When I consider how my light is spent," Fish notes the effect of ambiguous punctuation on centuries of exegetical controversy. Here and elsewhere, however, he pays no attention to the "interpretive communities" of editors, those specialized readers whose production of texts precedes and partly determines the strategies with which other readers "write" texts.[1] With similar insight and blindness, the reception theorist Hans Robert Jauss notes that printing and the formation of private libraries led to "the liberation of the secular reader from institutional reading" (60). What theorists have ignored is the process by which reading has been reinstitutionalized through critical editions whose separately published clear texts serve as the unstable groundwork of undergraduate literary studies. This neglect has an institutional cause. "With the virtual extinction of textual scholarship as a field of graduate [school] training," George Bornstein has observed in *Representing Modernist Texts* (1991), theorists seldom go beyond a perusal of Greg's classic, "The Rationale of Copy-Text" (5). As yet, theorizing about and reproduction of the literary canon remain largely separate tasks.

As the first complete recension of a major modern writer, the Cambridge Lawrence offers a test case in the intersection of textual theory and editorial praxis. *Editing D. H. Lawrence: New Versions of a Modern Author* takes the Cambridge project, now well more than half-way to its goal, as an occasion for theory. Our contributors, ten of whom have edited Lawrence for Cambridge or other presses, discuss a variety of genres: fiction, poetry, travel writing, and letters, each of which presents a unique editorial-cum-theoretical challenge. Cambridge editors and independent scholars reflect on the evolving theory that underlies the protracted editorial labors of the *Letters and Works* (1979–). For several Cambridge editors, this is the first occasion for theoretical reflection or self-criticism. They provide a glimpse of the institutional politics of editing. Several contributors testify that the edition's guiding principles have changed over time through a compromise between the Editorial Board and editors of individual volumes. In retrospect, others candidly express doubts about the process but endorse the product, while still others question the goal of producing eclectic and newly copyrighted texts.

The essays create a dialogue between practice and theory, intention and achievement. The experience of editors offers a critique of contemporary textual theory, already in flux, at the same time that theory mounts a critique of editorial practice. Though the research of the Cambridge project provides the bulk of the evidence, the critical focus widens to include the profession of editing and its unique product, the "critical edition." How well have Lawrence and his readers been served by the evolving theory and practice of the Cambridge Edition? How has the understanding of Lawrence's creativity and the nature of critical editing been altered by the Cambridge project? Has editing revealed or disguised the processes through which Lawrence's oeuvre reached its multifarious forms? Attention to such processes implies the "struggle for verbal consciousness" that Lawrence said "should not be left out in art." (*Phoenix II* 276).

The present is an auspicious moment to assess the re-editing of our most prolific English modernist in the context of a textual theory undergoing reconceptualization. Two recent eclectic anthologies have raised the consciousness of scholars. George Bornstein's collection *Representing Modernist Texts: Editing as Interpretation* surveys the re-editing of ten modernist authors, including D. H. Lawrence. Philip Cohen's collection *Devils and Angels: Textual Editing and Literary Theory* demonstrates that "Textual criticism is a theoretical activity."

Editing D. H. Lawrence: New Versions of a Modern Author explores not only the dependency of editing on theory but also the dialectical question:

"How can theory use editing?" The collection situates the re-editing of D. H. Lawrence in the overlapping contexts of literary theory and publishing history. What changes in textual theory will the re-editing of Lawrence's works likely bring about? In what ways have the assumptions of the Lawrencean interpretive community changed in the course of its work constructing critical editions of Lawrence? What have Lawrence's editors assimilated from the community of literary theorists?

An impending battle of the books adds urgency to our inquiry. Copyright on works by many of the great modernists—Lawrence, Conrad, Woolf, Joyce, Fitzgerald—has now lapsed. Freed from copyright restrictions and heartened by a ready market, publishers are sponsoring new editions or reissuing old ones. Controversy sparked by the innovative theory, methodology, and format of Hans Walter Gabler's *Ulysses: The Corrected Text* has not only filled many pages in learned journals but also led to further editions of Joyce (Mahaffey 188). The publishing scene features rival editions battling for financial or scholarly preeminence. Indeed, the financial stakes are so high that the Cambridge claim of new copyright in Lawrence may have to be settled in the courts and may have as far-reaching consequences for readers' access to texts as did the censorship trials of *Ulysses* and *Lady Chatterley's Lover*.

This intersection of theory and practice gives *Editing D. H. Lawrence: New Versions of a Modern Author* its point of departure. It is timely to ask how the Cambridge Edition of D. H. Lawrence reflects, refracts, and focuses the current ferment in textual theory, editorial practice, and publishing history.

NOTE

1. In Fish, *Is There a Text in This Class?* 147–73. No doubt there are more exceptions, but the general neglect by theorists of bibliographical evidence can be seen in popular anthologies of criticism. See, for example, *Reader-Response Criticism*, ed. Jane P. Tompkins (Baltimore: Johns Hopkins UP, 1980), and *Contemporary Literary Criticism: Literary and Cultural Studies*, 2d ed., eds. Robert Con Davis and Ronald Schleifer (New York: Longman, 1989).

WORKS CITED

Bornstein, George. "Introduction: Why Editing Matters." In *Representing Modernist Texts: Editing as Interpretation*. Ed. George Bornstein. Ann Arbor: U of Michigan P, 1991. 1–16.

Bowers, Fredson. *Textual and Literary Criticism*. Cambridge: Cambridge UP, 1959.

Cohen, Philip, ed. *Devils and Angels: Textual Editing and Literary Theory*. Charlottesville: UP of Virginia, 1991.

Fish, Stanley. *Is There a Text in This Class?* Cambridge, MA: Harvard UP, 1980.

Greetham, D. C. "Textual Scholarship." In *Introduction to Scholarship in Modern Languages and Literatures*. 2nd ed. Ed. Joseph Gibaldi. New York: Modern Language Association, 1992. 103–37.

Jauss, Hans Robert. "The Theory of Reception: A Retrospective of its Unrecognized Prehistory." In *Literary Theory Today*. Ed. Peter Collier and Helga Geyer-Ryan. Ithaca: Cornell UP, 1990. 53–73.

Kroeber, Karl. "The Evolution of Literary Study, 1883–1983." *PMLA* 99 (1984): 329.

Lawrence, D. H. "Foreword to *Women in Love*." *Phoenix II*. Ed. Warren Roberts and Harry T. Moore. London: Heinemann, 1968. 275–76.

Mahaffey, Vicki. "Intentional Error: The Paradox of Editing Joyce's *Ulysses*." In *Representing Modernist Texts*. Ed. George Bornstein. Ann Arbor: U of Michigan P, 1991. 171–91.

McGann, Jerome J. *A Critique of Modern Textual Criticism*. Chicago: U of Chi-P, 1983.

Tanselle, G. Thomas. "The Editorial Problem of Final Authorial Intention." *Selected Studies in Bibliography*. Charlottesville: UP of Virginia, 1979. 309–54.

Text and Context: The Cambridge Edition of Lawrence Reconsidered

Michael Black

In the United Kingdom, copyright subsists in an author's work for fifty years after death, or fifty years after first publication, whichever is the longer. Unpublished works remain the copyright of the author or the author's estate, and this copyright does not begin to run until publication takes place. To take the case of D. H. Lawrence, who died in 1930, copyright of works published in his lifetime, in the texts established in his lifetime, could have been expected to expire in 1980; but there were posthumously published works (for instance, much of the content of the two *Phoenix* volumes, published in 1936 and 1968; and the youthful poems collected in the Roberts-Pinto edition); and there were also unpublished works (the second part of *Mr Noon;* about three thousand letters; many drafts and fragments; the deleted portions of edited or censored works—all of these needed to be made available). The copyright situation in the United States was similar but more complicated, since the copyright term there has traditionally been longer, and the whole status of works published in both countries in the early years of the century can be very complex, depending on the place of first publication and the reregistration of copyrights after first publication.

Given that the project of publishing a complete edition of the letters and works in a carefully established critical edition conducted on scholarly principles was mooted in the 1970s, while copyright was still in force; given that it was essential to include the unpublished material, which would have remained in copyright even after 1980; given also normal ethical standards, it was clear from the outset that it would have been incorrect, improper, and unavailing for the Cambridge Press and the interested scholars to have said, "Let's wait until 1980, when we shall be free to do as we like." The approval of the Lawrence Estate was an essential condition, if only because the Estate retained control of the unpublished material. I make no secret of the fact that I considered it one strong argument in convincing the Estate of the desirability of such an edition that it would also constitute a new copyright and a new source of income: not, inevitably, as large as in the past, but worth having. As an editor controlling the literature list of a large university press, I was used to dealing with scholarly editions in which it was normal for the Press to claim copyright, and it was merely logical to extend to Lawrence what already regularly happened to Shakespeare and other classic authors.

This still surprises, indeed shocks, some observers—it even surprises some publishers who are not in the same kind of publishing; so I will explain the arguments. Since I am writing for a scholarly audience which I would expect to be jealous of the scholar's right to use important literary texts and hostile to any seeming proprietorial interference with that right, I point out at once that my arguments also protect the rights of scholars—those who do the work of editing. What concerns me most, as I indicate in the next section of this essay, is that scholarly editions of texts should continue to be undertaken, and especially the vast task of editing classical modern authors which has only just begun. I say undertaken: I can hardly say flourish, since it is my experience that they sell initially in small numbers and make their editors and publishers relatively little money. But they are a vital part of scholarly activity; more, they are one of our ways of conserving our literary tradition. Textual scholars spend years of their lives working on their texts; scholarly publishers invest a great deal of money in the setting of complex text and editorial matter. If that labor and expense are not protected by copyright, then any other publisher can at once reprint the new text, at no cost beyond that of printing; and so can undercut the original publisher, while the scholars would find their work appropriated, indeed pirated. It would follow inevitably that scholars and university presses would cease to publish scholarly editions of any author who commands a living readership. Do you want that to happen?

I have read, in reviews of or articles about the Cambridge Lawrence, remarks to the effect that the copyright claim represents mere greed on the part of the Cambridge Press or the Estate, even that the desire to secure copyright has led the Press to induce editors to make more changes to the text than they otherwise would. These remarks border on paranoia, or at least cynicism, about what was undertaken as a public service and an exciting venture on intellectual, not financial grounds. I have only to ask what reputable scholar would yield to that pressure, who would long be deceived, and what in any case would be the ultimate point? Why spend years and a lot of money doing less than the best-conceived job one can do? For money, it is implied.

It is the case that the paperback *Ulysses*, for example, has sold many thousands of copies, and I suppose that Viking-Penguin is happy with the sales.[1] But anyone aware of the true cost of reaching the point at which that edition could be produced—I mean the years of heavily capitalized work by the Gabler team—may reasonably doubt whether the total venture is substantially in profit. But at this point no volume of the Cambridge Lawrence text except *Mr Noon* and *Sons and Lovers* has sold more than 2,500 copies in hardback and paperback combined, and most have sold far less; so there is a simple misapprehension here, the fantasy of the scholar who likes to imagine exciting conspiracies out in the wicked world.

Copyright, like all law, is laid down as a matter of principle, in general terms. Its application must then be a matter of claim, of counterclaim, of eventual contest in the courts, of judicial decision. Pending those arbitrations, it is largely a matter of convention based on precedent: what is understood to be common practice among those who operate the system. There is no specific legal enactment to the effect that if the Cambridge University Press produces a new edition of Lawrence, it shall be copyrighted. This is a matter of claim, which could be challenged, and would be defended in the courts. The fundamental basis of the claim is threefold: convention and precedent in publishing itself; analogy with convention in other forms of editorial activity, especially music-publishing, where the concept of the "arrangement" has produced a whole structure of copyright dealing; and above all the basic appeal to equity mentioned above: that years of scholarly work and large investments of publishers' money and effort deserve to be protected. This is an argument about the balance of public interest: it is the point about scholarly labor that I expect to count with other scholars. Editors are not highly rewarded for their work; if they cannot even count on its being recognized as theirs, they have no incentive to go on.

As for publishing convention: to take the most obvious case, the works of Shakespeare (d. 1616) are in the public domain. You can quote or reprint the First Folio, or the successive editions of the eighteenth or nineteenth centuries. But if you want to make public use, beyond "fair dealing," of the New Cambridge Shakespeare, or the Oxford Shakespeare, or the Riverside Shakespeare, you will have to secure permission, and if your proposed use has a commercial element, you will have to pay a royalty or fee. These are copyrighted works: the copyright is vested in or administered by the publisher who made the investment, and the return is shared with the scholars who did the editorial work.

I point out that the differences between modern texts of Shakespeare are not, by crude statistical calculations, substantial; but nobody thinks of making crude statistical calculations there. The Alexander text, still much used in Britain, or the Dover Wilson text familiar to older readers, or the Arden text, are understood to embody a distinctive approach, which informs them as distinctive entities. It is the approach, the editorial principle, that matters: the fact that it issues in x% or y% of change, even if that were calculable, is merely a consequence of the principle.

Like copyright, to which it is related by my argument, this is a rather metaphysical domain, more familiar to classical scholars, who are used to talking of A's text of B, where A is an editor and B an author. They know the points at which A's text differs from another editor's; more important, they know why. They realize that A's text consists of the *whole* of the work concerned, not just the places where it differs from C's. The logic of this is simply that the editor has worked over and considered the entire text, and has made two kinds of decisions: not just what must be changed, but what stands unaltered—inevitably, the major part. Readers have to be confident that both kinds of decisions have been consistently made according to some stated principle, or they can have no faith in the text as a whole. Editors must consider every word, every punctuation mark or other feature; but do not examine these one by one, independently. Editors must apply principles, and the arguments about a text must start from the principles involved. Those being evolved in the Lawrence edition, in the case of *Ulysses,* in the case of Proust, are distinctively modern, in a way I outline below. It is not clear to me that the critics of these editions have wholly grasped what the principles are: certainly they do not seem to address them. This argument about principle is the really important one. Before I turn to it, I would like to deal further with the simple positivist argument about the proportion of change which might or might not constitute grounds for saying, "This is a genuine new edition, therefore a new copyright."

I start by saying there are slightly modified texts that do not in my view so qualify; but the ground for saying that would be consistent with what I have said above: to make a few changes that do not stem from the kind of fundamental examination I have been positing is to produce a corrected reprint only. I can conceive a fundamental recension that produced very little or nothing; in which case the received text is confirmed. The recension can hardly be copyrighted, despite the labor that has gone into it, for the simple reason that it cannot be distinguished from the received text. So minimal difference rules out copyright, for both theoretical and practical reasons. What point constitutes real difference?

There can be no statistical answer to this question. In the first place, although many people might suggest that it should be a proportion of the whole rather than a specific minimum number of cases, nobody would agree about the right proportion. Those unfamiliar with editorial work would fix it high. Experts would fix it low, since they know how little is needed to corrupt a text to the point where you simply do not know where you can trust it at all. Second, nobody would agree about *how* to compute the proportion. How many variants do you think there *can* be in any given segment of text? How do you account for recovered deletions or other features not *in* the received text? Third, the people who argue this way have simplistic notions of the nature and effect of a corruption: they are usually the people who think that changes of punctuation are trivial. Some are, of course. But consider this case, from *Sons and Lovers*, noted by Helen Baron, coeditor of the recent Cambridge text[2]:

> Then he glanced at Miriam. She was poring over the book, seemed absorbed in it, yet trembling lest she could not get at it. It made him cross. She was ruddy and beautiful. Yet her soul seemed to be intensely supplicating. The algebra-book she closed, shrinking, knowing he was angered; and at the same instant he grew gentle, seeing her hurt because she did not understand. (Penguin English Library text, ed. Keith Sagar, 1981, 206, repeating the first English edition, 157)

What Lawrence wrote was:

> [. . .] Yet her soul seemed to be intensely supplicating the algebra book. She closed, shrinking, knowing he was angered. And at the same instant [. . .] (*MS* 224; Cambridge *Sons and Lovers* 188)

One can see why the compositor Deacon, at Billings the printers in 1913, thought he was dealing with a scribal error in Lawrence's *MS,* and made the change. The original, the correct reading, is strange, and is accountable only as subtle authorial intention, indeed as metaphor. Helen Baron says, very finely, "Here 'closed' suggests a physical movement on Miriam's part, but is also a metaphor for her fear, as if she had been trying to absorb the mathematics by exposing herself to it like a wide-open eye, or a flower in the sunshine, or a snail exploring" (see note 2).

I point out, in passing, that the old distinction between accidentals and substantives, always dangerous, is in such cases exploded, and should not be used. On the other hand, Greg's fundamental argument about the tyranny of copy-texts is confirmed. The emendations above are made as a consequence of following a principle that Greg would recognize as a development of his own: that Lawrence's punctuation has to be recovered from a stage that is always likely to be earlier than first publication. His punctuation is, very often indeed, a crucial vehicle of his more subtle sense, especially his metaphorical and dramatic sense. As an example of the second kind, the dramatization of Hermione in *Women in Love* is frequently conveyed by the intonation-patterns of her speech; and the absence of question marks at the end of statements that would by others be spoken as questions is a mark of her insufferable (to others) superiority; and intended as such to those who can hear. Some cannot, of course.

To move to a more general overview, the cases that currently interest the academic and publishing worlds—the new editions of Lawrence, Joyce, Proust—need to be seen together in overlapping contexts. The interest in copyright, best seen as the interest in editorial principle, is, properly understood, an aspect of a whole phase of modern literary history.

The great writers of the first half of this century are all now long dead, and we have reached or can foresee the end of the posthumous copyright period. What typically has happened is that writers much praised and much criticized in their lifetime, such that their writings brought them more notoriety than wealth, usually began to see some financial success before they died. Death established them in the pantheon; they then began to sell very well indeed. The characteristic result is that for fifty years or so—the copyright term—the estates enjoy very large incomes. This money is divided according to contract, among the publishers, the agents, and the beneficiaries, usually children and grandchildren. (It is a familiar fact that Lawrence's posthumous wealth has been divided between the descendants of Frieda Lawrence's first and third husbands. This may seem ironical in a Hardyesque way, but is the natural result of property law.)

These families consist usually of ordinary people, not writers, lawyers, or scholars: to them the dead relative's works are a source of miraculous bounty, to be enjoyed while it lasts. They have, usually, no concept of a duty towards the heritage, and nobody points one out to them. After fifty years, or whatever, the cornucopia is empty, and that is that. The estate may often be administered by an ordinary legal firm with no special knowledge of copyright, and equally unconscious of any duty to the text. The publisher concerned is usually a general publisher; the agent is familiar with the ordinary business of publishing; but both parties may think, like the family, that this is a normal copyright, and when it runs out, there will be other authors to be getting on with. For all these people, the word "edition," perhaps preceded by the word "collected," means resetting all the works in a uniform format, perhaps correcting some misprints, and putting on a new jacket, to give the whole a new look. Textual scholarship, if the term enters their consciousness, is what happens to the classics, and is necessary because in past times printing and publishing were relatively primitive. The idea that their author actually presents a "textual problem" is strange and has no meaning. In this century we have had modern printing and publishing methods, so that an author can get the text "right" in a way that was not possible for Shakespeare. This bland and hugely mistaken assumption leads to the innocent cynicism that assumes that if textual scholars make a fuss, it is a self-aggrandizing to-do about trivialities. I remember the gloom and rage with which I read a dismissive letter from one of Pound's publishers, telling me that Pound too had been cynically prophetic about the way in which parasitic experts would crawl over his literary corpse after his death, making reputations at his expense, and how he, the publisher, shared the cynicism. Similarly, if a respected university press claims a new copyright in an edition of a modern classic, that is a naked attempt to continue to hold the public to ransom, buttressed by manipulation of the text.

The point that currently needs to be made is that all[3] the classic twentieth-century authors are badly in need of critical editions; and that it is actually the *duty* of the literary legatees, if they could only conceive it, to initiate and support proper critical editions without waiting for the term of copyright to expire. Simply to take the money while it lasts is not inert and cynical if one is not aware of the problem, but the effect is the same. Conversely, to encourage or to sponsor editions is to show a proper regard for what one inherits (as one would expect to maintain an estate if it were land or buildings, or conserve a work of art). It is not merely a source of income; yet, paradoxically, an enlightened approach increases or prolongs the return.

One must think with gratitude and respect of certain rare inheritors: Mrs. Valerie Eliot, herself a scholar; Madame Agathe Rouart-Valéry, a friend of scholars; the Princess de Rachewiltz and her half-brother Omar Pound (no literary text of our time stands more in need of an edition than the *Cantos;* may it finally appear). These are people who sense what it is they have inherited, beyond a source of royalties, and feel a proper responsibility towards it. I naturally include in this number the late Laurence Pollinger, a good friend of Lawrence and a good agent. Having been primed by pioneering scholars such as Harry T. Moore, Warren Roberts, Keith Sagar, and Jim Boulton, even he did not understand what I was talking about when I first broached the idea of an edition. Once he understood it, he supported it. It was not grasping in him as the conscientious and effective literary executor of the Lawrence Estate to see that it was also in the interest of the Estate, which it was his professional duty to advance: the fact is that duty and interest sometimes coincide.

The essential point of literary history involved here is that the texts of Lawrence, Joyce, Eliot, Pound, Proust, Valéry (I think especially of the *Cahiers*)—in short, the texts of most modern authors—have been peculiarly in need of a special kind of textual attention, a kind that derives from our growing sense that as twentieth-century authors, consciously in some cases and unconsciously in others, they were pursuing an aesthetic which we now identify as specifically modern, indeed modernist. There needs to be a relationship between this aesthetic and the way we handle their texts: in particular, modern textual scholars in their editorial procedures must make their starting-point a careful reconstruction, from the documents, of the compositional process followed by the author.

Editing Lawrence is not just a matter of grasping the external contingencies that affected his text from outside—his constant travelings, the controversial nature of what he wrote, and the consequent failures of communication or the censoring; of following those; and of "stripping out" the errors and interferences. Much more, one has to be attentive to the internal processes of prolonged composition and constant revision. It is this that links Lawrence, as modernist, to the others; that dictates the principles on which textual editors must work, whether on Joyce or on Lawrence. It is these principles that I think critics of the editions do not understand, so I devote the rest of this article to them. This takes us beyond points of detail to the heart of the matter.

Meanwhile, it is a conceptual obstacle that textual scholarship has been predicated on an over-simple concept of the individual text: too static and too closed. The associated shibboleth has been the "final intention." Textual scholars understand that this has often been frustrated or perverted, but go on believing in it; believing therefore that their task is to recover or reconstitute it.

Certainly the concept is not foolish in itself: one has to believe that writers want to put something before the public. If they do not do that, they do not sell, do not get read. In the discussion we are now engaged in, traditionalists have a certain shrewdness on their side, which needs to be interposed at moments when the modernist tendency becomes too absolutist. There is, in the end, a text to be identified. Yet the modernists have a certain shrewdness too: is *that* what Proust seems to have been doing, putting something before the public? Did he not in fact almost infinitely withhold it? Did the *Cantos,* after all those transformations, get finished? Is not Joyce another such writer? *Ulysses* did just manage to get published, *Finnegans Wake* even more narrowly, but it was a close-run thing; and the form of publication and the discussion now raging eloquently demonstrate how much his ideally endless elaboration and the toil of those years of composition were in fact broken off and roughly tied up rather than elegantly brought to term. Valéry is the supreme case: the *Cahiers* are simply the work he was never *going* to finish: it represented the constant interplay between the daily movement of his mind and the words he could each day get down on paper.

There is an apparent paradox here about form: modernist writers seem at first sight to exemplify either one extreme or the opposite one, and therefore not to be comparable. Joyce and Proust were endlessly revising one great work, or two great works: in Joyce's case, works of very formal structure. Nothing could seem more consciously elaborated: yet the constant revision produces the instability of the text. Valéry, at the other extreme, was constantly recording the spontaneous: down it went on paper, and the next day produced the next entry. Nothing could be less formal, more at the beckoning of today's spontaneity, even unconsciousness; and that produced the endlessly open form, true to the endless process within. Is that an inescapable polarity?—and where, between the poles, do Eliot and Lawrence fit?

It seems clear now that what look like single works in Eliot, in each of which the *apport* of spontaneity is drastically revised (as in *The Waste Land,* where we have the record provided by Mrs. Eliot's recovery of the early drafts) or in the *Four Quartets,* where we know something of the processes of composition—it is becoming clear that we have in each work something like the tension between two processes that Leavis once tried to express as "Ahnung" and "Nisus" (*Living Principle* 44, 62–69). The first, Ahnung, is the intuition of the moment, what Lawrence sometimes called the "inkling"; the other, Nisus, is the lifelong drive, something not fully conscious. In the case of Eliot, Leavis saw all the single works after *Ash Wednesday* as moments, points, in one long single creative aspiration, such that "the whole body of the poetry . . . affects us as one astonishing major work."[4] In respect of Lawrence, Leavis phrased a comparable insight more directly: dropping "Ahnung" and "Nisus," he used ordinary language to speak of "the emergence, as he [Lawrence] experienced it, of original thought out of the ungrasped apprehended—the intuitively, the vaguely but insistently apprehended: first the stir of apprehension, and then the prolonged repetitious wrestle to persuade it into words" (*Thought* 124, and cf. 122). The total effect is not dissimilar; the whole of Lawrence's work too struck Leavis as "a unity, a coherent organic and comprehensive totality" (67). Here is the paradox I have in mind: the tension between the sustained, spontaneous struggle with the individual works, so clearly recorded in the letters and elsewhere; and our sense after the event, that not only are the single works finally coherent, but they are part of a whole that was also found, but unplanned. This is the aspect of a characteristic twentieth-century aesthetic that I mentioned earlier.

With Lawrence, we are now almost fully able to follow, with most of the works, the extraordinary process of composition. A purely spontaneous start meant that he could often say things like "I am doing a novel which I have never grasped. Damn its eyes, there I am at page 145, and I've no notion what it's about. I hate it. F. says it is good. But it's like a novel in a foreign language I don't know very well—I can only just make out what it is about" (*Letters I* 544, letter of 23 April 1913 to Arthur McLeod). This was followed by the process of repeated and drastic revision, indeed rewriting and recasting. This revision was never the recovery or even the discovery of something which could properly be called a final intention, since that presupposes something held clearly in the mind: what was there was the "inkling," the "Ahnung." In no case in his mature work did Lawrence sketch out a plot, make notes on characters, ponder a "theme." It was inconceivable that he would produce the sort of novel where you can draw a diagram representing the course of a neatly executed preplanned action. The point of his revision is that it is always a return to an originating spontaneity, which this time might come out right.

These are intrinsic reasons for distrusting the textual scholars' innocent notion of the final intention, which fixes them immovably in the nineteenth century and earlier. The concept that I outlined elsewhere (see "Editing a Constantly-Revising Author") has a bearing not only on our sense of the modern aesthetic, but consequentially on our sense of how to edit a modernist text. There is a fundamental difference of gestalt. The old notion of the final intention implies that the artist felt at some point something much more specific than "that's right; that's it." The art-object is imagined as the achievement of a preconceived notion, a plan that exists outside the work and is applied to it. One classic analogy is with the painter working from a squared-up drawing and a number of studies and sketches, transferring the fully worked-out concept to the final canvas. Another is the musical analogy, in which the last notes of a symphonic work perfectly resolve a harmonic tension or a thematic transformation built up in the preceding whole.

The modern concept of continual revision correlates with the process to which Leavis gave such apt expression: the "ungrasped apprehended" yields finally to the "prolonged repetitious wrestle to persuade it into words." This struggle, I am suggesting, was not only (to take the most obvious example) the succession of rewritings which finally issued in *The Rainbow* and *Women in Love:* it is to be seen as continuous in the whole life's work, forever being undertaken afresh.

Lawrence scholars must have a sense of that total endeavor, but have for practical purposes to limit themselves to the text before them: it is important now that they should think as much of the process as of the result. This concept has now gone so far (I think, for instance, of the computer-generated synoptic text of *Ulysses,* and of Paul Eggert's interesting theorizations, as for instance in "Opening up the Text") that it is possible to contemplate the eventual generation by computer-graphic means of a text-in-process that is the scholarly equivalent of Duchamp's cubist painting of the nude descending a stairway, where every position of the figure in space is represented, or the Futurist paintings by Balla or Marinetti, which also rendered motion in space and time. If the old textual ideal was like a static portrait of the author drawing a line under his completed text, the new ideal is a video of the author at his table, revising, revising, revising, with the text forming and reforming as we read. This has been anticipated in those very interesting films (of Picasso or Pollock, for instance) where you see the painting grow before your eyes, from blank ground to finished artwork. If it is the process which is the real interest, I still find myself saying "finished": you certainly have the sense, with Picasso, that he could always have taken the work through another transformation, but also that he could choose to do that in another work: that is one secret of his prodigious creativity (and of Lawrence's, when you think how much he wrote in a short life). Hence my reservation, mentioned earlier, about absolutist (actually extreme relativist) interpretations of the modernist aesthetic. It does seem to me to have been one of Lawrence's undisputed intentions, despite his working method, to produce a rapid succession of works, which could be sent to a publisher, printed, published, and sold, since he had to make a living. He accepted the convention that the reader buys, owns, and rereads a completed book. If it does not seem "the same" the next time it is read, that is not because the text has changed, but because the reader has: by reading another book by Lawrence, for instance. The ordinary reader does not often reach the stage of being interested in how this writing achieved its form; but scholars and critics now must: and this is one reason why they should be seriously interested in textual matters.

The other reason is known: it has long been understood that the currently received texts are in various degrees corrupt. Critics have been at the mercy of these texts, and in constant danger of receiving as intention what is actually corruption. Ordinary readers, not interested in the aesthetic I have posited, of the constantly-revised text, ask for a "correct" one. A certain tension between these two interests is now becoming clear. A sophisticated reply would be, "You mean you want a reading text that takes account of the processes of composition, recovering what can be identified as Lawrence's intentions at every stage, and eliminating what can be identified as transmission error (including Lawrence's), or as editorial interference, including censorship." The two interests are not finally separable. All the evidence available to the Cambridge editors, or turned up by them, should convince readers that what Lawrence managed to get to his publishers was in various ways a compromise with what he had been struggling to realize, and that after it reached the publishers it was subjected to a quite different set of contingencies.

In the first stage, transferring the developing text from document to document, he was an imperfect transmitter or scribe of his own work, and never willing to take the time to compare one stage with the previous one, even to check the work of others, such as typists. It regularly happened that, faced with a transmission error, he would simply correct to a third form rather than check the first. This is characteristic: each phrase was not an opportunity to confirm or correct, but another occasion to revise, even to rewrite, often very freely. So much is this the case that we get the sense that an early draft, returned to later, could affect him as almost another work which he was replacing with a new one (cf. my remarks about "The Crown" in note 5). Familiar instances are provided by the early short stories. But it is true of very many of the poems, which will have to be edited accordingly. *Paul Morel* (the early form of *Sons and Lovers*) and *The Sisters* (the early form of *Women in Love*) constitute identifiable works in their own right, even though the relationship with the eventual form is strong. They need to be made available as separate volumes; not least because in the case of *The Sisters* the editorial apparatus will make available much material in underlying strata which lay too deep to be made available in the apparatus of *Women in Love*. The reader wanting the synoptic text of the work that finally became the two great novels of the Brangwensaga, must trace it, as the editors have, through the three texts in the Cambridge volumes.

At publication-stage, Lawrence was subjected to often gross inter-ference with his texts. At the end of the whole process of composition and publication, when the book came out (and I seriously doubt that he ever gave much time to reading his own books), he could never truthfully have said, "That's exactly what I wanted." It was always what he had to settle for. So, being engaged on a lifetime of renewed efforts, he turned to the next book in the same way as he had turned to the next revision of the last one.

The inherent paradox for textual scholars is that, to produce a reading text, they have in the best way possible both to represent this continuous process, to undo the damaging parts of it, and to distort it by arresting it at an ideal stage that never really existed. It is not so much a matter of freezing one frame in the continuous reel. You have first to choose the place at which to freeze the frame, and then very carefully to alter a lot of details, airbrushing some things out and painting some others in. The person who does not understand why you are doing this can with some show of justice say that you are producing a state of Lawrence's text which he himself never saw—to which the answer would be that if Lawrence had been his own editor (and he would not spend time on it) and if his publishers had realized they were dealing with classic works and had not been nervous about the reaction of readers and law-courts, then this pro-cess of producing the ideal first publication would not have laboriously and expensively to be done now. As well ask for the moon. I can say, as former publisher's editor who also writes, that all writers and all publishers suffer these contingencies in some degree; but not many produce work of such importance, few revise them quite so demonically, and fewer live in circumstances that so happen to corrupt their work.

The other objection, the theoretical one, is that if you posit a continuous process, it is a distortion both to freeze the frame and then to doctor the picture. The answer is, Well, do you want a reading text? This is the only conscientious way to produce one now. It was a reading text which was Lawrence's theoretical "final intention," and it would be wrong to be so hostile to that formula as to lose sight of realities. It might be reasonably argued by those who now favor synoptic texts that the Cambridge "Textual apparatus" is formulaic and dry, and the labor of reconstruction so great that readers can in practical terms only reconstruct single-reading-by-reading. The sense of whole stages of underlying text is imperiled or lost, except in those "Explanatory notes" which give consecutive underlying text for particularly interesting passages. To some extent this criticism will be met by the publication of supplementary volumes (*The Sisters,* for example) or by the reproduction of draft material in appendixes; but we have to concede the force of the criticism. Here the Press would say that there is a limit to what you can place in a volume; a limit to what it can finance; and a related limit, already painfully stretched, to what you can ask readers and libraries to pay. What we have is a defensible compromise.

The Cambridge text is therefore a construct, a critically established reading text, reached by a logical and historical process that takes full account of the processes of composition, and especially of continuous revision. To recapitulate: in the early stages Lawrence is composing through his revisions, typically producing a corrected manuscript, which incorporates one or more stages of revision, and then is converted into a typescript, which will again be revised—and may be retyped, and revised again. In none of these stages does Lawrence compare one state with another that is not before his eyes at that moment as a corrected form underlying a correction. Editors have to identify his lapses as scribe, and distinguish them from the errors of others as transcribers (especially his many and very fallible or strong-minded typists). One is screening out interference while recovering intention. I have touched on punctuation, which is often crucial. Lawrence's own pointing can only be recovered from early states that he inscribed, since there was a steady process of regularization (i.e., corruption) by others, which culminated in a blanket house-styling by the printers. What went as one copy of a revised typescript to the English publisher was rarely if ever identical with what went as another copy to the American publisher; these publishers proceeded to house-style differently, and very often to bowdlerize or to censor differently. The proofs were not corrected in identical senses in the two editions.

The editor producing a reading text is therefore obliged to be eclectic, facing the twin problems of shifting intention in the revising author, and constant degradation at the hands of the author, typists, would-be helpful friends like Frieda, publishers, and compositors. For matters of punctuation, only an early stage can be authoritative, most often manuscript. For the words themselves, one has to pick one's way through the sequence, discriminating between intention and interference. The frequent absence of proofs in Lawrence's case means that late changes of substance have to be weighed for authority, and one is often forced to judge by probability: Is this likely to be a proof-correction by Lawrence himself, and in that case was it a willing change or one imposed on him? Or did the publisher just intervene himself? Here is an element of judgment. At no time can the editor safely choose a reading on purely critical grounds: it was on those grounds that Mr. Deacon changed the punctuation in the *Sons and Lovers* passage mentioned above. It was quite a sensible judgment; it just happened to be wrong. If an unlikely reading can make sense, even a strange sense, it is much more likely to be what the author wrote than any more commonplace idea one can come up with oneself. The argument has to be based on a firm grasp of the chronological sequence, which determines that a carefully chosen state of the text is used as the base, and is emended in the light of earlier or later states according to an argued principle. That reduces to a minimum the element of eclecticism, and ought to reduce arbitrariness or personal taste to a related minimum. It cannot be altogether avoided, but cannot be embraced as overriding principle.

My photographic analogy might instead have been a natural one. What starts as a pure stream of authorial manuscript is swelled by tributaries of revision, is forced to change direction here and there by external obstacles, and reaches the sea of publication like a river heavily polluted by people living on the banks. With both analogies, the important sense is of something continuous, and continuously changing. The notion of a river, a flowing, has been used since Heraclitus to represent something of elusive identity, a continuous process that has a mysterious unity. At one point, and for all things a point in space is also a point in time, it is very different from what it is at another, yet it is the same thing, in evolution. There is something metaphysical about it, yet it is always physical. For this textual construct, Gabler has coined the expression "continuous manuscript text"; his reading text is "the emended continuous manuscript text at its ultimate level of compositional development" ("Afterword" to Joyce, *Ulysses* 1895, 1903). His synoptic text is the equivalent of my "nude descending the stairway" representation of the evolution of the text through time, and only lacks the kinetic element which interactive computer-video might add.

Commenting on the Cambridge Lawrence from a position of hindsight, my reaction is not to pick on details that one might now do differently or to list the errors that any human enterprise of large size and long generation will necessarily fall into (they seem to me to be small). My main point, and it surprises me now that I write it down, is that no member of the Editorial Board and no volume editor could at the outset have written about editorial procedure and principle in the way I have done above. What is remarkable is that our team and Gabler's, working far apart and with no communication between them, should have come up with comparable procedures and principles. I have no idea what concepts were in the minds of the *Ulysses* team before they started. I have to say that our minds were, if not entirely blank, very free from preconception. We knew that we were not going to adopt textbook concepts and traditional procedures. Apart from that, our only principle was that the materials themselves must dictate how they were handled, and the concepts and procedures had to emerge from relating the documents to each other as intelligently as we could manage. This was, in short, Anglo-Saxon empiricism or pragmatism; and if I were to learn that Gabler's team had reached the same procedures from an a priori principled argument or theory, I should feel that we had both been justified in our own ways. It is quite true that Gabler is the person who has supplied the concepts; and perhaps he started with them. As for us, when we read his "Afterword," it was very like Monsieur Jourdain discovering that all his life he had been speaking prose.

It is no accident therefore that similar arguments may be used against both editions; but we can be forgiven for feeling that the critics start from a disadvantage; such experience as they have is, we believe, predicated on outdated principles and an incomplete possession or understanding of the evidence; and the final argument in our favor and against them must logically be that our approach is the one that does justice to, as it is dictated by, the evidence. We have not produced a definitive edition, for there is no such thing, and never will be. Textual theory will advance in ways we cannot predict, and in future there will be other editions of Lawrence.[5] What we expect of our successors is that they will think we edited intelligently and consistently, and produced an edition which was principled in its very moderate eclecticism, which responded to a moment in literary history and to a comprehensible modernist aesthetic, and which has permanent value in a number of respects.

NOTES

1. The collaboration of Viking-Penguin in the Cambridge Lawrence would have made a substantial difference to the initial sales, since the Penguin imprint automatically commands a very large worldwide student market. The wide availability then of a cheap edition would have met early criticisms that the high price of the Cambridge books was in effect holding the public to ransom. The texts are now being made available in a Penguin series, with new introductions and notes for students and general readers, under the general editorship of John Worthen.

2. In "D. H. Lawrence: Mark my Words: The Relation of Lawrence's Punctuation to his Meaning" (unpublished talk given in Cambridge; text kindly communicated by Helen Baron).

3. A start has been made. Cambridge University Press has embarked on a complete Conrad and Scott Fitzgerald. The Abinger Edition of E. M. Forster was undertaken single-handed by the late Oliver Stallybrass and continued after his death by Elizabeth Heine. The Estate and the publishers were too diffident to claim copyright; had they done so, they would have been in a stronger position vis-à-vis the American holders of the publishing rights, who have, I understand, declined to handle the new edition or permit its circulation in their territory. The sales being thus drastically reduced, the edition has not been completed; and the American scholar is denied access to an important source. (This strengthens my view that copyright, properly exercised, is the friend of scholarship.)

  Oxford has produced some welcome texts of Henry James and Thomas Hardy. A start has been made on Virginia Woolf, though it seems to me to include, thus far, some ill-considered, indeed amateurish, items. But my main point stands: apart from *Ulysses* and the Cambridge Lawrence, what has been done so far is sporadic, a matter of skirmishes. Meanwhile, for instance, T. S. Eliot's prose is not even collected.

4. *Lectures in America* 55 (but this crystallizes a concept that Leavis had been developing since the Appendix in *Education in the University* [1943, reprinted from *Scrutiny*, Summer 1942]).

5. For instance, I can imagine that a future edition will choose *MS* as base-text in *The Prussian Officer* stories. Future editors may also reconsider volume-divisions. We started from the principle that we would respect Lawrence's own

decisions, without foreseeing all the difficulties: for instance, in the contents of *Reflections on the Death of a Porcupine* (1925). This contains, as is well-known, a heavily revised text of "The Crown," first published ten years earlier in *The Signature*. Characteristically, Lawrence drastically rewrote "The Crown" to make it fit his new preoccupations; and he eliminated or disguised what I take to be an element of self-revelation in which I detect a sexual crisis.

Given the task of editing *Reflections* as a whole volume, Michael Herbert, our editor, was bound to reproduce the later text of "The Crown." Fortunately, his apparatus gives the 1915 variants, which are in places substantial consecutive passages that Lawrence deleted. Effectively, the 1915 "Crown" is another work. More: when it is examined, it is seen to fall into place in that sequence of writings—actually rewritings, in which Lawrence is engaged in Leavis's "prolonged repetitious struggle"—all of them successive attempts to formulate what Lawrence called "my philosophy." These start with the "Foreword to *Sons and Lovers*" currently lost in Huxley's volume of the *Letters,* and now included, in a corrected text, in Helen and Carl Baron's Cambridge *Sons and Lovers;* this transforms into *Study of Thomas Hardy;* which transforms into both *Twilight in Italy* and "The Crown"; which transforms into "The Reality of Peace," which transforms eventually into *Studies in Classic American Literature.* Working on these texts recently for my commentary on *The Early Philosophical Works* (1992) has sharpened the sense that I try to convey in this essay, of the continuance, through revision and transformation, of Lawrence's one prolonged struggle.

To me now, therefore, it would make abundant sense to reorder these writings, breaking down the categories, and even infringing Lawrence's more opportunistic volume-divisions. *Study of Thomas Hardy* is not only or even primarily about literature, and should be separated from other literary criticism. *Twilight in Italy* has to be rescued from the inert category "travel-writing." In short, the nonfiction could well be recategorized; but it would be best to drop all categories and opt, so far as possible, for a single chronological sequence. Of course anyone who even attempts that at once falls into another set of difficulties. But a volume that contained the Foreword, the *Study,* "The Crown," and "The Reality of Peace," with notes which made clear the relationship both to *Twilight in Italy* and *The Rainbow* would advance Lawrence studies.

I ought to say also that I now regret the claim in the copyright notice, which consistently begins "This, the Cambridge Edition of [title], now correctly established. . . ." I drafted this in a moment of hubris when the first volume was about to be published, and it has been repeated ever since. The euphoric claim about "correctness" implies that there can be no further advance in textual scholarship; if one thinks a bit, this is self-refuting. I hope my former colleagues will reword this.

WORKS CITED

Black, Michael H. "Editing a Constantly-Revising Author: the Cambridge Edition of Lawrence in Historical Context." In *D. H. Lawrence: Centenary Essays.* Ed. Mara Kalnins. Bristol: Bristol Classical P, 1986. 191–210.

———. "The Works of D. H. Lawrence: the Cambridge Edition." In *D. H. Lawrence: The Man Who Lived.* Ed. Robert B. Partlow Jr. and Harry T. Moore. Carbondale and Edwardsville: Southern Illinois UP, 1980. 49–57.

Eggert, Paul. "Opening up the Text: The Case of *Sons and Lovers.*" In *Rethinking Lawrence.* Ed. Keith Brown. Milton Keynes, Eng.: Open UP, 1990. 38–51.

Gabler, Hans Walter. "Afterword" to Joyce, *Ulysses,* 1859–1911.

Joyce, James. *Ulysses: "A Critical" and Synoptic Edition.* Prepared by Hans Walter Gabler, Wolfhard Steppe, and Claus Melchior. New York: Garland, 1984.

Lawrence, D. H. *Sons and Lovers.* London: Duckworth, 1913.

———. *Sons and Lovers.* Ed. Keith Sagar. Harmondsworth: Penguin Books (Penguin English Library), 1981.

Leavis, F. R. (with Q. D. Leavis). *Lectures in America.* London: Chatto, 1969.

———. *The Living Principle.* London: Chatto, 1975.

———. *Thought, Words and Creativity: Art and Thought in Lawrence.* New York: Oxford UP, 1976.

Reading a Critical Edition With the Grain and Against: The Cambridge D. H. Lawrence

Paul Eggert

READING WITH THE GRAIN

Although reviewers have traditionally hailed critical editions of which they approved for their painstaking, more or less scientific methods and for their establishment of definitive texts which need never be done again, editors themselves are rarely so sanguine. Editors will usually maintain that they are producing *critical* editions and that the pursuit they are engaged in is textual *criticism*. The term draws attention to the editor's exercise of critical powers in establishing the text: a significant element of discrimination and assessment has always been a feature of editing. Nevertheless, there has been little disagreement until recently amongst modern editors that the primary aim of a critical edition, however well or badly achieved, is to establish the reading text of the work according to an argued standard, typically that of final authorial intention.

Yet, strictly speaking, it is impossible to arrive at such a text. Editors do not have a royal telephone line to the author's creative mind, and, even if the author is still alive, he or she would not necessarily recall what was intended at any particular point where the documentary texts disagree. In the case of full-length novels there may be thousands of such cases, most of them minor points of punctuation and the like. Any one of them, however, has the potential to influence tone, intonation, or sentence rhythm in one's reading—in short, to affect interpretation. Two, five, or twenty years after the event, the author may return to revise the work (say, when a new or collected edition is called for) but will return to the extant documents in the capacity of an outsider—a privileged one, it is true, and one whose rights to textual ownership of the work will be undisputed, but one who has inevitably changed in the meantime. So the forlornness of the task of that other, later outsider—the critical editor—need not be seen as crippling if even the author would not have been perfectly placed to perform it either. The editor works with the available tools: a familiarity with the author's works, a detailed knowledge of the circumstances of composition and production of the work in hand, a systematic collation of its various textual states, and research into the influences that bore on its composition and revision.

The editor's work is based on the postulation of a standard that has a certain convincingness among the audience for that the edition is prepared. The appeal is historical (restoring the text the author would have wished to see published), but the achievement of the standard usually involves the selection of readings from more than one lifetime state. The end result is one that the author never saw and that synchronically presents writing and revision that actually took place diachronically. Nevertheless, if readers want a single text of the work in which alterations made by parties other than the author—scribes, typists, typesetters, and nervy publishers—have been systematically eliminated, then the paradox that the establishment of an authorial text requires editorial mediation is unavoidable (see my "Textual Product" 33–38).

One method of intellectually defusing the paradox is to think of the text of the work as represented (but also, importantly, *mis*represented) by all the extant documents, so that the attempt to establish that text requires the editor to go, as it were, behind them. G. Thomas Tanselle's distinction between the text of the document and the text of the work is particularly helpful here: he writes of "the work that speaks to us across the generations [and that] will forever be a conjecture arising from those time-bound, vulnerable objects [the documents]."[1] Therefore the work can be thought of as having an ideal text that beckons but is never achieved: the efforts of the editor will, because of unavoidable reliance on critical judgment, always fall short, will never *quite* get there.

An advantage of this approach is that the implicit conception of the term "literary work" closely relates to the ordinary understanding of it—such as when we say *The Rainbow* and *Women in Love* became different literary works although they branched off a common stem, "The Sisters." Although we may realize that the particular printed copy that we have in our hands is apt to have all sorts of errors in it, the term "literary work" is too useful to do without. Usefulness demystifies its ideality, and familiarity with it makes us ready to accept the idea that the text of the work *ought* to be attainable in a critical edition in the form of a single sequence of words and punctuation—i.e., as a reading text. It seems too natural an expectation to question, especially in view of the linear form of reading that the physical book has encouraged (and for which authors have written) over the last five hundred years. It is also a commercial necessity given both the limited capacity of the hard-copy critical edition to present (rather than only to notate) multiple documentary forms of the text and also the need to make a reliable reading text cheaply available to a student and wider reading public.

Given this set of assumptions, the burning question for editors and for reviewers of their work is the method chosen to establish that text. The latter is usually the central bone of contention, and may be picked over in great detail. The (less central) apparatus may be commended or faulted for the fullness and accuracy of its record of editorial emendation of the historical document used as the basis of the reading text, and for the way in which it allows the reader to check how different the new edition is from the received one. Its record of textual variation may not be mentioned at all. If the edition contains explanatory notes, they are judged as helpful or supererogatory depending on how they clarify the reviewer's queries (or offend the reviewer's self-esteem) while reading the text.

How does the Cambridge series of critical editions of D. H. Lawrence satisfy this set of expectations? At first *sight,* they do so quite impressively. Ranged on the shelf in their solid respectability, the volumes seem to signify textual authority and rationality of argument. Their sheer bulk helps signify this (although individually they have an economy lacked by many critical editions); but, as one looks at them, there is more: the elegant black dust-jacket, a blurb that does not remind one even vaguely of the excesses of this typically overwritten genre, the insignia of the series on the half-title page, the assurance on its verso that this edition has been carried out under the supervision of an editorial board of eminent or established scholars. There is the sober page design quietly telling its own story, a story to which the solid binding and the hardback covers are contributing. And the extensive list of acknowledgments and the highly detailed chronology which comes next in the volume remind one that this edition was not the work of a single summer's vacation—not even of two. The fact that there are perhaps fifty pages of reading before the text of the novel starts is another signifying element, as is the presence of explanatory notes, a textual apparatus, and appendixes at the end. One becomes aware not only that the editor has put in a great deal of work, but that a great deal of work needed to be done. And this is all before one starts to read the words.[2]

One is, or at least upon reflection one ought to be, relieved then to find that the editorial matter has not been consigned to the back of the book as has been common in editions validated by the Center for Editions of American Authors or the MLA Committee for Scholarly Editions. This practice creates the misapprehension that the reader is being given an unmediated access to the author's text, whereas in fact the access is to an editorially established text—what can only be a collaboration of author and editor. At least the Cambridge introductions say this straight out before one arrives at the reading text; but should one skip the introductory matter and turn directly to the text, one will encounter line numbers which are there to key into the textual apparatus. Sooner or later curiosity will triumph and, turning to the apparatus, one will in turn feel the need to read the introduction to make sense of what the apparatus is recording and why the editor has made the textual choices he or she has. One will find then that the introduction frequently refers to entries in the textual apparatus and in the explanatory notes where particular textual decisions are justified: one then gets a dawning awareness that the volume is a mass of cross-references, that it is, despite the internal divisions of its editorial matter, working as a single unit. Everything seems to be there to document and justify the approach taken in the construction of the reading text, or otherwise to serve it by explaining its compositional history, its allusions, and by listing its rejected readings. The preeminence of the reading text—its singularity and authority—seems to be attested by the very design of the edition.

The singularity and authority of the reading text are also attested by the characteristics of style and argument used by the editors—by their scholarly rhetoric. The introductions have to account for how the work came to be written and published, the contexts in Lawrence's life and writings out of which it grew, and there must be a detailed consideration of all the extant manuscript and other material relevant to the editorial policy adopted. There can be a great deal of material of possible relevance. But in the introduction a story must be told and a case mounted.

The convention in operation here is, I suspect, actually a narrative one that is so powerful we do not stop to question it. The editor is telling a kind of story. It is at least partly a fiction because the editor never has *all* the evidence. The story's value is tested by its ability to encompass and explain without contradiction all the available evidence, to tease out and deal with all its implications, especially those that might seem to contradict the narrative thrust. The ideal reader raises every doubt, scours every footnote for an answer to the doubt, postulates alternative explanations and sticks with them till they prove unable to account for an extant piece of evidence and so do not tell as compelling a story as the editor's. Evidence is marshalled so that the appearance is given that the only possible or only defensible—the *inevitable*—conclusion has been reached. But having recognized this, one must also in fairness reflect that there are stories and stories: that the sustaining rhetoric also functions as a discipline. If the rhetoric is able to impose conclusions on the reader, that is partly because it has imposed prior obligations on the editor.

In the establishment of the reading text, the chosen standard is authorial—almost inevitable in a series devoted to editing the Works of a given literary author. The professed aim, as announced in the "General Editors' Preface" in each volume, is the preparation, as best as can be achieved, of the reading text which Lawrence would have wished to see published. This aim has the same air of ideality about it described above. Of the extant documents one is chosen to serve as base-text. This is the one over which the editor believes Lawrence had the fullest control, and it is emended in those places where Lawrence subsequently revised.

Tanselle's emphasis on critical judgment (which reiterates Fredson Bowers's) has its place in the Cambridge Edition too, except it gets nothing like the pride of place Tanselle gives it. Editorial judgment comes into play when a reading in the base-text is illegible or ambiguous, or when a reading in a later state may or may not be Lawrence's. The latter case typically occurs when his letters show him to have corrected proof but the proofs are not extant. The editor has then to decide when and according to what principle he or she will incorporate readings from the first English and American editions into the base-text. The tendency has been to minimize the scope of editorial judgment in such matters and to adopt a fairly mechanical approach by either, according to circumstances, maintaining the base-text readings in all but compelling cases, or to go the other way, as with *The Rainbow,* and to accept virtually all proof changes. The opportunity of some fine scalpeling of the reading text is thus foregone, but the attendant dangers of reliance on the editor's aesthetic judgments, of inconsistency, are minimized.

Choice of base-text has always to be sensitive to the circumstances of any particular case, and those circumstances are rarely the same. But, even taking this variable into account, the Lawrence Edition has shifted from choosing, as in some of the early editions, a late-state base-text such as a revised typescript or proofs (even where an earlier state is extant), to choosing manuscript as base-text. Because, where late-state base-texts were chosen, any miscopyings in them were corrected by reference to the earlier state, and practical effect of the change has been mainly on the comprehensiveness of the textual apparatus—which only records chronologically forwards from the base-text. If a late-state base-text is chosen, the apparatus will be considerably shorter; if an early-state base-text is chosen, then a much fuller textual disclosure is incumbent. Although one is really talking here only about tendencies rather than firm positions, the Edition can be said to have shifted from one somewhat akin to that of Philip Gaskell to one more like that of Sir Walter Greg as developed by Fredson Bowers.[3]

This labelling requires explanation. There are two authorial standards an editor must face. They are usually run together as one, but they are, I believe, very often separable (argued in my "Document or Process"). The first is what the author wrote initially and in revision; the second is what was done to that writing on his behalf, what he could have expected to happen as the book went through typing, typesetting, and in-house editing. The desire to run the two standards together runs very deep with editors who are frequently bibliophiles as well and who have an understandable desire to do the best by their author, to find a way of ironing out his inconsistencies of presentation and to polish up his writing—if only a little—for a modern audience. Thus Fredson Bowers, a firm believer in establishing the reading text according to the standard of what the author actually wrote rather than merely approved,[4] nevertheless regularized Nathaniel Hawthorne's spelling according to the 1813 dictionary Hawthorne is known to have used (discussed by Abbott 15). The temptation to do this sort of thing is strong, particularly if the editor is charged, as he or she nearly always is, with providing a single text of the work in the knowledge that this text will be reproduced in cheap format without the apparatus which would otherwise guarantee its bona fides. And of course Philip Gaskell, among others, has given support to the idea that, although, say, a manuscript exists, if the author is known to have carefully checked proofs, then they, or in the absence of them the first edition, should provide the base-text (e.g., 5–6, 207–8); and this, despite the fact that the proofs of a novel will be virtually certain to contain some thousands of non-authorial alterations, most of them ones of punctuation, the result of the normal processes of professional typing and typesetting.[5]

The Cambridge Edition's pragmatism has, I feel, been a strength in facing this problem. Although in the early editions, in a spirit akin to Gaskell's, the Edition was not as strict in observing the distinction between the two standards as I would have preferred, the temptation to clean Lawrence up for formal presentation has been largely resisted: what one gets is, as far as practicable, what Lawrence wrote. That is why, incidentally, I feel that the Cambridge edition of *Sons and Lovers,* given the aims of the series, *had* to restore the material that Edward Garnett excised. I have argued elsewhere that Garnett did a good job, but it is a valuable service for a critical edition to provide us with what Lawrence wrote, rather than what he acquiesced in, more or less under pressure, in order to get the novel published.[6] Were the two standards I mentioned to be run together in a critical edition and Garnett's cuts accepted, then there would have to be a frank admission either that the editor was offering an abridged authorial version on the grounds that many readers happened currently to prefer it; or, more defensibly, that he or she was editing a textual collaboration and thus having to reconcile two sources of intention within the reading text.

The demand for single reading texts of works puts, I believe, an artificially high stress on the standard used to establish them. The stridency of the reviews that critical editions sometimes attract suggests as much. I do not believe (as I argue below) that *any* single text can adequately represent a multistate literary work. But in a cultural and intellectual climate which, whether because of the inertia of custom and familiarity or because of sheer convenience, continues to call for the single reading text, the Cambridge Edition's way of catering to that requirement seems to me to make sense. The effort is made to preserve what Lawrence wrote, and to eliminate non-authorial alterations—systematically, accurately, and with as relatively little exercise of purely aesthetic judgment as is likely to be possible. The strength of the Edition, as I see it, is therefore pragmatic rather than theoretic.

READING AGAINST THE GRAIN

Tanselle's distinction between the text of the work and the text of the document may be read another way. If the text of the work is never perfectly witnessed by any document, then no one, including the author, can ever read it. We can only read texts that more or less imperfectly represent it. In other words, the "work" must exist, in one vital sense, beyond and outside the realm of the phenomenal where writing and reading take place. Comparison of literary to other works of art does seem to provide a philosophical rationale for this position. With tangible works of art such as paintings, the "work" is physically identical with the object (i.e., after due allowance is made for discoloration and other damage). But a literary work cannot be said to be identical with any one printing of it; and the singularity of the tangible work of art encourages an expectation of a singularity in the intangible—even if the latter has to be thought of as lurking somewhere behind its documentary representations.

However, this now-traditional line of argument derived from aesthetic philosophy is, as far as I can see, not supported by knowledge of the actual practices of painters' and sculptors' workshops over the centuries. Not only do traditions of apprenticeship disrupt notions of works of art being purely the creation of the artist, but there is abundant evidence of multi-versioned painting methods; and painted-over versions are now amenable to partial recovery by X-ray examination. In the area of sculpture, the making of cartoons, maquettes, and "limited editions" (casts or reproductions in another medium often not from the hand of the sculptor, but yet conventionally considered as "his" work) also tend to undermine the common assumption of the singularity of the work of art: awareness of production histories, in short, tends to overturn notions derived from the art gallery.[7]

Developments in editorial theory since the mid-1980s have in any case enforced an awareness of the versional nature of literary works of art and of the importance of documenting textual "process" (in addition to establishing the extractable "product"—the reading text). It *is* possible to accommodate these trends while simultaneously holding onto the notion of the "work" as singular: in a pluralistic gesture one acknowledges the legitimacy of critically editing versions *of* the work corresponding to the editor's location of textual authority: whether in the author, in a personal or professional collaboration, or in a specific audience (e.g., of the first edition, or of a specific magazine serialization). However, in countenancing widened grounds of disagreement about the object of critical endeavor, the literary work-behind-the-documents is tacitly acknowledged as multiple in everything but name. The idealist notion of the literary work is thereby reduced to something generated by convention, more a convenience than a robust existential category.

In this situation a promising alternative, I suggest, is to essay a definition of "literary work" that sticks to the level of the phenomenal. Such a definition would, I believe, need to maintain a distinction between document and work, but not in the way Tanselle sees it. Poststructuralist writings have made us all familiar with the idea of the instability of texts— i.e., the instability of texts when read. However, until they are read, while they reside as graphic traces, as ink on paper, they are stable; but when read by the author returning to his or her manuscript in revision, by the compositor when setting type, or by readers of printed documents, texts inevitably resume their unstable, dynamic existence. The work comes into a different kind of existence every time someone reads any one of its documentary forms; and every reading will be a distinct experience contextualized by its reader's location. Every reading is, therefore, partial—in both senses of the word.

This line of observation permits a nonidealist definition of literary work: it can be thought of as all (textual) dealings with the documents. As this definition would embrace what readers make of their experiences of reading the printed documents, and as most of this can only be known by report if at all, there can clearly be, by this (admittedly all-embracing) definition, no one text of the whole work. In this sense the "work" can never be finished unless the documents become entirely ignored, and so the work in its fullness can never be edited. But partial attempts can usefully be made. Although what went on in Lawrence's head as he wrote and revised is inaccessible, we can guess at this "reading" more profitably than most other people's by means of the more ample, and almost certainly more interesting, graphic traces—the documents— he and his printers left behind.

The definition of "work" I am entertaining here leaves the way open for editors concentrating on the phase up to the point of publication to present single or multiple texts according to argued standards and the purposes to which the edition might be put. What the definition rules out is any appeal to a "natural" editorial approach. There could be a series of legitimate editions of a single work by Lawrence. One would be the text read by the novel's original readers. In the case of *Lady Chatterley's Lover,* a variorum text could probably be prepared which presented the texts read by the various readerships of its Florence and Paris printings, the pirated printings, the expurgated printings, and finally the unexpurgated printings. Such an edition would provide valuable insight into what could and could not be printed and read in various countries over several decades of this century. But, in both these cases, the interest would be in the printed documents in their relationship to their various readerships. If one were primarily interested in the documents in their relationship to Lawrence's changing or refining conception of the work as it went through its various prepublication forms, then one might choose to represent the novel as it stood at, say, third manuscript stage or at a revised typescript stage. One might even produce a critical edition which gave the manuscript as the reading text and listed all Lawrence's textual changes at the foot of the page. Such an edition would be as uncompromisingly authorial as possible, and it would allow the reader to engage easily with the alternative authorial texts. But, as with the eclectic text of the critical edition, it could only achieve its aim through intrusive editorial re-sorting and partial re-presentation of the extant documentary texts. Perhaps the electronic environment will have the capaciousness and flexibility to respond to all these desiderata. If so, there will be more stress on the archival function of the edition and less on the reading text, even though it will doubtless continue to play a role—at the very least as an orientation device for the first-time user holding the (hard-copy) student edition in her hand.

One attraction to me of such a less-stressed approach to the reading text of a critical edition is its nearer correspondence to the actual experience of an editor. This must count for something. The editor has had his or her experience of, as it were, total immersion in the waters of intertextuality. He (in my case) has seen the author's text dispersed through a farrago of documents, seen aspects of it hitched to a hundred letters by Lawrence, heard many of its ideas and phrasings echoed in books Lawrence was reading at the time and in his other writings. The editor has read the work in all its states of development. He has perhaps regretted that Lawrence went on to change the text, or he has applauded the development but felt this has unfairly cast the "superseded" text out of consideration. He has observed the growth of the various states of the work out of the biographical-textual weave of Lawrence's life, has seen the work grow towards its first published form, and then has witnessed its only gradual abandonment as it merges into the biographical-textual weave of the next work. The editor has perhaps decided that what he has in the documents is a fascinating multiplicity of texts but must nevertheless acknowledge that what he has contracted to produce is a single one.

Mark Kinkead-Weekes puts the dilemma nicely in his introduction to his edition of the Cambridge *Rainbow* when he writes: "there are vital ways in which a work of Lawrence's *is* its process of becoming, which an edition should try to preserve in some fashion, however necessary it may be to choose between variants in order to produce a readable text" (lxiv). Read in the traditional way, the edition does not yield what Kinkead-

Weekes calls the work's "process of becoming," but read against the grain—not for what editions were set up to do but what they do in spite of themselves—the Cambridge editions, or at least many of them, yield a surprising multiplicity. When an early-state base-text has been chosen, the textual apparatus necessarily contains the readings, at every point of variance, of all states of the text.[8] Therefore reading against the grain, using the reading text to open up the textual apparatus rather than, as traditionally, using the apparatus to check the validity of the editor's decisions for the text, one can recover Lawrence's changes of mind and then trace significant patterns in those changes of mind. In other words, one can, wherever one wishes, construct alternative texts from the apparatus rather than considering it as just a repository of rejected readings. This form of reading is not easy, admittedly; but it can be done.

Similarly the explanatory notes. Although annotation is supposed traditionally to gloss difficult or allusive passages in the reading text and to defend its readings, the notes often do very much more. Take, for example, the note on Hermione Roddice in the *Women in Love* edition (531). It refers to the surname's being common in Eastwood, to Lawrence's mixing up the name in one of the typescripts of the novel with another name he had elsewhere used for fictional versions of Jessie Chambers, to references in the letters indicating that the character owes something to Lady Ottoline Morrell, to cross-references to other notes in the edition which confirm and extend this correspondence, and to Lady Ottoline's own view of Hermione and Lawrence's response as documented in one of his letters; the note finally quotes another letter where Lawrence contests as an oversimplification the idea that Hermione *is* Ottoline. All this, and more besides, is done in seventeen lines of type. No overtly literary critical opinion or ready-made interpretation is offered, and every statement is linked to a printed or documentary reference—even if the language, so packed with information, is less than elegant.

But the reader, following up the references, will find an ever-widening circle. The note unfolds "Hermione" into the politics of Lawrence's friendships, both personal and professional, and into some of his writings and his views about the sources of inspiration for all of his work. So the note's very effort of explanation, which is supposed to clarify and undergird a query the reader might have in reading the *text,* ends up equally working in the opposite direction. What is assumed to close down uncertainty if read with the grain, opens it up when read against; the name "Hermione" in the text becomes the temporary focus of a widening intertextual and biographical web. So an assumption of the need for singularity serves in the end to release multiplicity.

There is an objection to my line of argument that John Worthen voiced in a paper at the 1990 Montpellier Lawrence conference (where a version of the present essay was given): "I want to read what we will agree to call *Women in Love* rather than *in Women in Love*." I do too, at least sometimes; indeed when I read any text for the first and probably second time, I want to make use of the same convention ("what we will agree to call . . .")—for it is a helpful one. Texts—unstable in composition, revision, and production—are temporarily stabilized by the act of commercial publication or by critical editing and publication; but they resume their unstable dynamism when they are read. *That* is why the convention is necessary: not just as a personal convenience, but to give us a common point of reference from which to work. But neither consideration sanctions the elevation of a convention into an ideal conception of the work such as underlies the supposedly natural expectations about the singularity of texts of works referred to above. Indeed, if my definition of "work" and my descriptions of the reading text of a critical edition have any force, it is in stressing the very conventionality of the convention: the sense in which it is not possible to do *other* than read *in Women in Love*—whether one is reading the Cambridge text (or any other printing) from start to finish or whether one is reading "across" the novel, comparing a scene or attitude or motif or wording here with a similar one there, comparing them both with their counterparts in other versions of the novel, and reflecting on their differing contexts of composition. At such times I want to read, reflect, and re-read, but I do not want to allow myself to be intimidated by the convention into believing that I am reading something other than *Women in Love*. Why should I acquiesce, given the assistance of critical editions which say simultaneously (as I hope I have demonstrated) that I can—if I want to go on as in the past—but that I do not have to?

NOTES

1. "Textual Criticism and Deconstruction" 22. See also Tanselle's *Textual Criticism and Scholarly Editing* xi and *A Rationale* passim.
2. Argument in this and the next paragraph draws on Shillingsburg, "The Meanings of a Scholarly Edition."
3. Cf. the Cambridge editions of Lawrence's *Apocalypse* (1980), *The Prussian Officer and Other Stories* (1983), and *Mr Noon* (1984) as against *The Rainbow* (1989) and *The Boy in the Bush* (1990).

4. See, e.g., Bowers, *Principles* 197–98, where his approval of the choice of manuscript as base-text is unswervingly firm. This is the Bowers of the 1960s. However the older Bowers became more flexible. In his article of 1978 ("Greg's 'Rationale of Copy-Text' Revisited"), Bowers discusses the consequences of choosing an early state (Quarto) over a late state (Folio) as copy-text for an edition of Jonson's *Sejanus* (115–18). His preference is for the early state, though his argument runs along practical rather than a priori lines. But later in this densely argued essay, Bowers recants the firmness of his 1960s position, at least for the editing of eighteenth-century and later works. For a commentary, see my "Dealings with the Firm of Greg and Bowers."

5. On the superiority of Lawrence's manuscript pointing over that of a printed source, see my "The Reviewing of the Cambridge *Women in Love*" 300.

6. See Eggert, "Opening up the Text" 43–51; and cf. the editorial rationale in the Pennsylvania edition of Dreiser's *Sister Carrie*. In this, his first novel, Dreiser made substantial cuts suggested by a friend and literary mentor, Arthur Henry, "no matter what effect these revisions had on the novel. . . . In the strictest sense, his authorial function ceased after he inscribed the holograph draft of *Sister Carrie*. . . . Thereafter he acted as editor and revised his own prose and decided what non-authorial alterations . . . to adopt. . . . Dreiser undoubtedly agreed to make these excisions because he felt that they would make his novel more saleable" (West 579–81). The excisions (36,000 words) are restored in the edition.

7. For some examples and further discussion, see Eggert, "Textual Product or Textual Process" 19–22 and "Editing Paintings/Conserving Literature: The Nature of the 'Work.'" "Editing" of paintings is not restricted to restoration, as is commonly thought. The placement of a painting in a gallery or exhibition is a form of publication, and meaning is partly dependent on the gallery context. For the contemporary artist, or for the collector or curator, the necessity of choice of a version of a painting to represent the work can be a very real one. Opinions may differ as to what the work in question comprehends.

8. With the exception of the categories of silent emendation. These are an attempt to unclutter the apparatus by defining categories of variants which occur repeatedly or which are deemed so insignificant as unlikely to be of interest to anyone.

WORKS CITED

Abbott, Craig S. "A Response to Nordloh's 'Socialization, Authority, and Evidence.'" *Analytical and Enumerative Bibliography* 1 (1987): 13–16.

Bowers, Fredson. "Greg's 'Rationale of Copy-Text' Revisited." *Studies in Bibliography* 31 (1978): 90–161.

———. "Some Principles for Scholarly Editions of Nineteenth-Century American Authors." In *Bibliography and Textual Criticism*. Ed. O. M. Brack Jr. and Warner Barnes. Chicago: U of Chicago P, 1969. 194–201.

Eggert, Paul. "Dealings With the Firm of Greg and Bowers: A Personal Tribute to, and a Reconsideration of, the Work of Fredson Bowers, 1905–1991." *Bibliographical Society of Australia and New Zealand Bulletin* 15 (1991): 73–88.

———. "Document or Process as the Site of Authority: Establishing Chronology of Revision in Competing Typescripts of *The Boy in the Bush*." *Studies in Bibliography* 44 (1991): 364–76.

———. "Editing Paintings/Conserving Literature: The Nature of the 'Work.'" *Studies in Bibliography* 47 (1994): 65–78.

———. "Opening up the Text: The Case of *Sons and Lovers*." In *Rethinking Lawrence*. Ed. Keith Brown. Milton Keynes: Open UP, 1990. 38–51.

———. "The Reviewing of the Cambridge *Women in Love*." *The D. H. Lawrence Review* 20.3 (1988): 297–304.

———. "Textual Product or Textual Process: Procedures and Assumptions of Critical Editing." In *Editing in Australia*. Ed. Paul Eggert. English Dept., University College ADFA, Canberra, Australia. Distrib. New South Wales, UP, 1990. 19–40.

Gaskell, Philip. *From Writer to Reader: Studies in Editorial Method*. Oxford: Clarendon P, 1978.

Shillingsburg, Peter. "The Meanings of a Scholarly Edition." *Bibliographical Society of Australia and New Zealand Bulletin* 13 (1989): 41–50.

Tanselle, G. Thomas. *A Rationale of Textual Criticism*. Philadelphia: U of Pennsylvania P, 1989.

———. "Textual Criticism and Deconstruction." *Studies in Bibliography* 43 (1990): 1–33.

———. *Textual Criticism and Scholarly Editing*. Charlottesville: UP of Virginia, 1990.

West, James L. W., III, ed. *Sister Carrie*. By Theodore Dreiser. Philadelphia: U of Pennsylvania P, 1981.

Facts in Fiction: With a Short Argument About Authorial Intention

John Worthen

I

Editorial methods, while often claiming an origin in editorial principles, are in my experience as likely to be based on strategies as on principles: strategies addressed, among other things, to the different sections of the market in which editions are sold. The market for an edition, that is, may significantly alter the editorial practice used to establish it. I now propose to develop that argument, using examples from a number of the Cambridge University Press Lawrence volumes, and will show how it can also be used to illuminate the old topic of authorial intention.

My provocation to do so comes primarily from the long, fascinating, and important series of essays which G. Thomas Tanselle has been publishing annually in *Studies in Bibliography*.[1] Tanselle has argued consistently for editorial practice based on an understanding that the serious editor's job is firstly to distinguish four different kinds of textual concern (listed below), and secondly to recover the author's intention for the work in question. The four kinds of textual concern are:

The **document:** the inscribed or printed physical object descending to us out of history.

The **work:** the ideal concept which—according to Tanselle—is that intended by the author, though almost certainly never realized in any particular document or sequence of documents.

The **text of the document:** the arrangement of words, punctuation, etc., making up the document.

41

The **text of the work:** the arrangement of words, punctuation etc., which—as Tanselle sees it—as a result of the editor's work approximates to the author's ideal intention for the **work.**

The distinctions are clear and fairly useful. It is obviously the case that—in spite of what looks like a Platonic belief in "the work" as having no actual existence—we do regularly think of literary works in such terms. If I say that "*Women in Love* is one of the great twentieth century novels," I am obviously not referring to any surviving document: nor am I referring to the text of any surviving document: nor am I referring to any particular edited text of the work. I am referring to what we conveniently call *Women in Love,* and mean by it the work which Lawrence wrote in 1916 and 1917, but which nowhere exists exactly as he wrote it. I am perfectly happy to agree that the nearest we shall get to *that Women in Love* will be an edited text of the work: and I would argue that the Cambridge University Press *Women in Love,* without being a final or definitive edition, can for our generation represent the work *Women in Love.*

At least two of Tanselle's textual concerns, however—"the work" and "the text of the work"—are distinguished by his particular stress upon intention. And when he uses and distinguishes between those textual concerns in the course of his essays, he injects into them that same concept of intention, with at times rather strange results. On the first page of his 1990 essay "Textual Criticism and Deconstruction," for example, he remarks that "the texts we find in documents cannot automatically be equated with the texts of the works that those documents claim to be conveying" (1). Few documents (apart perhaps from scholarly editions) ever "claim" to convey a text. Normally, manuscripts and typescripts simply *do* or *do not* transmit texts. Tanselle makes the same point (and, I would say, commits himself to the same fallacy) when a few pages later he refers to "the relation of literary works to the documents that attempt to transmit them" (8). Tanselle's belief in "intention" infects the very way in which he conceives of documents; for him, the document wants to transmit the work and attempts to put forward its text for serious consideration—just as he conceives of an author intending and intentionally transmitting his work. Tanselle's textual/mental landscape is thus strangely peopled with the agents of intention, human and nonhuman.

The issue I wish to raise is how far the idea of intention is useful to the editor; and I want to approach this issue along the same route which

Tanselle took some fifteen years ago, in one of the most useful of his essays, "External Fact as an Editorial Problem." This essay sets out arguments and examples centering on the problem of what an editor should do about errors in historical references and in quotations which appear in surviving documents. Although the subject might appear of mainly technical interest, the essay firstly considers a question to which remarkably little informed attention has been given; and, secondly, as Tanselle rightly points out, a text's interpenetration with real life confronts us with some of the most basic problems of editing. How we deal with such problems turns out to reveal what we believe editions should be.

A good deal of what Tanselle says also relates directly to the Cambridge University Press Lawrence Edition. At some stage, every editor has faced the fact of Lawrence's notorious use of real-life people and places. Lawrence also regularly referred to and quoted his contemporaries; he wrote reviews and literary criticism referring to and quoting other authors; many editors also confront his inaccurate use of foreign languages; and some (especially the editor of *Movements in European History*) face the very real problem of Lawrence's use and misuse of historical facts.

II

Tanselle starts by drawing on a number of examples from Melville's *Moby-Dick,* of which he was one of the editors for the Northwestern University–Newberry Library edition ("External" 5–20). He shows that there are cases where errors of fact simply cannot be corrected. An author may go on to discuss his own (incorrect) quotation, for example; and we cannot correct the quotation without making the subsequent discussion of it ridiculous. The first thing to do, Tanselle sensibly suggests, is to ascertain whether an error *can* be corrected: the second, to decide whether it *should* be (44–46).

The literary "Extracts" that preface *Moby-Dick* show how, in many cases, Melville did not reproduce his original sources accurately. There is, for example, a citation from Montaigne that runs "the sea-gudgeon retires into it in great security" where Montaigne, in the translation Melville was using actually wrote "this little fish retires into it in great security." But the word "sea-gudgeon" appears in an earlier (and unquoted) part of Montaigne's sentence. Like many authors, at times Melville clearly adapted or modified his quotations to make them clearer, more explicit, or more striking; and thus effectively appropriated them. The phrase about the "sea-gudgeon" is not an error or an accidental misquotation, and we obviously should not correct it.

Our reasons for not doing so, however, will differ significantly. Tanselle will not correct the change because he believes he has ascertained the author's intention in "sea-gudgeon," and is therefore going along with it. I would say that there is, perhaps, evidence of the intention of the author, and I take that fact into account; but there is equally strong evidence of what happened to the text so that it took the form it did (we even know where "sea-gudgeon" came from). The change could not be a printer's error: it could not be a slip of the pen. It is not only (probably) deliberate; the text is singular, in the sense that there is no doubt that "sea-gudgeon" is what Melville actually inscribed. In such a case there is no obvious reason to print anything else than "sea-gudgeon."

In the case of another inaccurate quotation, however, Tanselle shows himself (I would say) dangerously ready to prioritize what he believes to be intentional authorial emendation. He makes a significant choice in the case of a quotation about Leviathan from *Paradise Lost* which runs, in the first edition of *Moby-Dick:* "and at his gills / Draws in, and at his breath spouts out a sea." Milton's text, in every edition upon which Melville is likely to have drawn—including that which he owned—reads (when modernized) "and at his gills / Draws in, and at his trunk spouts out a sea."[2] Tanselle considers that the word "breath" is probably a simple misquotation, or Melville's misreading of his own notes; he argues that divergences in quotations are quite likely to be "misreadings of handwriting or slips in copying," and concludes that

> it is difficult to see why Melville (or anyone else) would wish to make them intentionally. . . . Slips of this kind, which probably occurred in the process of transmission from authorial manuscript to printed book, call for emendation by the critical editor. ("External" 7)

That same policy (and that exact emendation) are adopted in the Northwestern-Newberry edition: "trunk" is printed, and the emendation (along with a number of others) explained as follows:

> In each case the correct word is one that might have looked like the erroneous one in Melville's handwriting, and there is no reason to

suppose in these instances that Melville was purposely altering his extract; it seems proper, therefore, to make the emendations.[3]

Tanselle may, of course, be right: "breath" for "trunk" may be an error. Human beings can make the most astonishing errors. I once discovered a compositor altering my word "autumn" to the word "summer" in typesetting (something which, if I had come across it when editing Lawrence, I would have argued strenuously for as proof of authorial emendation). And it is true that someone—almost certainly Melville—did correct some errors in the "Extracts" when the English edition of the novel was being prepared. Tanselle uses this as an argument that editorial emendation, pursuing the goal of authorial intention, should be used to carry the process still further ("External" 7–8; see also Melville 794–95).

Although extraordinary mistakes are possible, it is still hard to imagine how the handwriting which had copied the word "trunk" might later be misread as the word "breath." But that is not really the point. Tanselle is actually operating a very constricted version of human intentionality when he says, of what he regards as clear slips, that "it is difficult to see why Melville (or anyone else) would wish to make them intentionally." On the contrary, I find it very easy indeed to imagine how in this case "trunk" might carry associations both of elephants (the wrong kind of Leviathans) and of luggage: and I can easily imagine how a quick mind, aware of the potential fleeting ambiguities available to other quick minds, might have introduced a small change. All that Tanselle seems (unconsciously) to be demonstrating is that he finds "trunk" a simple and unambiguous reading. Some readers of this essay will doubtless side with him in his puzzlement over why anyone might *intentionally* have made the change from "trunk" to "breath." Other readers—I confess I believe they will be in the majority—will see the change as a potential clarification.

But all we can be certain of—so far as intention goes—is that Melville probably made the change. The argument from his work on the English edition is, unfortunately for Tanselle, as broad as it is long. The fact that Melville corrected some errors in the English edition, but not others, is not only evidence that he wanted his quotations correct; it is equally strong evidence that, where he did *not* correct his quotations, he effectively signalled his preference for the technically incorrect form in which they appeared: so an editor pursuing authorial "intention" should certainly not alter them.

I suggest, however, that we should not even be trying to argue whether alterations like "trunk" to "breath" were intentional or not. One point of view (my own) believes that the alteration could well have been intentional: another (Tanselle's) is confident that it could not have been. These are not good grounds upon which to edit our texts. The important thing in such a case, surely, is to recognize that although "breath" may certainly be unintentional, a mere error for "trunk," it is at least equally likely *not* to be an error. And in this useful test case, I would argue that the scholarly editor who believes in distinguishing authorial intention (or the lack of it) is up against a brick wall. The editor's duty, I suggest, is neither to emend "breath" on the grounds that it is an unintentional error, nor to preserve it because it is an intentional clarification, but to respect a prob-lematic documentary text which at this point remains opaque: where in-tention cannot easily be distinguished. If we allow the text that status— which we may be able to do, if we are producing an academic edition of the novel complete with apparatus and annotations, then in practice this will mean not emending but annotating the passage. In this case (to use Tanselle's definitions), the text (or texts) of the documents do not lead via intelligent editorial emendation to the text of the work: the latter must simply consist of the text of the documents, unemended.

Tanselle's confidence is disquieting, in this example and others, about what he thinks he can distinguish as authorial intention. He is not taking into account the possibility of a very wide range of human behavior pat-terns. He is also (incidentally) attempting to define the "intentional" as the product of a single act of will: when we are increasingly aware that inten-tions are normally complex concurrences of much less easily defined pat-terns of behavior. But his arguments as he has deployed them over the years—clear and wide-ranging, drawing upon a vast repertoire of examples—demonstrate his unshakable belief that the editor's job is to discover (and preserve) the intention of the author. He continues to believe that the editor should progress from the texts of documents, via a knowl-edge of the author's intentions, to the ideal edited text of the work. And although Tanselle is sometimes vastly sophisticated in his judgment of "intention" (he is alert, for example, to what conventions operate in the use of quotations at different periods of human history, and thus to what might or might not properly count as intentional), he is also committed to a belief in the recovery of an understanding of authorial intention by the editor working forward from the text of documents to the ideal text of the work.

It can come as no surprise, therefore, that he should attempt to make an absolute distinction between what he calls *transcription* of the texts of documents, on the one hand, and *editing* on the other. Editing, to him, involves the identification of intention: transcription does not. He tells us that we are woolly-minded (or worse) if we refuse to accept this distinction.

> The essential prerequisite to clear thinking on the matter is recognizing the difference between a transcription, in which the editor must faithfully reproduce the errors of a particular document, and a critical text, in which the editor is not bound to retain a factual error simply because it is present in an authoritative document. . . . The two approaches are distinct, and neither can be carried out competently if considerations applicable to one are allowed to intrude into the other. Errors of external fact often seem to provide the text cases for determining how well an editor has learned that lesson. ("External" 34)

Tanselle's distinction is made with characteristic clarity and dogmatism, but belongs to that species of human lawmaking which seeks prescriptive solutions to problems that are hardly ever clear cut. It is also primarily an argument for giving an editor power and rights over the texts of his documents, so as to turn them (according to his own rules) into the texts of works. We have seen this power used and, I would argue, abused in the case of the Milton quotation. The clear distinction Tanselle seeks to make between editorial approaches to documents and to editions is obviously likely to produce such results.

If we choose *not* to correct an error of history or quotation in a text, we may in fact be doing any one of a number of things. We may be attempting as editors to preserve what Tanselle calls the "intended features of a literary work" (he himself adjusted that phrase to read "the intended features of an author's work" when he reprinted it in his *Selected Studies in Bibliography* [357], presumably to play down the bizarre concept of a work itself having an intention). This means printing what we may believe and can argue that an author intended to inscribe, however erroneous it may have been when compared to the facts or the vocabulary of the external world. Sometimes, there is nothing else we can do: or we might start to consider *Finnegans Wake* simply a badly proofread book.

But another way of putting this point—with which Tanselle would certainly not agree—is that we may choose to preserve in our editions errors of fact and history present in the texts of our documents not just because they are unavoidable features of those documentary texts, and cannot be emended, but because the matter of emendation simply does not arise: we simply do not know what authorial intention might be.

In, for example, the Cambridge University Press edition of Lawrence's novel *The Rainbow*, Ursula Brangwen is seen standing outside Ilkeston station, waiting at the tram terminus for a tram to take her up the hill to Bath Street (342). The fictional date is, without question, 1900, given the rich and careful chronology Lawrence has invented for the novel. Ilkeston station existed where the novel says it did: the tram terminus was indeed outside it: but that particular tram route up to Bath Street did not open until 1903, giving Ursula an unconscionably long wait for her tram (see explanatory note on 342:6, 526).

Significantly, without even considering Tanselle's idea of intention, we can all agree that this divergence from external fact must be preserved in the text of the work: it is what the texts of the surviving documents say, and we are, in a dramatic way, obliged to reproduce them literally. There is no conceivable way of emending the text that could deal with the case. The chronology of the novel cannot be emended; and it is equally obvious that an editor could not rewrite the sentence so that Ursula got herself to Bath Street on foot (the passage goes on to describe her reaction to her tram journey).

All that is perfectly plain, without any consideration of Lawrence's intention at all. His intention was (presumably) for Ursula to catch a tram up to Bath Street in Ilkeston in 1900. But what *kind* of intention that may have been is utterly unclear. We cannot tell whether he *knew* he was being historically inaccurate or whether he thought he was right or whether he did not much care, either way. I am, for example, not at all sure whether, from the perspective of the spring of 1915 (when he actually wrote this passage), Lawrence had any way of knowing the exact year of the starting of a tram service which he himself would have had no occasion to use before 1904.

The novel's CUP editor, Mark Kinkead-Weekes, says however that the error was "deliberate."[4] I suspect that such an assertion of an error's intentionality is offered as a logical justification for preserving a piece of text which could not actually have been dealt with in any other way. Editors, in our culture, prefer not to admit that they are in the hands of fate, fortune, and the vagaries of surviving documents. But in this case we do not need the support offered by a belief that we can ascertain Lawrence's intention in order to know what to do. I would argue that in such cases (which are many) it is *not* to the author's intention that as editors we respond but to the ineluctable nature of a piece of documentary text.

Another example. The CUP edition of Lawrence's *Movements in European History*, edited by Philip Crumpton, does not correct the numerous historical errors in the book. For instance, Lawrence remarks that "The great St. Bernard once sailed down the beautiful lake of Lucerne without even glancing around him, his mind so bent on his own affairs" (146). The episode actually happened on Lake Geneva; "Lucerne," however, is there in the first surviving text. What Lawrence's intention was, however, is more than slightly problematic. We can, in this case, be certain about the source of the mistake: he took the reference from a history book (Kenneth Bell's *Mediaeval Europe*) which made the same error.

Now it might be argued that Lawrence could not have intended to reproduce (or for us to read) a mistake; if he had known that Bell was wrong, he would not have reproduced the error. Tanselle would presumably print "Geneva." And yet—we should not be quite so quick to emend. Lawrence himself took a steamer down Lake Lucerne in September 1913, on his way back to Italy; and though he came within thirty miles of Lake Geneva in June 1914, his route took him away from it, and he never saw it. But Lucerne caught his attention in a very particular way: "irritating as ever—like the wrapper round milk chocolate," he called it in *Twilight in Italy* (271). He had good reason to enjoy and to reproduce Bell's factual error: St. Bernard had no eye for the ostentatiously or even the grandiosely picturesque.

If we emended the text, we would lose the particular point which Lucerne came to have in Lawrence's version of the world. We would, furthermore, also lose a significant link with *Lady Chatterley's Lover*, where Constance travels through Switzerland and muses "I'm like Saint Bernard, who could sail down the Lake of Lucerne without ever noticing that there were even mountains and green water" (255). As with *The Rainbow*, it would not be possible to emend the "error" in the novel: the editor would have to explain why Constance's train diverts to Geneva *en route* to Venice. But this later reference to Lucerne confirms that "Lucerne" was part of a complex of meaning in Lawrence's writing, where "Geneva" simply was not; and such created meanings are arguably far more significant than historical errors. Both texts with Lucerne in them are richer with meaning than they would be without: even though what they reproduce is not fact and not history. The editor who believes in the primacy of "intention" would, however, want to correct both, and certainly would correct the history book. Again, Lawrence remarks that Russia "invaded Poland in 1791" (216): the invasion took place in 1792. The error (suggests the Cambridge editor) may have been a result of Lawrence's misinterpretation of one of his authorities (see Explanatory note at 216:27, 305). What his intention may have been, however, is thoroughly problematic. He may have intended to agree with his authority; he may have believed for reasons we do not know about that 1791 was right; he may even have meant to write 1792 and made a slip. But 1791 was what he undoubtedly wrote: and that fact is more significant than any intention we are ingenious enough to credit him with.

Tanselle is absolutely right in one respect, however. What we actually *do* in such cases will reveal what we think the nature and function of our edition is. Are we editing a book of historical facts? Are we editing a work by Lawrence in which errors of fact and history are significant in demonstrating an author's mental and literary predilections—and are (thus) more significant than the so-called facts are?

Clearly, our editorial choices in such cases are directly linked to the role of the edition we are creating. The important thing to say is that Tanselle's arguments show him seeking to transform the edited text into a certain kind of (ideally authorially but certainly editorially controlled) domain. He sees the editor as the author's collaborator in seeking out and determining intentions that lie behind words: and he wishes to reduce the significance of the text of the document by describing a belief in its peculiar integrity and authority as concealing a desire to "transcribe" it, not to edit it. In that way, he prioritizes the role of the careful editor over and above not only that of the frequently careless author but also over the primitive and unreformed text. The editor, so to speak, colonizes the unpromising domain of the text and, by scrupulous intervention, brings it up to the standards of his own editorial culture. Once colonized, it is never allowed to revert to its bad old ways. But it is never granted self-rule: it remains under the control of the colonizing power.

III

To step outside Lawrence and external fact for a moment, and to broaden the argument, how would Tanselle cope with the spelling of the name "Evens" in Edward Bond's play *The Sea*? The pronunciation puzzled me, so—as I was directing a production of the play—I wrote to Bond to ask him how one should say it. His reply staggered me: "Evens is the normal Evans. Its just that Im not very good at spelling and no one pointed it out to me in time. So it got printed" (Bond to Worthen, 1 March 1980). In such a case, we happen to "know" what the authorial intention was: and I imagine that Tanselle would be happy that the intended spelling "Evans" could be so unquestionably established. He would presumably print that spelling if he were creating an edition of the play.

The pronunciation of the name on stage (the problem I had in mind when I wrote to Bond) is perhaps settled: there can really only be one standard pronunciation of the name in the course of a performance, though of course individual characters may pronounce a name in their own way: and some characters might conceivably wish to say "Evens" rather than "Evans." I would, however, argue for the retention of "Evens" as the spelling in an edited text of the play. There are layers of ambiguity in that name which are simply not present in "Evans": the only evidence against the spelling "Evens" (so far as I know) is a postcard written seven years after the play had first been produced, and even longer after it had been written. An author may at some stage wish to remove an ambiguity which has become a significant part of his text: and has, of course, every right to attempt to do so. If the play were reprinted under Bond's guidance (something which has not yet happened), it might perhaps appear with the spelling "Evans" in place: though the spelling was not changed when Methuen reprinted the play with some authorial alterations in their second volume of Bond's collected plays.

A new edition with the spelling "Evans" would inevitably become a new and significant documentary text. But only one of the play's texts. Works have historical dimensions as well as local manifestations in the forms of documents; and *The Sea* belongs to the moment of history at which it first appeared as well as to the present moment in which it is read, as much as it does to its author—an author who might later want to change it. In history, as well as in the documents, the name is "Evens" as well as "Evans": the "error" cannot simply be obliterated, even if an author tries to obliterate it. Texts, or parts of texts, regularly evade their authors' intentions for them. Any informed discussion of Dickens's novel *Great Expectations* will not only take into account the original ending of the novel, which the author (following the protests of Bulwer-Lytton) rejected: criticism may well choose to treat the rejected ending as "the" ending. Even an editor of the novel might conceivably restore the original ending and relegate the revision to an explanatory note: or at least print both endings side by side, giving priority to neither. All we can say is that Dickens's behavior was complex and his intention not easily articulated when he agreed to alter his ending: and that the work's text of the ending is as a result multiple, not single. We can certainly not simply assert that what finally appeared in *All the Year Round* was what Dickens intended, and that what had appeared in the proofs (as recorded by John Forster) was a superseded intention.[5]

   T. S. Eliot was relieved that the original (and considerably longer) manuscript of *The Waste Land* had disappeared. He did not want readers inquiring into his deletions: rumors of the manuscript's reemergence are reported to have "depressed" him. In fact, the poem surfaced in 1969, and has been edited (by Eliot's widow) in a facsimile edition with a beautifully readable transcript: thereby indicating that the reader's job is (now) to examine the deletions at least as carefully as the undeleted passages.[6] What in this case we can rightly see as an author's intended text has been joined and in some ways superseded by the publication of an unintended text in the shape of the facsimile. I think, too, of the republication against its author's wishes of W. H. Auden's poem "Spain," which for many years he had forbidden.[7] Texts have the habit of taking on another life than that in which they are controlled by their authors' intentions for them. To allow them that life is by no means the same as to wish only to transcribe them in certain particular historical manifestations; it is a reflection of their peculiar and complex nature—a nature I think Tanselle seeks to play down.

IV

   Above all, however we employ it, our policy of emendation or non-emendation—as Tanselle makes very clear—necessarily brings up the problem of what the edition is *for*. Is it attempting a diplomatic transcript of a manuscript or (in the case of *Moby-Dick*) a printed text, so that the reader may treat the edition as in effect providing a facsimile of one or more documents? Is it attempting to reproduce what are arguably its author's intentions, to create an ideal text of the work? Is it treating the text as an entity lying beyond any understanding we can have of the intentional role of its author—so that we may well produce an eclectic text, never seen, never even intended by an author but making sense of the different states of the various documents, and offering editorially a logical consequence of the text's developments and vicissitudes? And, above all, what *kind* of compromise between those various positions should an edition try to reach?

An appropriate answer to this question will, very often, be found not in a rehearsal of editorial principles but by understanding the kind of market for which the edition is designed. If Lawrence's *Movements in European History* were being produced by Cambridge University Press for use in schools, it would clearly be desirable for the historical record to be set straight and the numerous errors in the text corrected: St. Bernard should sail down Lake Geneva: 1791 should become 1792 in the account of the Russian invasion of Poland. We should not countenance errors being passed on in an edited text to those likely to be influenced for the worse by them. But as the book has been edited as one of the Works of Lawrence in the CUP edition, there is an equally strong argument for leaving "Lucerne" and "1791" uncorrected. Tanselle would doubtless describe such a text as the text only of a document, and would call me a mere transcriber for promoting it. But the text of the edited work is in this case what the author certainly wrote: not only does it reveal Lawrence's use (and misuse) of his sources and not only does it demonstrate his particular interests and concerns as well as his capacity for inaccuracy, but—above all—it is the text of the work in which his intentions are simple, problematic, and ultimately (I would say) unrecoverable.

I would, however, suggest that we might consider printing that text only if the edition were an appropriate place to do so. An edition that appeals to a specialist market might well produce a text with clear and obvious errors in it, warts and all; such an edition might in some cases take the form of a photographic facsimile, or—in particular—a grouping of facsimiles, which may be an exceptionally good way for an editor to transcribe a text faithfully. Philip Gaskell indeed once argued for this approach as a serious editorial possibility for an edition of *Ulysses* (237–38, 240–43). The edition of *Movements of European History* by Philip Crumpton did not correct factual and historical errors but explained them in its explanatory notes. A text designed for a popular market and for easy reading—let alone one produced for school use—might well, however, ensure that its readers are not troubled by things like apparent errors (coupled with necessary explanatory notes) and editorial explanations. A popular edition might well tidy up things which in more specialist editions will be left as they are but explained. An acting edition of *The Sea* might spell the name "Evans" throughout: a scholarly edition (with annotations) could spell it "Evens." All the different texts—the academic, the popular, the playscript, and the school textbook—would have been edited; all would have good reasons for existing in the form in which they did; and none of them would be "better" than the others, as they would serve different functions, different sectors of the market, and different users.

v

The problem may again be neatly focused by an example (once more of external fact) taken from a CUP edition. What should we do in our printed texts—which even in the case of scholarly editions will rarely be multiple—about the Italian that Lawrence's 1916 self-typed typescript provides for Hermione in *Women in Love*? There are numerous errors. A striking example is Hermione looking at the cat "Mino" and saying "Ti imparano fare brutte cose, brutte cose——".[8] She obviously wishes to say "They are teaching you to do bad things, bad things," but "imparano" means "learning": she needed to say "insegnano."

The commercial publisher—and the printer working for the commercial publisher—would probably have no doubt about their attitude to the problem, if their attention were drawn to it. They would correct "imparano" to "insegnano": the error is palpable. Lawrence (it may further be argued) could not have intended to print or us to read incorrect Italian, any more than he would have intended to write incorrect German to his mother-in-law (his wife Frieda on at least one occasion altered his German when an error—or a Freudian slip—meant that he was actually being rude [see Lawrence, *Letters V* 62–63]). No printer would willfully print a foreign word inaccurately, any more than he would willfully misspell an English word or use a word that was a clear mistake for another one.

The academic publisher will, however, have more of a problem. It could certainly be argued that "imparano" cannot have been "intentional," and many editors would be unhappy about producing a text that—if unemended at that point—might appear to have been carelessly edited. It could also be fairly argued, however, that Hermione's Italian is incorrect not because of Lawrence's ignorance but because of her ignorance: that her pretentiousness is revealed to us when she commits the classic howler of confusing "learn" and "teach" while pretending to speak Italian like a native.

That may be true. In the nature of the case, however, it is impossible to tell whether "imparano" is Lawrence's or Hermione's error; both cases may be argued with equal vigor. There is, *pace* Tanselle, no way of establishing authorial intention—except insofar as we know what it was that

Lawrence actually *typed:* "imparano." I would suggest that, in such a case, we should accept that the text of the document is, as it were, impenetrable: it is unavailable for emendation: the editor's hands are tied: and in the scholarly edition, "imparano" should be printed, with an explanatory note. (An edition of the novel designed for sale in Italian-speaking countries might, however, well alter the word to "insegnano.")

The CUP Edition editors and the Editorial Board have necessarily considered many such cases. Fifteen years ago the Editorial Board would, I believe, have had no doubt that such errors should be corrected; the CUP text was appearing in a commercial form as well as in an academic one, and (it was hoped) it would also be a commercial proposition. The CUP Board in 1985, however, accepted that the error "imparano" should remain uncorrected: because the Edition had found itself (for one reason and another) selling almost entirely at the academic end of the market. CUP has abandoned the idea of producing a paperback of each and every one of its Lawrence editions—something that made at least an attempt to appeal to another market sector. The standard hardback edition will only appeal to, and be bought by, specialists and specialist libraries: and this has arguably changed the nature of the Edition.

We should see editions such as those in which Tanselle believes, too, not as the ideal editions of works but also as *local* editions, appropriate to a particular sector of the market: appropriate to those capable of dealing with the work of the academic editor, and those able to understand the vagaries of documents, texts, and mere transcripts. One might, unkindly, think of them as university library editions: not as editions that should take over and dominate the marketplace. Tanselle, however, sees texts edited according to his principles as single embodiments of principle and skill that can channel a diverse flow of documents into the controlled flow of a great cultural river: he thinks of culture as something supported (and improved) by its classic, edited texts. It is worth pointing out that even the CUP Lawrence Edition is doing a rather different—and particularly difficult thing—compared with (say) the Northwestern-Newberry *Moby-Dick,* of which Tanselle is one of the editors. The CUP Lawrence has chosen to produce texts that (as expensive hardbacks) sell to the tiny academic sector of the market—and so may (in theory) be as idiosyncratic and as heavily annotated as they choose—but that also have to appeal to the American market (words used in a different sense in North America are singled out for special treatment in the Explanatory notes): and that also appear in an unannotated form in the purely commercial market. Grafton and Viking have in the past produced commercial volumes using the CUP text. As of 1995, there is also a Penguin student edition of many of the CUP Lawrence texts, appealing to yet another kind of market and arguably necessitating still other editing strategies. Every significant textual decision has been reconsidered by the Penguin editors; and some (for example, the reading of *The Trespasser* at 217:4, where "scared" was chosen by the Cambridge editor but "seared" is the reading of the Penguin editor) has been changed.

VI

Everyone concerned with the editing of Lawrence should read Tanselle's essays, especially "External Fact as an Editorial Problem"; but they should also judge whether they can accept the arguments in those essays about the recovery of authorial intention as the main basis for editorial judgment. I am arguing neither for textual conservatism nor for editorial passivity; but there are times when a text manifests such a complexity of possible intentions that it is in essence impenetrable—so that to attempt an entry into it, by asserting that its author's solitary intention might be recovered in order to emend it, would be to impose one's judgment upon it in an unhelpful way: to colonize and subjugate it, to use my earlier metaphor. Editorial emendations, it must be said, frequently show editors more concerned with being editors than with considering the problematic nature of their enterprise, or with discovering appropriate strategies for the actual production of texts that different kinds of readers use.

NOTES

1. See Tanselle, *Selected Studies;* see too his *Textual Criticism since Greg: A Chronicle, 1950–1985* (Charlottesville: U of Virginia, 1987) and *A Rationale of Textual Criticism* (Philadelphia: U of Pennsylvania P, 1989).
2. *The Poetical Works of John Milton,* ed. Helen Darbishire (London: Oxford UP, 1958), 158: "and at his Gilles / Draws in, and at his Trunck spouts out a Sea" (*Paradise Lost,* bk. vii, ll. 415–16). Melville owned the Hilliard, Gray edition of the *Poetical Works* (Boston, 1836).
3. See Melville, *Moby-Dick* xx, 795.
4. See Explanatory note at 342:6, 526: "the Ilkeston tram service did not begin until 1903, but DHL would have known this very well, so the licence is deliberate."
5. See John Forster, *The Life of Charles Dickens* (London: Chapman, 1872–74),

335–36. See too *Great Expectations,* ed. Angus Calder (Harmondsworth: Penguin, 1965), 494–96; and Edwin M. Eigner, "Bulwer-Lytton and the Changed Ending of *Great Expectations.*" *Nineteenth Century Fiction* 25 (1970–71): 104–8.
6. Peter Ackroyd, *T. S. Eliot* (London: Sphere, 1985), 324; T. S. Eliot, *The Waste Land: A Facsimile and Transcript of the Original Drafts Including the Annotations of Ezra Pound,* ed. Valerie Eliot (London: Faber, 1971).
7. Auden's "Spain" reappeared in Robin Skelton's anthology *Poetry of the Thirties* (Harmondsworth: Penguin, 1964), 133–36. Skelton noted: "I have agreed to make it absolutely clear that 'Mr W. H. Auden considers these five poems to be absolute trash which he is ashamed to have written.' I am most grateful to Mr Auden for putting the needs of this anthology before his own personal wishes in this manner" (41).
8. Corrected *TS* (University of Texas), Roberts E441d, 367; *Women in Love* 300 (line 35).

WORKS CITED

Bell, Kenneth. *Mediaeval Europe.* Oxford: Clarendon P, 1911.
Bond, Edward. *Plays: Two.* London: Methuen, 1978.
Gaskell, Philip. *From Writer to Reader.* Oxford: Oxford UP, 1978.
Lawrence, D. H. *The Trespasser.* Ed. John Turner. London: Penguin, 1994.
———. *Twilight in Italy.* London: Duckworth, 1916.
Melville, Herman. *Moby-Dick, or, The Whale.* Vol. 6. *The Writings of Herman Melville.* Ed. Harrison Hayford, Hershel Parker, and G. Thomas Tanselle. Evanston and Chicago: Northwestern UP and the Newberry Library, 1988.
Roberts, Warren. *A Bibliography of D. H. Lawrence.* 2d ed. Cambridge: Cambridge UP, 1982.
Tanselle, G. Thomas. "External Fact as an Editorial Problem." *Studies in Bibliography* 32 (1979): [1]–47.
———. *Selected Studies in Bibliography.* Charlottesville: U of Virginia P, 1979.
———. "Textual Criticism and Deconstruction." *Studies in Bibliography* 43 (1990): [1]–33.

Some Theoretical Issues Raised by Editing *Sons and Lovers*

Helen Baron

I *have* patiently and laboriously constructed that novel. (19 November 1912)

—*Letters I* 478

I sit in sadness and grief after your letter. I daren't say anything. All right, take out what you think necessary—I suppose I shall see what you've done when the proofs come, at any rate. (1 December 1912)

—*Letters I* 481

Edward Garnett, literary adviser to the publishing firm Duckworth, insisted on crossing out 10 percent of the *Sons and Lovers* manuscript before he would accept it for publication. Was Lawrence grateful to Garnett or did he submit to an ultimatum? Should a modern edition of the novel contain the whole text of Lawrence's final manuscript or only Garnett's 90 percent?

This is the most important theoretical question presented to an editor of *Sons and Lovers,* but it is not the only one. If an editor decides to accept the full manuscript text, should he/she then incorporate into that text the proof revisions that Lawrence made to the edited text? Are there any circumstances in which an editor ought to suppress proof revisions? On the other hand, if an editor decides to accept Garnett's 90 percent of the text, together with Lawrence's proof revisions, should he/she take the first edition as base-text, together with its four to five thousand alterations to Lawrence's punctuation, which pervasively alter his meaning, tones, and nuances?

59

This first step is not quite a stark choice between the manuscript (*MS*) and the first edition (*E1*); there are four main choices:

1. 100% *MS* text, *MS* punctuation.
2. 100% *MS* text, *MS* punctuation, proof revisions.
3. *E1* text, *MS* punctuation.
4. *E1* text, *E1* punctuation.

What are the theoretical arguments that help an editor decide amongst these options? Clearly there would be little support at the present time for an editor who wanted to accept some of the passages crossed out by Garnett and reject others on critical grounds. Suspicion of and hostility to such "eclecticism" has been one of the main driving forces behind the move in this century to erect principles, tenets, agreed methods of procedure. A general assumption exists that while the reading public would like the corrupt reprint of a modern author replaced by a "correct" text, they do not want to be left to reconstruct it themselves from a comprehensive so-called variorum edition, but at the same time they certainly do not want *X*'s Lawrence or *Y*'s Lawrence. Thus there is an implicit suspicion of editors, a fear that they wish to give the public *their* Lawrence and not *the* Lawrence. Meanwhile the editors labor for years, hoping to be of service to their author, knowing that there can never to an absolute standard of correctness or certainty, but endeavoring always to make the best judgments in the circumstances.

What matters of principle enable editors to avoid this opprobrium and yet to make these difficult decisions?

Eclecticism has been effectively disgraced. An editor may not decide to affirm or reject Garnett's cuts on the grounds that it is a "better" novel without or with the passages in question, because "better" means in effect "preferred by me" on aesthetic, critical, or moral grounds.

The long reaction this century against eclecticism has taken two main directions, the "best text" theory denounced by Greg (*Art and Error* 18–19, 21), and the "rationale of copy-text" propounded by him. According to the first, an editor should choose the best—most final or least corrupt— surviving document as copy-text and print a diplomatic transcript of that with manifest errors tidied up but with variants from other documents confined to an apparatus. According to the latter theory, an editor should choose the earliest of the finished states of a work for his copy-text, as representing most faithfully the author's punctuation, and reproduce that, edited to incorporate any substantive variants from later states of the text that can be argued to be authorial revisions, on the grounds that this will more accurately represent the text the author intended to produce.

A further view has emerged, in reaction to the emphasis on authorial intentions, that after publication or after decades as established classics, the works have entered the public domain, they have become in some sense the public property of the author's society, and therefore his "intentions" no longer count. In the case of *Sons and Lovers,* this view would tend to lead to a tidied-up transcript of the first edition. It is in effect a straightforward argument that Duckworth's first edition *is Sons and Lovers* as it has been known and read for nearly a century. That text has been established by historical fact, and for an editor to intrude gobbets of material into it that have never been part of it would be anachronistic and spurious.

While this position conveniently cuts the Gordian knot of theoretical complexity, there are several important counterarguments to it, of which, in my view, the chief one is that some authors have waited several centuries for the texts, and indeed in some cases the *canon,* of their works to be established. A second counterargument is that the decision to reprint the first edition has the effect of tying an editor's hands from ever reversing the manifestly antiquated censorship of Lawrence's text, made progressively by Garnett on the manuscript and proofs. However, for those readers to whom the view is persuasive, I would like to take some space to illustrate what has not generally been appreciated: the extent to which the repunctuation of Lawrence's prose in *E1* produces a different meaning from Lawrence's own punctuation of the same words in *MS.* This is not a trivial consideration: it must be emphasized that the compositors altered Lawrence's punctuation on average once every four lines.

THE PRINTED REPUNCTUATION OF LAWRENCE'S PROSE

One of the most striking examples comes from a dialogue between Paul and Miriam in chapter 12, in which they compare Clara's failed marriage with Mrs. Morel's, and Paul tries to describe the "big and intense" passionate foundation he thinks a marriage needs if it is to succeed. Miriam's perception of what Paul means is rendered thus in print:

> Miriam pondered this. She saw what he was seeking—a sort of baptism of fire in passion, it seemed to her. She realized that he would

never be satisfied till he had it. Perhaps it was essential to him, as to some men, to sow wild oats. . . . (Ch. 12, "Passion," *E1* 318)

In Lawrence's manuscript the last sentence here reads:

Perhaps it was essential to him—as to some men to sow wild oats. (*MS* 452)

As Lawrence wrote the sentence, Paul's ideal of passionate experience is placed by the dash in a *distinct qualitative contrast* to "sowing wild oats," but as it was printed, the two have become equivalent, even identical.

This example of house-styling shows vividly how the mere replacement of a dash with commas can make the words mean the opposite of what was intended. How is it possible for such small changes to have such a drastic effect on the meaning? It is because Lawrence's use of syntax was significantly different from current orthodoxy: his meaning was not impregnably embedded in his sentence structure but depended peculiarly on his punctuation.

For example, he used dashes a great deal in speech to create the impression of a character thinking out loud, to indicate hesitation, uncertainty, sudden changes of direction or subject matter, inability to complete a thought, and so on. The printers used dashes according to a quite different principle: strictly for parenthesis. Therefore they removed many of Lawrence's dashes and inserted many where he had not used them. By replacing a dash at the end of speech with a full stop, the printers made Lawrence's characters often appear more confident and assertive than they seem in *MS*. In addition, the printers introduced a large number of exclamation marks, making the characters in effect more emphatic, even more strident, than they appear to have been in Lawrence's conception.

Another of his regular techniques for nuancing conversation was so unconventional that even some modern editors have been tempted to mistake it for an error. He frequently omitted the question mark from a speech which he described as a question ("he asked"), while at the same time ending other speeches with a question mark where the accompanying verb was not "he asked" but "he said." Invariably these alleged errors were tidied up by the compositors, but with a resultant alteration of the implied tones of voice.

Lawrence also broke with convention when he used "And" or "But" to begin sentences. It was not a case of careless writing but a deliberate method of comparison, which he exploited in order to organize the structure of a paragraph and to produce a kind of argumentation that was not within the conventional rhetorical mode. Contemporary house-styling, however, required that sentences should not begin with conjunctions, and such sentences were often joined to those preceding them.

Finally, the other major difference in practice, with a more subtle effect on Lawrence's prose, was that he made widespread use of commas but was sparing of colons and semicolons, whereas the compositors frequently changed his commas to semicolons. This seems to me to reveal a fundamental structure of his prose: that it was paratactic rather than syntactic.

THE EFFECT ON THE READER: A COMPARISON OF PASSAGES

The first proofs printed directly from the manuscript were galley proofs, a set of which was corrected and revised by Lawrence. Only a very few of these survive,[1] but those that do, fortunately, came from the set that Lawrence revised, and so they bear his handwritten alterations, as well as some made by the printer's reader and by Edward Garnett—who went through the proofs before sending them on to Lawrence and made small censoring excisions. The surviving galley proofs are equivalent approximately to the first edition pages 359–68 and 401–23, that is, the last chapter and parts of the two previous chapters.

The first galley begins a quarter of the way through chapter 13, "Baxter Dawes," describing Paul's impersonal treatment of Clara at work despite her passionate preoccupation with him. Lawrence had written:

> It maddened her to hear his mechanical voice giving orders about the work. She wanted to break through the sham of it, smash the trivial coating of business which covered him with hardness, get at the man again. But she was afraid, and before she could feel one touch of his warmth, he was gone, and she ached again. (*MS* 486; *E1* 353)

The compositor, Moore, joined the second and third sentences with a semicolon ("man again; but she was afraid") and removed the comma after "warmth." Neither change distorts the overt meaning, but by contrast they highlight Lawrence's usage. His second and third sentences present the flow and ebb of Clara's urge to caress Paul: the counter-rhythms are suggested by the juxtaposed sentences. Lawrence's comma after "warmth" is not grammatical so much as rhetorical; it has the effect of slowing down the sentence and providing a pause before "he was gone"—almost mimicking a storyteller's cadence. This seems to me a frequent and characteristic feature of Lawrence's prose.

Similarly, Moore removed another comma when, a page later, Clara asked Paul what he would do if he made a lot of money with his painting. Lawrence wrote Paul's reply as follows: "Go somewhere in a pretty house near London, with my mother." The omission of the comma after "London" in the printed texts changes the rhythm and such meaning as depends on that. In the printed version, Paul is repeating a decision he had come to some time before. As Lawrence wrote it, Paul's tone is more thoughtful, and his last three words have a quietly ominous emphasis for Clara.

A few moments after the exchange just quoted, Paul bursts out to Clara—at least he does in manuscript:

> "Don't ask me anything about the future," he said miserably. "I don't know anything.—Be with me now, will you, no matter what it is—."
> And she took him in her arms. (*MS* 487)

When Moore set this, he omitted the dashes but added a question mark:

> . . . "I don't know anything. Be with me now, will you, no matter what it is?" (*E1* 354)

Lawrence's dashes indicate that Paul is not delivering a considered speech but blurting his appeal as a sudden demand not completable in words. By contrast, Moore's changes, including the grammatically correct question mark, make Paul calm and reasonable, more like an E. M. Forster character putting a decent proposal to a friend.

A few lines after this passage Moore *removed* a question mark. Lawrence's manuscript reads:

> After a moment he lifted his head, as if he wanted to speak.
> "Clara?" he said, struggling.
> She caught him passionately to her, pressed his head down on her breast with her hand. She could not bear the suffering in his voice. (Ch. 13, *MS* 487; cf. *E1* 354)

For readers of *E1* and subsequent editions, Paul's utterance appears without a question mark, and therefore "the suffering in his voice" has a different sound. Moore also omitted the comma after "head." Like those after "warmth" and "London" already discussed, this comma had served to slow the pace, but it also seems to me to alter viewpoint. I read Lawrence's text as presenting the movement of Paul's head in terms of Clara's dawning perception of Paul's activity and intention. I read the repunctuated version as describing Paul's intention from *his* point of view. The reason such different interpretations arise, it seems to me, is that the comma, by slowing the movement of the sentence and introducing a pause, would, if read aloud, suggest the idea: "he lifted his head—*it was* as if he wanted to speak." The observer of the action is placed at a distance from it. But without the comma, the grammar would be different. It would then be Paul, the subject of the verb, who controlled the phrase "as if": "Paul did (a) to give the impression he wanted to do (b)."

It would come as no surprise to a teacher of English as a foreign language that such distinct differences in meaning are conveyed in English by slight pauses and shifts of tone. But is there no other way to capture them in print than relying on a little comma? Why did Lawrence not anchor his meaning more tangibly in his sentence structure? He could for example have said something like: "and she realised he wanted to speak." But Lawrence's art-speech did not spell out every nuance: it was remote from the syntax of the essayist, and close to the diction of the poet.

Lawrence's commas are more problematic than his question marks and dashes—and much more frequent. My last two examples show that a considerable amount of subtle meaning can depend on commas.

> She [Clara] was afraid in her soul. He might have anything of her, anything. But she did not want to *know;* she felt she could not bear it; she wanted him to be soothed upon her, soothed. She stood clasping him and caressing him, and he was something unknown to her, something terrible, almost uncanny. She wanted to soothe him into forgetfulness. (*MS* 487)

Lawrence presents Clara as being aware of a set of feelings that more or less constitute an argument: she wants to soothe Paul physically without making any mental effort to understand his problems. The third sentence ("But . . . soothed.") is an important rhetorical unit presenting the paragraph's main antithesis of soothing *in apposition to* understanding or knowledge. This antithesis is taken up in the fourth sentence, with "clasping" and "caressing" (as equivalents for "soothed") set against the idea *not know* repeated in the word "unknown." The antithesis is continued in the fifth sentence, where this time "soothe" is repeated and set against "forgetfulness" as the equivalent of *not know.*

Moore therefore broke up the clarity and unity of Clara's inner debate when he tried to eradicate a sentence beginning with *But:*

> . . . He might have anything of her—anything; but she did not want to *know.* She felt she could not bear it. She wanted him to be soothed upon her—soothed. (*E1* 354)

This new shaping: "He might have anything of her—anything; but she did not want to *know*" introduces the doubt: what precisely did she not want to know? It suggests she did not want to know "what he had of her." It seems to present a woman sacrificing her body to a man's needs but wanting to shut off her mind and not register what was happening to her body. But Lawrence had set "*know*" in apposition to "soothe" to indicate that Clara wanted to respond passionately to Paul's need but did not want to analyze the causes of his misery. Because of the punctuation changes, not only is "*know*" no longer presented in its intended apposition to "soothed," but the emphasis of the supporting italics has become unanchored; and in addition, the italics have then been reinforced with the introduction of dashes. The result is that Clara's tone has altered from somewhat insistently self-persuading, to stridently incoherent and even anxiously repelled—in fact, more like the sexual psychology attributed to Miriam in the novel than to Clara.

A final example follows on in manuscript directly from the previous. Here, some of the punctuation changes damage the overt meaning, and I quote the whole paragraph because it demonstrates the way in which Lawrence's characteristic appositional dialectic depended intimately on his punctuation.

> And soon the struggle went down in his soul, and he forgot. But then Clara was not there for him, only a woman, warm, something he loved and almost worshipped, there in the dark, something wonderful. But it was not Clara. And she submitted to him. The naked hunger and inevitability of his loving her, something strong and blind

and ruthless in its misery, made the hour almost terrible to her. She knew how stark and alone he was. And she felt it was great, that he came to her. And she took him simply, because his need was bigger either than her or him. And her soul was quiet and strong within her. She did this for him in his need, even if he left her. For she loved him. (*MS* 487)

The main points here—all lost in the typesetting—are that after the third sentence, "But it was not Clara," the dialectic switches from Paul's point of view to Clara's, the contrast being introduced with the word "And." In addition, in Clara's part of the paragraph, her perceptions are kept separate. By his use of a sequence of sentences beginning "And," Lawrence contrasts her reasoning and her feeling while keeping them on a par: neither is syntactically subordinated to the other.

But Moore was as tantalized by these sentences beginning "And" as he had been by "But" previously: so he joined the third and fourth sentences: "But it was not Clara, and she submitted to him." This not only erased the antithetical shaping of the paragraph, but it subsumed Clara's submission into the presentation of Paul's viewpoint. Then by running together the next three sentences beginning with "And," and removing a comma after "simply," Moore changed the meaning of Clara's motivation:

She knew how stark and alone he was, and she felt it was great that he came to her; and she took him simply because his need was bigger either than her or him, and her soul was still within her.

(The verbal change from "quiet and strong" to "still" represents an authorial revision on the page proofs.)

Repunctuated, her motivation becomes: "simply [=merely] because his need was bigger . . . and her soul was still," whereas Lawrence had written that "she took him *in a simple manner* because of his need; and *meanwhile* her soul was quiet," the latter being a feeling and not a reason. As a separate sentence, it remained a feeling; joined up, it was subordinated to "because" and became a reason.

Lawrence's use of "And" here to begin sentences appears to be characteristic of his syntactic structure. It is perhaps paradoxical that he *contrasts* the two people with "and" instead of "while" or "but." I interpret this usage as intended to leave the two characters in parallel, related but distinct. It avoids implying any hierarchical ordering according to some value system. Similarly the other "Ands" in this passage present Clara's feelings and thoughts in parallel: their logic resides in their coexistence, it is presented by juxtaposition, instead of by systematization into the logic and subordination of complex grammar.

If viewed as a challenge to the conventional way of ordering prose, Lawrence's apparently wayward punctuation may turn out to be a subversive move: to use juxtaposition as a technique for breaking up the reader's syntactically embedded presuppositions in the hope that the reader will see experience afresh, with new interconnections. This interpretation may not produce instant or universal assent, but I trust that the examples themselves do impress upon the reader the unavoidable fact that the repunctuation of Lawrence's novel was so comprehensive and drastic that in reading the printed text hitherto the general public has not had full access to Lawrence's meaning.

Why did Lawrence not correct the punctuation when he saw the proofs? What was his attitude to punctuation? Very few overt comments are extant, but most of them amount to a shrug of indifference, which is best represented by his humorous Introduction to McDonald's first bibliography of his writings (*Phoenix* 232–35). But he could also protest at mangled publication of his works: "The [poem] 'Violets' is printed all wrong—you see I had no proofs or anything" (*Letters I* 324).

It must be significant that nearly all the punctuation Lawrence did enter on the surviving gallery proofs had been in his manuscript. He made eight interventions, of which three were essential to the meaning, while the others affected rhythm and nuance. These tiny examples appear to show a minute attention to detail on Lawrence's part and a precise concern with his own punctuation. They appear to, until the statistics are considered. The surviving galley proofs amount to 1,630 lines of type and in them there are 437 differences of punctuation from manuscript, slightly more than one every four lines (counting pairs of brackets and inverted commas as one). In none of the passages quoted above did Lawrence correct the compositor's repunctuation of his manuscript.

It may seem to be an indictment of Lawrence that he did not correct the punctuation, but there were many reasons for this. The chief problem was that at this stage in his career he had very little control over the publication of his work. All of his first three novels were cut and censored by his publishers, as well as heavily repunctuated. It is a moot point to what extent he was aware of how much difference the house-styling made to his work. He probably was. He appears to have begun to reverse much of the printer's repunctuation of his first novel, *The White Peacock,* but gradually to have given up the unequal struggle. It would have been a massive labor to attend to the four to five thousand such changes in *Sons and Lovers.* As it was, the pruning and censoring of his manuscript, together with his own habitual urge to revise and improve his texts at the proof stage, gave Lawrence more serious alterations to think about.

Some bibliographers would argue that because Lawrence revised the proofs of his novel and because he corrected some of the errors in punctuation, he in effect or de facto accepted all the rest of the printer's punctuation. The argument runs that because he did not alter the thousands of punctuation changes on the proofs back to his manuscript readings, he endorsed them. But this argument, it seems to me, falls down because it does not take into account either the sheer quantity involved or Lawrence's inflamed irritation that his book was not already in the shops.

GREG THEN?

The demonstrable alteration of Lawrence's meaning by the housestyling of *E1* persuades me that, at the very least, an editor must accept *MS* punctuation. Does this indicate that the most appropriate theory for an editor of *Sons and Lovers* is Greg's: choice of copy-text based on fidelity to author's punctuation?

An important argument against erecting Greg's theory to a universally applicable set of rules is vividly illustrated for me in the citation given by James Thorpe in *Principles of Textual Criticism* (148) of William Butler Yeats's request to his editors and publishers to punctuate his poetry for him: "Do what you will. . . . I write so completely for the ear that I feel helpless when I have to measure pauses by stops and commas."

Theory is a necessary finger in the dam against the horrors of eclecticism, but any theory must exist in a creative tension with the exigencies of circumstance: the character of the author, the work in question, the surviving artifacts.

The apparent flouting of Tennyson's "intentions" by Christopher Ricks received unmitigated praise from one reviewer who believed that, in riding roughshod over Tennyson's desire to suppress early drafts and parallel examples, Ricks satisfies "the present age['s] . . . interest in the processes whereby art comes into existence" (Killham). Such editorial disregard of "intention" on the grounds that Tennyson's work has entered the public domain, is acceptable in the current climate because it errs in the direction of inclusiveness, multiplicity. In the case of *Sons and Lovers*, the "public domain" approach might persuade an editor to publish the first edition text and supply all the deleted *MS* passages in an apparatus.

But the exigencies of circumstance must be taken into account. An essential difference between Lawrence and Tennyson is that Tennyson had more control over the publication of his works than Lawrence had. Individual states of the text do exist that come close to representing Tennyson's intentions. But Lawrence's control over *Sons and Lovers* was in effect removed by Garnett. Or was it? Was their relationship one of mutually acceptable collaboration?

COLLABORATION OR CONSTRAINT?

Lawrence began writing "Paul Morel," which was to become *Sons and Lovers,* in September 1910. He had promised Heinemann his second novel, and had sent a finished draft of what later became *The Trespasser* to Ford Madox Hueffer before forwarding it to Heinemann. But Hueffer's criticisms were so severe that Lawrence decided to send Heinemann "Paul Morel" instead. He struggled to complete a draft of it while working as a teacher in Croydon during the bleak year that followed his mother's death in December 1910; and when he failed, he turned to Jessie Chambers for advice on how to proceed. In a famous judgment she told him to dispense with the fictional elements in his plot, and start the novel again, keeping it "true to life" and incorporating the story of his older brother's life and death (Chambers 192). He agreed, but had barely begun the new task when he fell ill with a serious bout of pneumonia which resulted in his resignation from teaching.

It was while convalescing in December 1911 and January 1912 that he received his first crucial assistance from Edward Garnett, who read the rejected *Trespasser* manuscript, discussed it with Lawrence, made critical notes to guide him in his rewriting, and proposed to offer it to Duckworth for publication. This experience was important to Lawrence: when in July 1912 Heinemann declined to publish the manuscript of "Paul Morel" (which Lawrence had completed at the third attempt and then carefully revised in Germany), Lawrence was enraged, but as soon as he learned of Garnett's interest in the book for Duckworth, he was so encouraged that he volunteered immediately to Garnett: "Anything that wants altering I will do" (4 July 1912) and "I will make what alterations you think advisable. It would be rather nice if you made a few notes again" (8 July 1912;

Letters I 423). Garnett's criticisms on this manuscript addressed not merely wording and detail but larger issues such as authorial stance. Lawrence welcomed them and agreed with them (*Letters I* 426).[2]

At this early stage in his career, Lawrence was grateful for criticism from advisers like Hueffer and Garnett, and from women friends like Louie Burrows and Jessie Chambers. And it is clear that they contributed generously to his rethinking and revising of this novel. However, in my judgment their contributions fall short of what would reasonably be characterized as "collaboration," in the sense of working together on the novel, since it was Lawrence each time who sat alone and produced the pages of manuscript.

Moreover, while Lawrence solicited, appreciated, even depended on this kind of outside help in the process of writing during the early years, he also manifested a rapidly increasing access of confidence as a result of his move to Germany and his contacts with European intellectuals. Compare his letter to Heinemann's reader Walter de la Mare from Eastwood on 13 March 1912, "And this novel—it won't be a *great* success,—wrong sort" (*Letters I* 375), with his description of the same manuscript (*MS3*, revised but not rewritten) from Germany on 10 June 1912, "Now I know it's a good thing, even a bit great. . . . Some Germans who really know a good thing when they see it speak in high praise" (416–17).

Accompanied by continuous conversations and arguments with Frieda—who must have come closer than anyone else to "collaborator" on this novel—Lawrence produced the bulk of his fourth and final manuscript between 7 September and 18 November 1912. He sent it off to Garnett for publication by Duckworth and wrote an impassioned, articulate, and artistically confident letter (with a forceful supporting postscript by Frieda) informing Garnett that the new novel had "form," and a "development—which is slow like growth." He insisted that the novel as he had now completed it was a unified whole as a result of his labor of "pruning it and shaping it and filling it in." It had inner coherence because he had "worked out my theme, like life." Indeed, his claims for it went beyond form, it was "a great tragedy, and I tell you I've written a great book. It's the tragedy of thousands of young men in England" (*Letters I* 476–77).

Lawrence's tones of voice toward Garnett in this letter demonstrate the extent to which Lawrence's confidence in his own creativity and in his artistic purpose had increased as he wrote this last version of his autobiographical novel. Although his account of the plot may not appear to tally perfectly with the *published* version of the novel, Lawrence is defending with passionate conviction the coherence and significance of his manuscript of the whole novel. If his tones are over-insistent in places, it is surely because he realized that for his artistic purposes, Garnett, in his obsession with "form," was dangerously similar to the Hueffer from whom Lawrence had been glad to escape. They shared, against Lawrence, a critical position coherent with the practice of Henry James but consciously based on the practice of French nineteenth-century novelists, and in particular Flaubert.

It is a real question why Garnett did not send the manuscript back to Lawrence with the instruction to shorten it by so much, by a given deadline. But he did not. Certainly he knew Lawrence was eager for publication and desperate for the income; and certainly Lawrence admitted a month *after* Garnett had announced his decision, that he could not have done any more to the novel for at least six months (*Letters I* 501). However, it is evident that Garnett simply decided to cut the manuscript himself, and informed Lawrence in terms that did not brook discussion.

At this point in the history of the creation of *Sons and Lovers*, "collaboration" is not a meaningful concept. Garnett's action bears no comparison with his contributions to Joseph Conrad's early novels (Jefferson 55–70). Nor was his role analogous to that of a theatrical producer who collaborates in the modifying of a play text.[3] Nor is there a viable comparison with the assistance given to T. S. Eliot by Ezra Pound when he typed up, criticized, praised, and revised the heterogeneous and unfinished manuscripts of *The Waste Land,* until, as Eliot explained to John Quinn: "when I say *MSS,* I mean that it is partly *MSS* and partly typescript, with Ezra's and my alterations scrawled all over it" (Eliot xxiii). Pound left the manuscripts of *The Waste Land* in Eliot's hands, having offered his observations upon them as a fellow artist; Garnett worked on Lawrence's finished manuscript without negotiation and then forwarded it direct to the printer.

Historically, Garnett's decision to cut the novel was an ultimatum. Lawrence had no option but to comply. This is clear from Lawrence's reaction: it was not one of welcoming further constructive criticism, but of "sadness and grief."

Garnett was now speaking to Lawrence as a publisher constrained by the current fiction market, which he and Duckworth believed could not support a novel so long and so explicit (Jefferson 150). Such length was not only economically unviable, but readers would object. Indeed, more than one reviewer did object, even to the length of the pruned version. But what is the evaluation of this historical fact in the late twentieth century when length and sexual explicitness are viewed very differently?

Garnett may, on the other hand, have expressed his objections to Lawrence less in commercial terms than in the codes of the prevailing convention as to "form." In the months that followed, Lawrence made revealing remarks about "These damned old stagers" who "want me to have form: that means, they want me to have *their* pernicious ossiferous skin-and-grief form, and I won't" (*Letters I* 492). He went so far as to tell Garnett: "your sympathies are with your own generation, not with mine. I think it is inevitable. You are about the only man who is willing to let a new generation come in. . . . But I don't want to write like Galsworthy nor Ibsen, nor Strindberg nor any of them, *not* even if I could. We have to hate our immediate predecessors, to get free from their authority" (509). It is clear that the subsequent collapse of his relationship with Garnett during the creation of *The Rainbow* was the logical conclusion of his reluctance, indeed refusal, to submit to Garnett's authority and his notion of form, as well as of Lawrence's growing belief that he could now find other publishers.

Other, apparently more adventurous, publishers had been approaching him for a long time. While on his journey from Germany to northern Italy, Lawrence received a letter from Hueffer urging him that Martin Secker, a publisher who was just establishing his business, wanted to make Lawrence an offer for a novel, and Lawrence was very tempted to send him straight away the third manuscript of "Paul Morel" (*Letters I* 434). But it was the problem of "a bird in the hand," and Lawrence hastened to apologize to Garnett for the suggestion: "Don't be cross with me about Secker. I know you don't care much for the Paul Morel novel, that's why I thought you'd perhaps be glad to be rid of it" (*Letters I* 439–40). However, in the very postcard (1 December 1912) on which he responded to Garnett's decision to cut *Sons and Lovers,* Lawrence warned: "D[uck-worth']s terms are quite gorgeous—But I'm so afraid you'll repress me once more, I daren't say anything. Still another man wrote this morning that one of the most enterprising of the younger publishers wants the next novel I can let him have, at very satisfactory terms.—They comfort me after your wigging" (482). This appears to have been the literary agent Curtis Brown (perhaps writing on behalf of Martin Secker) to whom Lawrence wrote in 1921, "I wish I'd come to you ten years back: you wrote me just too late" (482n2).

Lawrence bowed to necessity. He was constrained by his obligation to Edward Garnett and by the virtual certainty of publication. He had many reasons. He was under enormous pressure prior to the publication of *Sons and Lovers*. He had resigned from teaching and committed himself to the life of a writer but had published very little and firmly believed that the third novel was crucial in terms of public awareness. Having decided permanently to support Frieda, he was living without an income on the shores of Lake Garda in northern Italy. He was awaiting Frieda's divorce proceedings in England, the legal settlement of which would almost certainly mean a financial penalty against himself as co-respondent. It was therefore by this time financially and otherwise urgent for him to put a third novel out into the world. He had expected *Sons and Lovers* to be published after he had finished correcting the galley proofs, and was rendered almost desperate when Duckworth proposed further censorship and a round of page proofs: "I don't mind if Duckworth crosses out a hundred shady pages of *Sons and Lovers*. It's got to sell, I've got to live" (*Letters I* 526). This explosive reaction can hardly be taken as a considered expression of his textual "intentions" any more than his resigned response had been, in December 1912, on learning Garnett's decision to shorten the novel. In fact, his freedom of maneuver was so limited that "preference" is a more suitable word than "intention." He "intended" to get his novel published by hook or by crook, but his clear "preference" would have been for his *MS* to be published at once and in full.

There is no question that he was grateful to Garnett for letting him "come in," albeit in reduced size; and he expressed his gratitude to Garnett frequently and generously in the letters of this period. The spiritedness of his thanks has led some commentators to conclude that Lawrence positively preferred the abridged text. It is, of course, possible to find quotations to justify any editorial line of action among the welter of contemporary documents. Ideally, full weight should be given to all Lawrence's utterances. But that is clearly impossible here, and indeed there is always the problem of the thoughts that went unrecorded. However, the above account is not intended to represent an assemblage of *proof* that one editorial approach is *correct*, but to illustrate this editor's understanding of Lawrence's prevailing attitude in the circumstances of late 1912 and early 1913.

My own weighing and pondering of Lawrence's utterances and circumstances at the time have led to the conclusion that it is impossible now, in a scholarly edition of the work, to let Garnett's judgment continue to prevail over Lawrence's. The manuscript whose coherence and greatness Lawrence advocated with such passionate conviction cannot seriously in 1995 continue to be judged to contain 90 percent essence and 10 percent superfluity.

100% MS TEXT, MS PUNCTUATION—WITH OR WITHOUT PROOF REVISIONS?

Rejection of the author's proof revisions may be a serious option in the cases where an author is revising a poem, tale, or novel many years after it was first published, and in effect creating a different work. But there is no such lapse of time in the case of *Sons and Lovers*. Lawrence had spent approximately two years writing the novel, from *c*. September 1910 to November 1912, writing it four times in intensive bursts of a few months and leaving it alone for months in between. Having posted the final manuscript to Garnett on 18 November 1912, he received the galley proofs less than three months later and revised them from 5 February to 3 March 1913. The page proofs arrived a fortnight later, and he revised them from *c*. 22 March to *c*. 11 April 1913.

Furthermore, it was Lawrence's regular practice to revise proofs when he received them, attending chiefly to verbal clarification and adjustment, as well as to errors. Therefore his substantive revisions are normally interpreted as representing his preferred readings. In the case of *Sons and Lovers*, he made a few alterations to rectify lacunae produced by Garnett's excisions (and these are rendered redundant once the excised passages are retained); but by definition the vast majority of his revisions were to text left untouched by Garnett.[4] An editor hardly has the right to overrule his author and declare these substantive changes invalid. To do so seems to me to make the "best text" error that Greg decried: "the tyranny of the copy-text, a tyranny that has, in my opinion, vitiated much of the best editorial work of the past generation" (*Art and Error* 24).

CONCLUSION

Readers of this essay will have noted that no arguments have been mounted in respect of the editor's aesthetic or critical evaluation of the deleted passages, the quality of the prose, the role of each scene, or the shape of the whole. The case mounted here is purely bibliographical. Now that the new Cambridge edition is available, criticism can play its part. It is this editor's belief that an eighty-year-old tradition of reprinting a botched, censored, and butchered text can now be interred, and the whole body of Lawrence's text can at long last be put before the public. Perhaps skeptics would be well advised to allow Lawrence's full text a balancing eighty years of exposure and consideration before readers are asked to vote on whether the offending passages should be removed again.

NOTES

1. They are deposited by their owner, Guy Collings, at Nottingham University Library. They are described and analyzed in Baron, "Surviving Galley Proofs."
2. A few notes related to this manuscript have survived in Garnett's hand: see Baron "*Sons*" 319–21.
3. As exemplified in "Stoppard, *Travesties*, 1974," in Gaskell 245–62.
4. Sexton argues that some of Lawrence's proof revisions present stages in the development of Paul's relationship with Miriam, which are designed to replace different versions of the same stages found in some of the passages "justifiably" cut by Garnett. Arguments of this kind, based on critical interpretations of individual passages, cannot provide an editor with a sound basis for adjudication on the treatment of proof revisions. Sexton's case is also undermined by his assertion that no proofs survive and therefore no information is available as to whether variants between *MS* and *E1* originated with Lawrence or the compositors. This does not inspire confidence, since both galley and page proofs are listed in Roberts.

WORKS CITED

Baron, Helen. "*Sons and Lovers:* The Surviving Manuscripts from Three Drafts Dated by Paper Analysis." *Studies in Bibliography* 38 (1985): 289–328.
———. "The Surviving Galley Proofs of *Lawrence's Sons and Lovers.*" *Studies in Bibliography* 45 (1992): 231–51.
Chambers, Jessie. "*E.T.*": *A Personal Record*. London: Cape, 1935.
Eliot, T. S. *The Waste Land, a Facsimile and Transcript of the Original Drafts Including the Annotations of Ezra Pound*. Ed. Valerie Eliot. London: Faber, 1971.
Gaskell, Philip. *From Writer to Reader*. Oxford: Oxford UP, 1978.
Greg, W. W. "The Rationale of Copy-Text." *Studies in Bibliography* 3 (1950–51): 19–36; rpt. in Gottesman, Ronald, and Scott Bennett, eds. *Art and Error*. London: Methuen, 1970. 17–36.
Jefferson, George. *Edward Garnett: A Life in Literature*. London: Cape, 1982.
Killham, John. "*The Poems of Tennyson* Edited by Christopher Ricks" (review). *The Yearbook of English Studies* 1 (1971): 302–3.

Lawrence, D. H. *Phoenix: The Posthumous Papers of D. H. Lawrence*. Ed. Edward D. McDonald. New York: Viking, 1936.

——. *Sons and Lovers*. London: Duckworth, 1913.

Roberts, Warren. *A Bibliography of D. H. Lawrence*. 2d ed. Cambridge: Cambridge UP, 1982.

Sexton, Mark S. "Lawrence, Garnett, and *Sons and Lovers:* An Exploration of Author-Editor Relationship." *Studies in Bibliography* 43 (1990): 208–22.

Thorpe, James. *Principles of Textual Criticism*. San Marino, CA: Huntington Library, 1972.

Editing as Interpretation: Self-Censorship and Collaboration in the Cambridge Edition of *The Rainbow* and *Women in Love*

Charles L. Ross

Just as the heart of editing is emendation, so the basis of emendation is interpretation. Because the Cambridge Edition aims to produce texts that D. H. Lawrence "would have wished to see" ("General Editors' Preface" vii), it must attend to acts of revision. Who rewrote a passage, with whose help or advice, under what sorts of pressure? As interpretations, the answers to these questions will persuade readers by their probability rather than mere possibility. The truism that meaning is indeterminate acquires a fresh relevance for editors whose creations—critical texts—will always be underdetermined in regard to documents and overdetermined by possible motives.

Hence, my reservations about Cambridge decisions to emend stem not from their status as interpretations but from their insufficiently self-critical treatment of "fact" and "authorial intention." In difficult cases, I shall argue, Cambridge invokes an "authority" that is unavailable except through the interpretive acts it purportedly grounds.[1] Cambridge editors seem unaware that they are trapped, for better and worse, in a hermeneutic circle or interpretive community. Their rhetoric mystifies the nature of editorial choice, thereby undermining the avowed purpose of a critical edition, which is to enable readers to construct alternate texts or versions of a work.

THE RAINBOW: SELF-CENSORSHIP

Consider the Cambridge Edition of *The Rainbow* (1989), edited by Mark Kinkead-Weekes. The available documents include a complete autograph manuscript (*MS*), a heavily revised typescript (*TSR*), and the first edition (Methuen, 1915). Author's proofs have not survived. From letters to his agent, J. B. Pinker, we know that Lawrence was compelled to "cut out" phrases on slips and pages sent to him separately from the main proofs. Lawrence claimed to have stood firm against altering "passages and paragraphs," but Pinker testified at the obscenity trial that Lawrence had altered all except one passage about which the publisher had complained (Ross, *Composition* 39–41). Many revisions made in the lost proofs occur in sexually explicit passages and therefore raise questions about forced self-censorship. Moreover, the published revisions often alter effects that Lawrence strove to create in heavy revisions of the typescript. Woman becoming independent and taking her own initiative, the recognition of a sexuality beyond good and evil, and a Blakean rejection of any distinction between sexuality and spirit—these are the themes and variants at stake.

The Cambridge editorial strategy in assessing the possibility of self-censorship in such revisions follows four linked moves:

1. The editor examines the proof changes, sometimes conceding an aesthetic loss.
2. The editor advances Lawrence's intentions as the ground of his interpretations, arguing that the final reading represents those intentions. Theoretically, this is a circular and self-confirming maneuver. Having posited intention interpretively, the editor ascribes it retroactively to the author.
3. The editor presents an explanation that he claims is "equally poised" with a counterargument that he leaves unexplained, uncited, or both. (As a rule, the Cambridge Edition cites only itself on editorial issues.) This move assumes that an editor, working on a given text, can invent two equally persuasive arguments from the same interpretive practices. What Stanley Fish calls the "situated" nature of practitioners in an interpretive community, however, casts doubt on the possibility of equally poised arguments.[2]
4. In cases that retain what the editor calls "any doubt," he defers to the readings of the published text rather than those of the typescript. This deference is based on a rhetorical privileging of the authority of the Methuen first edition. Thus Methuen is called "the novel to which [Lawrence] gave his imprimatur" (Kinkead-Weekes lxiii), as though the penurious pacifist in wartime England, whose previous draft of *The Rainbow* had been refused by Methuen for indecency, were in any position to object to publication. On

the other hand, Lawrence defended the integrity of the typescript version and expressed resentment at having to censor the proofs (Ross 39–41). So "imprimatur" creates more authority than warranted by the history provided in the edition's "Introduction." To elevate the authority of the first edition even further, the editor understates the effect of revision in the lost proofs. Though Lawrence "was proof-correcting, or rather, revising extensively yet once more in proof. . . , [t]here are no major alterations in this last revision" (Kinkead-Weekes xliii). How alterations differ from extensive revisions is not clear, but the implication is that adjudicating dubious revisions will not appreciably alter the overall aesthetic effects of the Cambridge Edition.

Let us see how this combined editorial and rhetorical strategy works in practice. Consider the scene in "Anna Victrix" where the pregnant Anna dances naked in the privacy of her room as homage to the Lord and "in exemption from the man," her husband, who has been forcing his will upon her. Lawrence later recalled that exception "was particularly taken" to this scene by publisher and prosecution. In the typescript, moreover, Anna's motivation and attitude toward the Lord have a plausibility that seems compromised in the first edition (*proof deletions in this and subsequent quotations are surrounded by square brackets and substitutions by angled brackets*):

She had her moments of exaltation still, re-births of old exaltations. As she sat by her bedroom window, watching the steady rain, her spirit was somewhere far off [, with David. She had always loved David. It had haunted her, how he danced naked before the Ark, and the wife had taunted him. And David had said "It was before the Lord: the Lord hath chosen me, therefore will I play before him"]. . .

Suddenly she realised that this was what she wanted to do. Big with child as she was she danced there in the bedroom by herself, lifting her hands and her body to the [Lord, to the unseen Lover whose name was unutterable] <Unseen to the unseen Creator who had chosen her, to Whom she belonged>.[3]

Without the reference to David, the dance comes abruptly; and without the reference to God as a "Lover," the characteristically Lawrencean link between married love and religious emotion is less striking. In the same scene, "was in love with" became "liked"; "shamelessly" became "exultingly"; and "Lord" was changed inconsistently to "Unknown," "Unseen," and "Creator."

How does the Cambridge editor proceed? Having first established probable self-censorship ("These might well be changes for which [Lawrence] had been pressed"), the editor reverses himself in the rhetorical question: "And even if there was [pressure] . . . might [the changes] represent a significant change of imagination?" (Kinkead-Weekes lxvi). He then ascribes Anna's impulse to a mere "youthful 'crush' or an erotic memory of David dancing naked" that Lawrence probably thought better of. This interpretation justifying inaction, however, is less than fully persuasive. "Crush" hardly describes the feelings of a married and pregnant woman in a chapter titled "Anna Victrix." Though the editor concedes that the religious dimension of the scene has been strengthened at the "expense of the erotic," he suggests that "there is at least much room for argument" (lxvi). Nevertheless, he avoids mentioning published scholarship that argues the case for restoration with reference to the original sources (Ross 44–46). Finally, he defers to the authority of the first edition, since "any doubt" that Lawrence might have had a "change of imagination" gives the benefit of the doubt to the first edition.

This example provides a microcosm of editorial practice in the Cambridge Edition. Although Kinkead-Weekes is writing a volume in "The Cambridge Biography" of Lawrence covering the years of *The Rainbow*'s composition, he does not acknowledge the similarity between biographer and editor in the instance of speculative decisions to emend. As Richard Ellmann has observed, the biographer must bring to bear "a pattern of explanation" on the data of a writer's life (15). An editor too must recognize that so-called changes in imagination arise through acts of interpretation that, in turn, aim to be probable and inclusive. The Cambridge editor, in contrast, resorts all too often to the merely possible and piecemeal.

Consider another example of dubious revision that changes a central theme, despite the editor's assertion of "no major alterations." While composing the novel, Lawrence announced that its "germ" was "woman becoming individual, self-responsible, taking her own initiative" (*Letters II* 165). The Cambridge editor, however, does not restore passages cut from the proofs that provide a woman's perspective and that at the time might have been considered too outspoken.

One such scene describes young Tom Brangwen's sexual adventure at Matlock with a young woman who has become the mistress of a foreign gentleman. The cut passages explain that she provokes Tom to the affair so as to assert an independence that has been compromised by social circumstance, and that she does not encourage Tom after their fling because she values her freedom of action:

> ["It was dissatisfaction and anger that had led her to her form of life. Yet she had always seemed jolly"] (*TS* 25)

> She gave him an intimate smile, which made him feel [that what was between himself and her was the right sort of thing, and what was between the other man and her was not the right sort of thing. So he wanted her to come with him. But she was too fair, and she wanted her hard, brutal freedom. She would be no man's woman. She wanted her price only. He was dark with anger.] <confused and gratified.> (*TS* 28)

The editor sees no loss in these cuts because he assumes that Lawrence was interested exclusively in Tom Brangwen: "None of these is wanted if the emphasis is to fall on a single exciting and liberating adventure, which appears to be what Lawrence finally decided" (Kinkead-Weekes lxvii). This judgment perfectly illustrates the circularity in reasoning by final authorial intentions. Even granting the self-confirming assumption, however, the deleted passages may be thought to ring true for Tom's character, which is morally and sentimentally conventional.

Consider, for example, Tom's thoughts after seducing or being seduced by the young woman, a passage that makes his success plain:

> His heart thumped and he thought it the most glorious adventure, and was [madly in love with the girl. By gad, she was a tanger. He admired her to extremity, he almost loved her. But he did admire her, and it *was* a success.] <mad with desire for the girl.> (*TS* 28)

The editor argues that these deletions "hardly" affect the explicitness of what happened and, additionally, that the treatment of Tom's "love" for the girl was "self-contradictory" in the typescript: "The revisions from *MS* to *TSR* [revised typescript] show that Lawrence was himself uncertain about how he wanted to handle the episode (Kinkead-Weekes lxvi). Here the editor has actually assigned his own sense of the text to Lawrence. His negative judgment on the coherence of the typescript version assumes that "madly in love" and "almost loved" contradict each other rather than reveal the young man's ambivalent feeling after intercourse. Characteristically, the Lawrencean third-person contains several voices, that of the excited youth ("madly in love") and that of a more detached, summarizing third-person ("admired . . . almost loved"). Note, too, the consistency between the editor's interpretation here and in the previous scene about Anna's love for the Lord. The married Anna Brangwen was judged to have originally harbored an inappropriately "youthful 'crush'" on Jesus Christ, and now bachelor Tom cannot be allowed to entertain love for the handsome girl without falling into self-contradiction. The editor refers obliquely to other interpretations in the statement "It is possible to imagine objections here," but neither summarizes nor cites any published "objections" or rival interpretations.

Consider the most difficult case of all—the expansion of "The Child" chapter in typescript. Here Lawrence inserted many handwritten pages and later returned to make the very last revisions in the entire typescript. Seized by inspiration, he conceived two linked scenes that focus on the uninhibited, even "immoral" sexual activities that first Will and subsequently Will and Anna pursue and that somehow break through the stalemate of their marriage. The typescript shows a heightening of the exorbitant, deliberately shocking nature of this lovemaking, which is also an assault on repressive consciousness. Yet certain proof changes reverse the direction toward excessiveness in the typescript additions and revisions.

The Cambridge strategy of emendation is predictable. The editor admits that "the difficulty here is that the excessiveness of the passage is unquestionably part of its meaning." But he still finds justification for keeping hands off by pointing to the cutting of a "sermon" in Ursula's much later section of the novel. This, he contends, implies that Lawrence was worried about "too heavy an underlining" of the sexual practices in "The Child." This is a possible though hardly compelling interpretation. Reading the lengthy inner monologue originally given to Ursula in the middle of biology class, one may conclude simply that Lawrence cut it as dramatically unconvincing. And, in fact, the gist of the monologue was rewritten first as lengthy revisions in *Twilight in Italy* and then as a full-scale pronouncement, "The Crown." (See, for example, the interpolations in "The Lemon Gardens." If the editor has noticed these similarities, he does not mention them.) Moreover, Lawrence did not tamper in proof with the outspoken language of lovemaking between Ursula and Skrebensky on the Sussex and Lincolnshire downs, scenes whose conception had likely inspired him to create the sensual revels of Will and Anna in

"The Child." The editor does not mention this direction in typescript revision—from the end of the novel back to "The Child"—though it has been discussed earlier in published commentary. If Lawrence had become worried about the end of the novel, he might be expected to have cut something from those scenes in typescript; but he did not do so.

The editor simplifies his task by, first, isolating two changes from a baker's dozen having to do with Will and the "warehouse lass" and, second, providing an explanation that seems plausible for those changes but not for many others. A passage describing Will's behavior and the response of the "warehouse lass" he has picked up, for example, was changed:

> She would be small, almost like a child, and pretty. [There would be pretty little places in her body, that he wanted to discover. He wanted to know them and enjoy them. He wanted to have his fill of them.] <Her childishness whetted him keenly. She would be helpless between his hands.> (*TS* 344)

In the typescript, this reference to "pretty little places" found its echo in Will's subsequent appetite for "each tiny beauty" in Anna's body, so its elimination disrupts that symmetry. Cambridge judges that the change, though possibly forced, "points to a different kind of sexuality than thoughts of places in the body; the kind that depends on a sense of power and makes some men 'whetted' by rather childish girls" (lxviii). This seems plausible for the two changes cited, but does not account for numerous others in the scene that look like euphemisms and that are not defended.

Far more than censorship of a few sexually explicit passages is at stake here. If Lawrence toned down the ending of "The Child," he may have also changed the consequences of the self-censored sexual practices. This suspicion follows from the assumption, in the editor's words, that Lawrence "nearly always did more than bowdlerise" (lxix). As the editor does not recognize, however, this assumption may imply more than one consequence with regard to self-censorship. The editor means that Lawrence voluntarily made changes beyond those necessary to bowdlerize a sexually explicit passage. In the context of suspected self-censorship, the assumption may also imply that so-called voluntary revisions stemming from bowdlerization have led to revisions that might not otherwise have been made. That is, the ramifications of self-censorship may spread beyond its origin. And when we look at the nature of the proof changes in "The Child," a pattern leaps into view. In proof revisions, the socially subversive consequences of the exorbitant sexuality, which had been the raison d'être of his typescript revisions, were muted. The editor misses this pattern because he has already committed himself to a story and selects facts that fit it. For example, he mistakes the chronology of revision, implying that Lawrence wrote "a sensuality violent and extreme as death" in the typescript as part of the revised conception of "The Child." In fact, Lawrence substituted those words for others ("a sensual voluptuousness") in the lost proofs, perhaps in an act of self-censorship. That is, the related emphases on "death" and the "purposive" self paradoxically created through extreme sexuality were substituted or added in proof. At the same time, the typescript's attack on the domestic virtues was muted by two cuts:

> [She too absolved herself: she absolved herself from her "goodness," from her connection with the Ten Commandments of our ordered life.]. . . . [She was far more interested in him as a self-seeking stranger than in the aforetime good, responsible husband.] (*TS* 350)

And finally for this reconstruction, Lawrence emphasized the "free," "new," and "purposive" man as opposed to the originally less promising "disengaged," "superficial," and "public" man liberated by sensual activities. Lawrence summed up this trend by adding the unusually sententious sentence: "He wanted to be unanimous with the whole of purposive mankind."

Put together, all these changes in proof support an alternative interpretation. While euphemizing the revitalized sexual practices of Will and Anna, Lawrence also made them less threatening to domestic life and more compatible with the public realm. This process of thematic accommodation may have resulted from Lawrence's recognition of civilization and its discontents. It may also be the result of prudence, especially considering the direction toward exorbitance in the typescript revisions and the publisher's subsequent pressure to censor the proofs. Put theoretically, the end of "The Child" is indeterminate in meaning because it is underdetermined in regard to documents and overdetermined by possible motives. In this situation, it is vital to give readers probable interpretations that account interpretively for the greatest possible number of variants. To refrain from citing, much less engaging, other published interpretations of the evidence deprives the reader of the impetus and means to construct other versions (Ross, "Revisions").

In sum, the Cambridge edition of *The Rainbow* treats self-censorship as a relatively minor aesthetic concern. The new text restores only a paltry number of words and one phrase, despite Lawrence's testimony that he cut out "phrases." The editor's rationale of emendation vacillates between probability and possibility, ultimately deferring to the exaggerated authority of the first edition. The strong pull of the Methuen edition, based on the editorial concept of "final intentions," is also reflected in the circular argument that the published text is "what Lawrence finally decided" (Kinkead-Weekes lxvii). This strategy short-circuits interpretation. Lost to view is the simple fact that Lawrence's manuscript contains voluntary, uncensored artistic expression, whereas the first edition contains self-censored "phrases."[4] Finally, the editor never cites the rival interpretations of self-censorship against which he is tacitly arguing. This omission undermines his final gesture of reasonableness to "readers who consider that this edition errs too far on the side of caution" and who can "judge for themselves by consulting the textual apparatus, and make their own restorations" (Kinkead-Weekes lxix). Earlier, however, the reader was told that "there are no major alterations in this last revision," hardly words to stimulate curiosity. So we may wonder what sort of Common Reader, unversed in specialized scholarship, will pick through 130 pages of apparatus in search of several dozen variants? And if that extraordinary reader does attempt to "reconstruct" meaning from the apparatus, will he or she recognize that different interpretations produce quite different texts?

WOMEN IN LOVE: COLLABORATION

All revision may be considered part of the larger phenomenon of collaboration, as Gary Taylor has argued (41). Collaboration includes an author's explicit or tacit acceptance of help from individuals and the publishing institution. Editorial treatment of collaboration depends primarily on the stories editors tell about the authority of their authors. Editors cannot appeal to a standard outside interpretation to privilege their stories. Instead, they establish authority by narrative means and subsequently shape texts embodying that inferential authority.

The editors of the Cambridge *Women in Love* (1987)—David Farmer, Lindeth Vasey, and John Worthen—never ask whether a revision that resulted from collaboration makes better or worse sense in artistic terms. Instead, Cambridge typically treats all nonauthorial contributions as "corruptions" that should be expunged from the text whenever possible.

This assumption of authority undervalues Lawrence's working control during revision—discounting the likelihood that in revising he responded to the text before him, under his eye. The editor of *The Rainbow*, for example, aims "to present Lawrence, revising the [typescript] with the accurate transcription he never received" (Kinkead-Weekes lxiv). For *Women in Love*, the question of accuracy becomes mixed with that of collaborative advice and emendation by Frieda Lawrence and several typists in the prepublication history of the work. By deciding that Frieda's collaboration should be accepted only where Lawrence's revision "precludes" a return to an earlier state, for example, Cambridge retroactively disrupts Lawrence's control of his own revisions (554n209:26). To "circumvent" Frieda as often as possible, rather than accepting her contributions whenever not improbable, Cambridge must often eliminate Lawrence's ingenious responses and revisions, thereby casting doubt on his grasp of the sentence, paragraph, page, or version (591). The ideology of the Cambridge Edition, moreover, is at odds with itself—referring meaning to an author but overruling many of his acts on the assumption that he mistook the text under his own hand.

The manuscript trail offers some clues to various possible stories of authority. We have for inspection, in chronological order:

1. Handwritten notebooks comprising roughly the last one-third of the novel. Those for the first two-thirds are lost.
2. Duplicates of a first typescript (*TSIa* & *TSIb*), heavily revised in both Lawrence's and Frieda's hands, and sorted into separate wholes late in the process of revision and transcription.
3. A second typescript (*TSII*), prepared from one of the duplicates (*TSIb*) and heavily revised by Lawrence.
4. The Seltzer (American) first edition, set from a typed copy of the heavily revised *TSII*.[5]
5. One revised set of duplicate proofs of the Secker (English) edition, but not the one used by the printer for setting the published novel.[6]
6. The English first edition and its second impression (1921), both of which incorporate censorship by Lawrence and the publisher, Thomas Secker.[7]

Two links in the chain from *MS* to print are missing: a typescript copy of *TSII*, prepared by Seltzer for his compositors but never seen by Lawrence; and the proofs Secker used to set his English edition. The loss of the first is minor, since any unauthorized changes can be deduced by comparing typescript and first edition. The loss of the second, however, forces Cambridge to rely on inference in choosing between readings from the lost setting-copy proofs and variant readings in the surviving proof, which was not used for setting. This necessary strategy illustrates that editorial choices cannot be checked against the facts of the text, as Stanley Fish argues, "because it is only within our accounts . . . that the text and its facts, or, rather, *a* text and its facts, emerge and become available for inspection" (144).

How do our accounts of Lawrence at work shape the facts and editorial choices in *Women in Love?* Lawrence heavily revised *TSIa* & *b*, calling on Frieda's help in transcription and evidently also accepting her advice in matters of style, such as the choice and spelling of French and German. Lawrence and Frieda worked on the duplicate typescripts in no discernible order, putting them together as units late in the process of revision and transcription. Then Lawrence chose *TSIb*, either because he assumed that the duplicates were identical (they are not) or because he preferred *TSIb*. In either case, *TSII* was prepared from *TSIb*. Unable to find a publisher, Lawrence kept *TSII* with him for three years and revised heavily several times. According to Cambridge estimates, he revised over 90 percent of the *TSII* pages and completely rewrote 10 percent. Then he sent the typescript to Seltzer in America and had no further part in the preparation of the first edition.

Let us stop there for a moment. Since *TSIb* was the exemplar for *TSII*, Cambridge argues reasonably that Lawrence's "own revision in *TSIb* should take priority over those he made in *TSIa*." Yet transcriptions and/or changes from *TSIa* to *TSIb*, made by both Lawrence and Frieda, are considered questionable on a variety of inferential grounds. For example, Frieda may have mistranscribed, changed, or added something without Lawrence's approval. Therefore, Frieda's handwritten contributions are judged collaborative and retained only if they appear in both typescripts (not merely in *TSIb*), and not always then. Thus Cambridge establishes the authority of *TSIb* only to undercut it. This is the thin end of a long wedge, followed by all sorts of exceptions that are based on inferences, not facts. Throughout the tortuous reconstruction of "authority" from readings in the fragmentary *MS* and/or *TSIa* and/or *TSIb* and/or *TSII* and/or Seltzer and/or the proofs of Secker and so on, Cambridge never credits the control Lawrence had over any one version. In short,

Cambridge never vests authority in the author's creation of *a* version of the work. Despite their quantitative evidence of thorough and repeated revision of *TSII*, Cambridge leaves unexamined the possibility that Lawrence exercised authority over *TSII* by virtue of his revision of the whole and that consequently *TSII* may have more authority than an eclectic text.

There is no extra-interpretive evidence by which to adjudicate these rival claims; but Occam's razor may be invoked ("What can be done with fewer [assumptions] is done in vain with more"). The Cambridge eclectic text reconstructs authority, on the one hand, from several "original" authorities (in *MS, TSIa* & *b*, and *TSII*) and, on the other, from several "final" authorities (in Secker proofs and printed editions). The result is a purportedly single authority operating through no fewer than seven material states over five years in two different publishing environments. A very different notion of "authority" would follow from an account of Lawrence as an artist controlling his medium in *TSII* through wholesale revision, undertaken without any external pressure and resulting in a version with its own raison d'être. In fact, my Penguin English Library edition of the novel is based on just such a definition of authority. I would assert that both accounts have coherence, but only one meets the principle of parsimony. And though parsimony is not decisive by itself, it joins probability as a factor in the inferential and highly rhetorical invention of authority.

Consider more closely the role of Frieda in revising and transcribing. Though her additions and corrections are often accepted, she is referred to as an impediment: "Explanatory notes alert the reader when it has not been possible to circumvent Frieda's influence" (591). Yet evidence of her sympathy and tact far outweighs evidence of her errors. While working along with Lawrence to prepare duplicates of *TSI*, for example, she added a line at page 142:9, substituted a word at page 184:31 and page 187:39, merged several revisions at page 189:4, revised a clause to avoid redundancy at page 198:6, altered Birkin's appearance at page 269:32, changed a metaphor at page 280:14, corrected Lawrence's French at page 237:27–28 and his English idiom at page 230:10 ("he felt a dislike [to] <at> the thought of them"), and clarified Lawrence's typing at page 147:17. This evidence suggests that Frieda not only edited well but responded creatively to Lawrence's revisions, and that Lawrence was alert to her interventions, sometimes rejecting them in *TSIb* or later in *TSII*. In any case, the category of "mistranscription" is interpretive, not objective, and depends on how a change is judged.

Although all the above collaborations by Frieda are retained in the

Cambridge edition, the editors' disposition against her leads to rejection of readings that seem more likely than not to have met with Lawrence's approval. Thus a substitution in German that makes better contextual sense and that Lawrence likely accepted from a native speaker is overruled because it appears only in *TSIb*. Here are the circumstances. Following Loerke's mimicry of an old Cologne woman and a railway guard, which convulses the Reunionsaal audience, the German Professor, "crying loudly," says: "Ja, das war merkwurdig, das war famos" in the *MS*[8] but "Ja, das war ausgezeichnet, das war famos" after Frieda's revision in *TSIb*.[9] Cambridge reinstates "merkwürdig," editorially adding the umlaut that Lawrence left out, on the ground that the word is "old-fashioned but (for a Professor before the war) perfectly acceptable" (575n406:37). As usual, Cambridge ignores context. These are the Professor's first words after laughing so hard that "the veins in [his] neck were swollen, his face was purple, [and] he was strangled in ultimate silent spasms of laughter." So Lawrence may well have considered it more appropriate for the Professor to say "ausgezeichnet" ("excellent" or "splendid"), as Frieda contributed, than "merkwürdig" ("remarkable" in the sense of "peculiar"). It is more likely than not that Lawrence welcomed Frieda's collaboration in modifying the German exclamation. Note that the choice between "merkwürdig" and "ausgezeichnet" depends entirely on inference, the probability of the story—Ellmann's "pattern of explanation" or Fish's "account"—that produces "facts."

The story that Cambridge never credits in emendation is that Lawrence's versions have holistic meanings and his revisions build on each other. Hence Cambridge never worries that restorations are anachronistic in the context of a version from which they were absent when Lawrence was revising. Take what may seem at first a valid restoration. While lying naked, recovering from the wrestling bout in "Gladiatorial," Birkin and Gerald sort out their feelings. Birkin says in *TSIa*:

". . . One ought to wrestle and strive and be physically close. It makes one sane."
"You do think so?" [Gerald replied.]
"I do. Don't you?"
"Yes," said Gerald, "it's life for me—"[10]

It seems Frieda left out "for me" when transcribing this into *TSIb;* then, the typist of *TSII* put a period instead of the dash; finally, Lawrence himself crossed out "it's life," leaving only "'Yes,' said Gerald."[11] Cambridge restores the phrase from *TSIa* without considering that in *TSII* Lawrence had been radically revising the friendship between Gerald and Birkin, making it less conscious—that is, more repressed—and thereby more intense. On the page in question, Lawrence not only struck out "it's life" but also added "The wrestling had some deep meaning to them—an unfinished meaning." There are, in sum, several interpretive reasons to keep *TSII* as it stands (that is, without either "it's life for me—" or "it's life."). First, Lawrence thoroughly revised *TSII* more than a year after finishing work on *TSI*. He had tried hard to place *TSI* with a publisher; so the version had its own integrity. Second, this revision joins another on the same page and many more throughout *TSII* that fit an interpretation in which Lawrence changed his presentation of the male friendship while rewriting *TSII*. According to this interpretation, restoration of the original reading would be inappropriate because it is creatively outdated. One published study of the manuscripts has suggested as much, but Cambridge does not cite it (Ross, "Homoerotic Feeling").

As though to confirm an account crediting prepublication versions with integrity, Cambridge plans to publish an edition of *TSI* with the title *The Sisters*. What will be their rationale for adding to the canon? Presumably they will argue that *TSI* is a very different "novel" and that Lawrence thought of it as finished when he sent it to publishers, who rejected it. By that rationale, however, the revised *TSII* also becomes a discrete novel with a raison d'être that argues against conflating readings of earlier and later versions.

The allegiance of the Cambridge Edition to the theory of an eclectic text also predisposes editors to see "error" where an assumption of coherence in *TSII* yields perfectly good sense. "Error," that is, follows from the preference for one interpretation over another. Cambridge is disposed to seek explanations in a speculative history of composition, as opposed to coherent meanings in the chosen base-text (that is, *TSII*); as a result, Cambridge exaggerates Lawrence's carelessness so as to justify saving the artist from himself. For example, Cambridge unnecessarily changes the name of a servant from "Simpson" to "Crowther" in the "Industrial Magnate" chapter. This is the scene in which Mrs. Crich sicks the dogs on her husband's workers, whom she considers "foul human beings who come crawling after charity." Cambridge notes that Lawrence "varied between Crowther and Simpson" in earlier typescripts (*TSIa* & *b*) and that both servants have the same name "Thomas." Therefore, they assume, Lawrence actually meant Crowther when he wrote "Simpson, drive them away." Here history obscures the clear sense of the text. Whereas Crowther, the elderly butler, is mentioned earlier in the same paragraph, the "Simpson" to whom Mrs. Crich gives her order is identified clearly as the "groom" in the next paragraph: "And she would stand watching with an eye like the eagle's, whilst the groom in clumsy confusion drove the lugubrious persons down the drive . . . " (216). The perfect intelligibility of the text, its distinction between butler and groom and their respective duties in the Crich household, gets lost in speculation about origins; as a result, Lawrence is made to appear careless when he was actually in control of his materials.

Indeed, Lawrence's control over central themes in the novels is brought into doubt by editorial decisions that rest on unexamined interpretations. For example, almost all decisions to regularize or normalize a repeated reading in a long text will be interpretive. Consider the key trope of the "sons of God" from Genesis, which Cambridge normalizes with a capital "S" in "Sons" in preference to the small "s" of the King James version.

The topos of the "sons of God" from Genesis has great importance to Ursula—first in her adolescent mixing of religiosity and eroticism, then in her rejection of Skrebensky as a husband, and finally in her acceptance of Rupert Birkin. Though Cambridge claims to cite the Authorized Version of the Bible in all commentary, it emends the biblical "sons of God" (small "s") to the unauthoritative "Sons of God" (capital). No explanation is given. Yet the choice of upper-case "S" misrepresents not only the usage in the Authorized Version that Lawrence knew well from boyhood but also many examples of Lawrence's own handwriting in *The Rainbow*, *Women in Love*, and elsewhere (e.g., in *Apocalypse* and *Lady Chatterley's Lover*, where lower-case "sons" is preserved by Cambridge, again without explanation). There is a lot of lexicographic evidence, none of which is reported. At times Lawrence's handwriting of "sons" makes it difficult to distinguish between upper-case and lower-case. However, several instances of the initial "s" in "sons" are clearly lower-case and most of the others only appear upper-case because Lawrence wrote a print "s" at the beginning of words. Nor does Cambridge cite evidence from the surviving proofs of Secker's English edition of *Women in Love*, which Lawrence corrected and in which he left the lower-case "sons" untouched.

The crucial interpretive point is that the Cambridge decision has disastrous consequences on the coherence of the novel. By capitalizing

"Sons of God" in both *The Rainbow* and *Women in Love,* Cambridge not only disrupts the parallel between the "sons of God" (small "s") and the "daughters of men" (small "d") but also blurs the distinction, both biblical and thematic, between the numerous sons of God in Genesis and the unique Son of God (capital S) in the *New Testament.* Whereas the singular Son of God (like the "Son of Man," capitalized in *The Rainbow* on 266:17) makes grammatical as well as doctrinal sense, plural Sons of God are bad grammar and bad religion. Thematically, Lawrence needs the distinction that Ursula herself draws in *The Rainbow* when she asks, "Who were the sons of God? Was not Jesus the only begotten Son?" (257:11; in fact, here the Cambridge editor inconsistently keeps the small "s," without explanation). Ursula is precisely right and gives the best reason for regularizing "sons of God" in the lower-case. In *Women in Love,* moreover, the choice to capitalize "Sons" has given some readers the impression that Ursula is paying obeisance to a patriarch when she recalls "the old magic of the Book of Genesis, where the Sons of God saw the daughters of men" (312:35–36; in fact, Lawrence clearly wrote a lower-case "s" here, but Cambridge normalizes it to a capital letter). This capital "S," then, has distorted Lawrence's view of women and has fueled charges of "sexism" that are, in this case, groundless.

Editorial restoration in the Cambridge edition extends beyond spelling or punctuation that a scribe or typist may have mistranscribed. Cambridge routinely restores the substantive readings of pre-*TSII* states that were revised by Lawrence himself in *TSII*. According to the Cambridge rule, any revisions associated with errors in punctuation must have been responses to errors and therefore do not count. They explain, for example, that they have restored an "original reading, before the transmission errors which provoked his revision" (547n136:31). This rule discounts a priori Lawrence's authority in revising a "corrupt" text, interpretively revaluing opportunism or discovery as "error." Paul Eggert, a Cambridge editor himself, has approvingly described the practice: "Where Lawrence has revised a passage that had been miscopied, the editorial tendency is to reinstate if possible the earlier reading on the grounds that the novelist did not have the opportunity to revise his own work" (71). But this "tendency" is evidently quite flexible; for, "where such a revision is linked thematically to other changes . . . then it will also be accepted." What Eggert hails as a "pragmatic compromise" is really another self-confirming interpretation. After all, a thematic link between revisions can always be found or, conversely, denied. Hence, Cambridge inconsistently but wisely accepts the interventions of typists. When some emendation to the earlier texts (*MS* or *TSI*) must be made, Cambridge accepts the *TSII* typist's correction on the ground that "Lawrence tacitly accepted this reading" (545n110:29). Once, for example, the typist left a blank space to remind Lawrence to finish a sentence (Lawrence filled in "glistening," 111:24). Here the typists acted collaboratively and are treated as collaborators. Evidently, human and material agencies of transmission can be useful.

Indeed, as Jerome McGann has urged, literary works may be considered not merely as "channels of transmission" but as "particular forms of transmissive interaction" (11). McGann's assumption contrasts sharply with Cambridge's belief that Lawrence must be saved from his medium. An account like McGann's encourages the retention of readings that arose from or included nonauthorial transmissive factors. It becomes legitimate to credit Lawrence with a holistic response and to ask whether a revision makes artistic sense, no matter what its origin. After all, this is what Cambridge does in effect when it decides that Lawrence "tacitly accepted" a typist's correction or that he revised a mistranscribed passage in such a way as to "preclude any return" to an earlier reading (554). An assumption that Lawrence often collaborated with the means of production, in turn, leads to different but coherent editorial choices. For example, a revision that was partly attributable to an error in punctuation but that seemed more colloquial could be kept (127:7 and 184:23), or a revision initiated by "error" might be accepted as truer to developing characterization (239:11 and 272:30). Where an unknown hand thrice underlined "disquality" and Lawrence erased two emphases but kept one, an editor might decide that Lawrence had endorsed the advice of the unknown agent for the obvious reason that the word is a Lawrencean coinage (225:17). And so on.

To sum up, editorial treatment of collaboration is founded on an inferential portrait of the artist at work. The portrait of Lawrence at work implied by Cambridge seems improbable. On the one hand, Cambridge believes, Lawrence revised creatively in the midst of self-censorship. Cambridge assumes that Lawrence was capable of keeping the holistic meaning of the work in view even as he censored himself; consequently, any other "voluntary" changes done during this process of self-censorship carry full authority. In this view, Lawrence's resilience or opportunism even extended into the bowdlerization of the published editions, as in Secker's English editions of *Women in Love*. In all cases of doubt, authority is invested in published editions, even though such deference to print means accepting the likelihood of unrecognized authorial self-censorship.

On the other hand, according to Cambridge, Lawrence always fell victim to collaborators in the prepublication stages, rarely profiting from the advice of others—Frieda, editors, and typists. Whereas the Cambridge Edition rarely saves Lawrence from himself, or the tale from its teller, in the context of self-censorship, it intervenes consistently to save Lawrence from his collaborators and his own ingenious responses to the vicissitudes of textual transmission.

CONCLUSION

The preceding critique has been based on the belief that there are no objective rationales of editing, only more or less inclusive interpretations that are persuasive by virtue of their rhetoric. Editors privilege some rhetorical principles over others, usually in the name of their authors. Then, in the act of constructing narratives to justify their decisions, editors impute these "intentions" to their authors with the avowed goal of "restoring" or "reconstructing" a text or, in Cambridge's rhetoric, *the* text of the work.[12] Such self-confirming interpretations seem the inescapable and enabling context of editing; or, in the words of Jerome McGann, "All editing is an act of interpretation" (27).

NOTES

1. See discussion of authority in my "Note on Nomenclature," pp. 189–92 in this collection.
2. Fish, *Doing What Comes Naturally* 194: "An interpretive strategy produces the object of its attention, an object that will be perspicuous to those who share or have been persuaded to share the same strategy."
3. Lawrence, *The Rainbow,* Corrected Typescript: 280, now owned by the University of Texas, Austin, and listed as E331b in Warren Roberts, *A Bibliography of D. H. Lawrence.* Subsequent quotations will be identified as *TS* followed by page number.
4. There are curious exceptions, one of which provides a rationale for a very different strategy of emendation. Where the manuscript contains a crossing-out that was restored in the first edition, Kinkead-Weekes decides to keep the *MS* reading on the grounds that "the *MS* crossing out is the only firm evidence" of Lawrence's intentions (Explanatory note at 346:38). Indeed, this is a convincing reason for always giving the *MS* presumptive authority over the Methuen first edition. Had Kinkead-Weekes followed this logic in regard to the controversial, erotic passages that were deleted in the lost proofs, we would have a substantially different text.
5. Lawrence, *Women in Love* (New York: Privately Printed [Thomas Seltzer], 1920).

6. Lawrence, *Women in Love* (London: Martin Secker, 1921). [Corrected proof copy for first English edition, published by Martin Secker in 1921, now owned by University of Texas at Austin, and listed as E441g in Roberts.]
7. Lawrence, *Women in Love* (London: Martin Secker, 1921).
8. Lawrence, *Women in Love,* Holograph Manuscript: 242; listed as E441c in Roberts.
9. Lawrence, *Women in Love,* Corrected Typescript: 541; listed as E441e in Roberts.
10. Lawrence, *Women in Love,* Corrected Typescript: 334; listed as E441d in Roberts.
11. Lawrence, *Women in Love,* Corrected Typescript: 430; listed as E441f in Roberts.
12. See my "Note on Nomenclature," pp. 189–92 in this collection.

WORKS CITED

Eggert, Paul. "Textual Product or Textual Process: Procedures and Assumptions of Critical Editing." In *Devils and Angels: Textual Editing and Literary Theory.* Ed. Philip Cohen. Charlottesville: UP of Virginia, 1991.
Ellmann, Richard, *A long the riverrun: Selected Essays.* New York: Knopf, 1989.
"General Editors' Preface" to Lawrence, *The Rainbow* and *Women in Love* vii–viii.
Fish, Stanley. *Doing What Comes Naturally.* Durham: Duke UP, 1989.
Kinkead-Weekes, Mark. "Introduction" to Lawrence, *The Rainbow* xix–lxxvi.
Lawrence, D. H. *Women in Love.* New York: Privately Printed [Thomas Seltzer], 1920.
———. *Women in Love.* London: Martin Secker, 1921.
McGann, Jerome J. *The Textual Condition.* Princeton: Princeton UP, 1991.
Roberts, Warren. *A Bibliography of D. H. Lawrence.* 2d ed. Cambridge: Cambridge UP, 1982.
Ross, Charles L. *The Composition of "The Rainbow" and "Women in Love": A History.* Charlottesville: UP of Virginia, 1979.
———. "Homoerotic Feeling in *Women in Love:* Lawrence's 'Struggle for Verbal Consciousness' in the Manuscripts." In *The Man Who Lived.* Ed. Robert B. Partlow Jr. and Harry T. Moore. Carbondale and Edwardsville: Southern Illinois UP, 1980. 168–82.
———. "The Revisions of the Second Generation in *The Rainbow.*" *Review of English Studies* 27 (1976): 277–95.
———, ed. *Women in Love.* By D. H. Lawrence. Harmondsworth: Penguin Books [Penguin English Library], 1982.
Taylor, Gary. "The Rhetoric of Textual Criticism." *Text.* Vol. 4. Ed. D. C. Greetham and W. Speed Hill. New York: AMS Press, 1988. 39–57.

Editing *The Plumed Serpent* for Cambridge: Or, Crossing the Communication Gap

L. D. Clark

The remarks offered in this essay represent conclusions that have accumulated little by little during the long, tedious, and often frustrating task of editing *The Plumed Serpent* for the Cambridge Lawrence. My comments fall into two categories. The first takes up disagreements between Editorial Board and volume editor which better foresight would have avoided—and which if nothing else caused great delay. The second touches on a larger question of how conformity to orthodoxy in our statement of editorial principles led in establishing the text to a disparity between declared theory and actual practice unconfessed by the editor and apparently unrealized by the Board. That is to say, in my "Note on the text" the Board and I did not arrive at a statement that truly describes the steps I followed in creating the new text. Furthermore—another but related problem—in the "Textual Apparatus" we did not record in its clearest form the progress of Lawrence's revisions.

From what I have gathered in conversation and from correspondence, other volume editors have experienced adversities similar to mine in their relationship with the Cambridge University Press Board: in which case this early part of the discussion may contribute to an improvement of mutual understanding between editor and Editorial Board as the Cambridge endeavor moves on into future volumes.

Let me say at once that in spite of the difficulties gone into here, I believe collaboration between the Cambridge Board and myself produced a text of *The Plumed Serpent* that will stand up under examination by critics, the general reader, or anyone else. If the product is thus satisfactory, then it may seem no more than quibbling to take up now the issue of how to describe the means by which this desirable end was achieved. I

99

suspect, however, that the outcome might not always be as fortunate as it was in this instance: that flaws in a description of principles and clashes of opinion often imperfectly resolved by compromise could damage the results in dealing with other works. And who knows, perhaps we could have turned out an even better text of *The Plumed Serpent* if the communication gap between the Board and myself had not often been so wide and demanded so much time and effort to bridge.

Before attempting to elucidate what may be taken as contradictions in what has been stated so far about my editorial procedure, I will outline some of the divergences between what was said and what was heard back and forth across the gap. Misunderstandings plagued us from start to finish. I began work in 1975—through a twelve-year span to publication in 1987. Though well-versed in Lawrence's Mexican period, at the outset I knew little about textual editing; and such articles as W. W. Greg's little gospel, "The Rationale of Copy-Text," offered less help than I had expected from it: in part because I was a puzzled beginner but also because even after I had learned from long experience, Greg's theories as presently interpreted did not seem fully adaptable to the practice of what I was engaged in. Not much guidance did I receive, either, in response to the proposal to edit the volume that I submitted to Cambridge. The evaluator—unidentified to me but I take it not a member of the Editorial Board—gave faint approval to my suggested editorial strategy, then went on to his greater interest in challenging my account of Lawrence's American connections. For one representative example, this: I had occasion to quote what Lawrence once wrote to Mabel Dodge in Taos: "I shall be so glad if I can write an American novel from that centre" (*Letters IV* 260). This, in the eyes of my evaluator, amounted to no more than a courteous comment to a prospective hostess.

Now here yawned a communication gap indeed, not so much between the writer and myself as between him and Lawrence's own words before his eyes!

Next—even though, as I say, the evaluator offered no serious objection to my technical methods—for reasons obscure to me, Cambridge asked that I submit a new proposal. I declined. At which point Michael Black, at that time the press director, stepped in with the sort of mediation that was to fill the breach more than once: to the effect that this was not so much a disagreement in principle as in how one put the case. After some delay, all parties concerned agreed to settle for this saving of face on both sides, and I went ahead with the edition.

Still, in spite of debate back and forth, the essential textual problems on which I badly needed advice remained unaddressed. There was no scarcity of material. All states of the novel's text had survived except Lawrence's final corrected proofs, and the chronological relationship between texts was unquestionable. We had the autograph manuscript (*MS*); the typescript made from it (*TS*)—which carried Lawrence's revisions (*TSR*); two sets of uncorrected galleys for the first English edition (*G*); and the published texts of the first English (*E1*) and the first American (*A1*) editions. Variants between the uncorrected *G* text and the published *E1* of course made most of Lawrence's final revisions easy to extrapolate.

Not fully conversant with editorial practice as presently conceived, which is purportedly based on Greg's theories, I went a different direction in choosing what Greg calls a "copy-text" from what Cambridge University Press had decided to designate as a "base-text." It appeared logical to my half-informed state of mind to assign this role to *E1*. My reasoning was that since this text is the most authoritative in substantives—that is, wording—after two stages of revision by Lawrence, and since substantives contribute far more to fullness of meaning than accidentals—that is, punctuation etc., then *E1* must take precedence over a text like *MS:* although the latter did contain Lawrence's original, uninfluenced punctuation, and it seemed a good plan, as I will later explain, to restore that. So, on the apparent good sense of my reasoning, I prepared a sample chapter and submitted it to the Board.

Now textual experts may wonder how I could ever have entertained such naive assumptions about editorial principles, and why I should risk embarrassment now by admitting to once having dwelt in such darkness. In answer, I hope to demonstrate that my premises were not so benighted as they may sound: not when the matter of how to reconstruct a text of this novel is weighed from all angles. At the moment I will say only that the other rim of the gap lay in the hazy distance as I waited, almost a year, for comments from Cambridge on my sample chapter—this delay, let me add, occurred while I was on a grant from the National Endowment for the Humanities and spending full-time on the edition, though not yet knowing where I stood with the Board. All I could do was push on in blind faith and growing uneasiness, for during that year I became better informed on the editorial theories that reign in our time.

When the reply from the Board came, the as-yet overlooked matter of a base-text was inevitably at the center of it. The Board, as textual scholars will already have guessed, required that we pick a text from early in the composition process, and in this case we had the earliest: *MS*. By now I was prepared to accept this as the base-text, knowing that protest would be futile, but I will not say that I had achieved the conviction on the subject that I knew the Board to hold. However, in anticipation I had already come to practical conclusions as to how the labor so far expended could be modified to fulfill the conditions that I had correctly expected the Board belatedly to set down. Let it remain an open question for the moment whether what I saw as the two demonstrable superiorities of *MS* over other texts warranted declaring it to be the one and only underpinning for a new edition.

Aware, then, that my own reservations about the Board's opinions on the interrelationship among texts would have no bearing on the actual work of editing, I forged ahead. Another common-sense observation from Michael Black helped to confirm my private attitude as well as my working methods: no matter at which end of the textual history I started, in his opinion I would probably reach about the same conclusions in judging the most acceptable readings. This indeed turned out to be true: with the pleasing advantage that my apparent obedience to declared editorial principles did not mean sacrificing the eclectic text that I was preparing, which is what the evidence seemed to me to demand.

But the slow unfolding of discord between the Board and myself was far from over. When I eventually submitted my nine hundred-page manuscript, I was in for new shocks. The most arresting of these was that the explanatory notes and appendixes came back to me unraveled and restitched with patches of wrong or outdated information hurriedly gotten together. To this I could only object that if illumination of one of Lawrence's most enigmatic works was so easy to whip up out of a couple of reference books, then why call in an expert to do it? So sparks flew back and forth across the chasm this time, until on this particular score the Board in the end came around to sweet reason—that is, to my point of view—and I won back the bulk of my notes and appendixes.

Another crisis arose over my introduction: one that led me to realize, as I often have before, that a natural mental barrier prohibits mutual understanding in almost any dispute. —Was it Conrad who said that our reason was given us to justify our desires? Another way of putting the same thing would be that our conclusions are contained in our assumptions, and all the rationalizing expended in between counts for little. The prospectus of the Cambridge Edition had instructed me to reconstitute the "genesis" of *The Plumed Serpent* and place the novel in the context of Lawrence's life and work. Now to me, "genesis" meant—as it still does—the growth of the work in the author's imagination from conception to maturity: analysis of which is attainable for *The Plumed Serpent* as it is for few other works by Lawrence, with a body of evidence reaching back at least to his first fascination with American literature in early 1916. But the Board's perception of "genesis" was far different from mine. To them it meant an account of contextual circumstances and details of the author's activities from about the time when he began composition of the physical text. My "genesis" was described by the Board as "intellectual background"—to be considered interesting but not essential to presentation of a volume in this series. Here we soon came to a nice distinction—the greatest narrowing of the communication gap, maybe, but still a cleavage: the distinction between critical analysis of the novel as literature—which I agreed would be out of place in this edition—and imaginative background essential to comprehending Lawrence's fictional purpose. My contention was that this disagreement need never have occurred if the prospectus had been clear. Of course nothing was to be done about that now—even if the Board had admitted to the ambiguity, which it did not—and the upshot was that I had to rewrite the introduction: retaining, by way of compromise, a minimum of the "intellectual background." The time and energy consumed in this repetition of a task thought to be already completed may well be imagined.

But then I see no need to go on belaboring contentions that are over and done with: which, as I say, resulted in no lasting damage to the text; and through which, as far as I know, all persons implicated survived in good health and in almost equable temper. The purpose for bringing up the dissension at all is by now evident: to suggest that ways be sought for closer cooperation, early on, between Editorial Board and volume editor.

What I do intend still to criticize goes beyond friction between individuals to my quarrel, mentioned above, with certain editorial principles accepted as unquestionable among many textual scholars. Let me reiterate that in my judgment a divergence in the understanding of concepts had no ill effect on the text of *The Plumed Serpent* as achieved. I wish I could speak with equal confidence of the "Textual apparatus." Here, I think, we were confronted by and never overcame a difficulty inherent to textual criticism as to most scholarship: a sound practice is hardly established before it becomes overextended, a convention adhered to even when circumstances call for a different approach, an orthodoxy: all of which is due to the natural conservatism—pedantry, often enough—of the world of learning. The "critical apparatus," the good old *apparatus criticus,* was devised, as we all know, for biblical and classical literature. The variants in dealing with texts of classical provenance are many. Manuscripts for any one work may run into the hundreds, but whatever the number of discrepancies between them, these are in most instances small: a word or a phrase, a few variations in accidentals traceable to the quirks of scribal transmission. All extant manuscripts of ancient works are far removed from the one the author himself wrote, manuscripts copied and recopied for centuries during which time documents with major differences in the text either disappeared or else were recognized as separate works. As for biblical texts, I assume that from the beginning the Holy Ghost was not given to revising or excising long passages, although the jots and tittles were pored over with rabbinical diligence.

When it came to adapting the traditional apparatus to more modern literature, some modifications had to be made, of course, but these have been minimal and done in fear of violating the traditions of our fathers. In the main, editorial policy still clings to the view that the long-revered textual apparatus is a wonderful machine for providing a complete history of any text.

Not so, I feel, with *The Plumed Serpent*. Here eleven lengthy excisions occur, either as deletions in *TSR* or as passages struck out in final proof and therefore absent from *E1*. Some of these were partially revised in *TSR*, and then have disappeared between *G* and *E1*. Some in *TSR* or in *G* were replaced by newly composed passages, some not. As it turned out, what had occurred here in the complicated transmission of text could not be recorded in the form of the textual apparatus adopted, not without a clutter of ellipses and other symbols that would hinder any reader in following the shift of Lawrence's thought from text to text. At first I elaborated a system of relegating these passages to an appendix, each entry headed by a thorough discussion of its place in the scheme of composition; and wherever thought necessary, an entry in the explanatory notes was to be supplied as well. The Board dismissed the idea out of hand: every variant was to go in the textual apparatus, *period*. Yet, once they truly looked into the problem, they too saw the predicament. Suggestions on what to do passed back and forth across our gap, none of which stood up under close inspection. Finally, sensing an impasse, I proposed setting up these passages in the apparatus in wider columns than those of the regular entries, with variants recorded internally—within braces, as someone else added. This we agreed on, though like many compromises, I consider this one only half-successful. I was even less pleased when it was decided, without consulting me, to print in wide columns only those passages over three hundred words—a mere mechanical adaptation that only confused the original purpose of setting these passages apart. And I cannot fail to add that the last remark crossing the gap in this controversy—when the volume was already in proof—came from Michael Black. And it was— guess what!—that maybe we ought to have printed these passages in an appendix.

Now while I think the reader's study of Lawrence's revisions would have been better assisted through a method less bound by custom, in any event the explanation in the heading to the textual apparatus is a true account of how it functions. This is not the case with the claims made in the "Note on the text," because what is asserted there is not how I under- stand what I did in assembling a text for this edition. And since a con- scious disparity between statement and practice may appear unforgivable in scholarship—even if I contend that it did no harm to the outcome in the text itself—let me hasten to explain. Speaking admittedly from experi- ence with a single volume, I must question the wisdom of having taken the prevailing editorial principles of today, widely revered though they are, as a theoretical groundwork. To clarify my position, let me glance at the evolution of textual criticism in recent years.

Work on the Cambridge Lawrence began in the midst of a contro- versy over the editing of American literature texts that dates from the 1960s and still goes on today.[1] Although not directly involved in the conflict, the Cambridge project has proceeded on criteria drawn up under its influence, addressing the same textual issues and relying on the same theoretical source: the Greg article already cited, "The Rationale of Copy- Text." Greg's arguments and the much-debated ramifications of these can be summarized as follows. In examining the habits of compositors who set new editions of Renaissance plays over the years—and who worked from earlier printed editions for which no authors' manuscripts were known to survive—Greg found that while they readily altered the punctuation of the source-copy, they were not prone to take such liberties with the wording. It was to distinguish between form and substance in these texts that Greg suggested the term "accidentals" for punctuation and other conventions of form, and the term "substantives" for the wording. His conclusion con- cerning accidentals was that in each successive edition they move farther away from whatever they may have been in the author's original. Conse- quently, the accidentals of the earliest printed text should be nearest to those of the author's lost manuscript, and thus the most "authoritative."

Greg recommended that this earliest printed text serve as the basis for any new edition of the work—for accidentals, remember—and borrowing a term first employed by R. B. McKerrow over forty years earlier, he called this the "copy-text." He added a cautionary point which under the circumstances would not even seem necessary, yet one which has not always been heeded: "The copy-text should govern (generally) in the matter of accidentals, but . . . the choice between substantive readings belongs to the general theory of textual criticism and lies altogether beyond the narrow principle of the copy-text" (Greg 26).

Unfortunately, Greg shifted the meaning of McKerrow's term, and thereby, as he should have foreseen, opened the way to disagreement and dispute. McKerrow had designated as "copy-text" the most authoritative text to be located—"authoritative" in both form and substance.[2] He was concerned—and so was Greg—about haphazard and arbitrary methods widespread in the discipline in choosing a text to rely on for a new edition. An all-too-prevalent practice came to no more than circular reasoning whereby an editor attributed to his chosen text authority whose chief source was his own preference for that particular text. Recognizing that those with least reason to be dogmatic are often the first to be so, Greg denounced this practice as "tyranny of the copy-text" (26) and advanced as a prime objective the abolition of such "tyranny" by restricting the powers of the despot.

The course of textual criticism in the McKerrow-Greg tradition has been expansive and tumultuous, and attended by a certain measure of irony. For better or worse, the scholars who formulated procedures for the large-scale project of editing major authors in American literature adopted Greg's "rationale"—not, to be sure, without widespread objection, since the theory was being applied to a body of texts far different from those Greg was analyzing. The contention has in fact ranged much farther afield, into whether there can ever be any such thing as an "authoritative text"— or even any such thing as an "author." All of that is outside the scope of the present paper, but the effects of the quarrel on the whole field of textual criticism, including the Cambridge Lawrence, have led to a curious situation, and this is where the irony lies. In the hands of its defenders, Greg's essay has been elevated to near-scriptural sanctity, with "copy-text" as the word at the sacred core. So that in spite of Greg's emphatic limitation on the status of such a document, and the protestations of Gregians that they do indeed abide by the "general theory of textual criticism" in the treatment of substantives, many an editor today assumes that the proclamation of his "copy-text," supported by elaborate and learned argument, is his most erudite task, and on difficult points in the actual editing of the work will appeal to the "copy-text" as the court of highest resort, sliding back into what editors were often guilty of in the days before the progress wrought by McKerrow and Greg, in effect revitalizing the "tyranny of the copy-text."

In light of these recent adventures of textual crusaders, let us return to the Cambridge Edition. In the hope of circumventing wars and rumors of wars raging around the field, Cambridge substituted the term "base-text" for "copy-text." For all that, the new identity appears to have done little toward reforming the culprit. I wonder, even, whether the new name has not led, at least in the case of *The Plumed Serpent,* to a greater unwarranted assumption of the importance of one text over another, to a classification of texts dictated by scholarly rigidity rather than by the nature of the material available. To wit, my "Note on the text" reads: "The base-text for this edition is DHL's autograph manuscript (*MS*), . . . *MS* has been emended as follows: (1) from DHL's revisions (*TSR*) in a typescript (*TS*) made from *MS;* (2) from the first English edition (*E1*), which incorporates DHL's changes in the unlocated final proofs. . . ." What this infers is that *MS* lies not merely at the beginning of the novel's creation, but is a summit of the author's creative power to which the editor has ascended to recapture the essence of the work; that *MS* is the sovereign document in a hierarchy, subject only to limited improvements by implanting fragments from later stages in the history of the text: as though the author went often astray in striving toward a finished work in the form envisaged and must be recalled by the editor to the pristine stage of creation and guided forward, as it were, under his direction.

But no—this does not truly depict what happened in the history of the *Plumed Serpent* text. *MS* is valuable as a source from which to retrieve elements lost in transmission that do much to enrich the Cambridge text, but to assign it a greater role is to exaggerate its rank in the great chain of composition. Where this and all other states of the text stand in Lawrence's grand design can best be appreciated by reviewing all the stages of composition, before as well as after *MS.*

Lawrence wrote a first version of his novel in Chapala, Mexico, in summer 1923. Although he gave it an ending, he called it unfinished, saying that he would return to it when his soul was calmer (*Letters IV* 465). This manuscript was typed at his New York publisher's and remained untouched until Lawrence went back to work on the novel in

Mexico more than sixteen months later.[3] Once he had looked over the Chapala version, he rejected it as a whole, and so removed it from any but a distant textual relation to the definitive novel (see Brett 181). Yet this move does exemplify the tentative nature of Lawrence's approach to the writing of this work. The first form of the second version is *MS*, which Lawrence turned out in Oaxaca in about ten weeks, during late 1924 and early 1925. By his own testimony he fell desperately ill on the very day he finished the manuscript (*Letters V* 230). The early chapters of this text were transcribed most inexpertly by Dorothy Brett, who was in Oaxaca during part of Lawrence's stay (Brett 204, 207), and the rest of it was eventually typed in Curtis Brown's New York office, with the punctuation "corrected" to conform to commercial secretarial standards.

With all of this before him, it is incumbent on the editor, in my opinion, to make decisions relying on external as well as internal evidence: taking account, for example, of Lawrence's attitude toward the novel brought on by his near-fatal sickness: that is to say, his condition certainly influenced his initial revisions. After his return to New Mexico, still far from well, he spoke of not daring so much as to look at the covers of the manuscript notebooks, because they brought to mind his revulsion against Mexico (*Letters V* 230). And then, when all of *MS* had been turned into typescript and sent to him, he delayed for weeks even reading through this text: although his task as he saw it just then was merely to "prune and correct" (*Letters V* 245, 254, 256). Once underway, he did do some "pruning" by excising passages here and there, but what he might have foreseen as "correcting" became a much more complex operation of revision and addition, extending from *TSR* on into the lost *G* proofs, until the substance of key portions of the novel as published stand altered out of recognition from what they were in *MS*. Through all of this, even after he had regained his health, Lawrence's feelings about the novel remained ambivalent. Most critics rely on one facet only of the contradictory evidence—Lawrence's more arresting assertions to the effect that *The Plumed Serpent* was his supreme accomplishment—while his real enough doubts about it go unrecognized.[4] The tone of these magnified claims is itself defensive, and they do not square with a remark dropped while he was revising galleys for *The Plumed Serpent:* that *Women in Love, The Rainbow,* and *Sons and Lovers* were his favorites among the novels (*Letters V* 314). Hesitation to advance toward publication is obvious in his communication with publishers. Martin Secker on one occasion consented to a request from Lawrence to "work freely" on the galleys—implying revision in depth, and Lawrence was not sure he wished Alfred Knopf to see the manuscript until he had done more work on it. In seeking reassurance of his achievement, he went so far as to ask friends expert in Mexican culture to read the galleys—though none ever did because of the publishing timetable. His reluctance to publish the novel at all, his protestations that it was too good for the public, may well have been a mask for uncertainties, and these are evident too in the sometimes aggressive warnings to friends that they would not like the book.

Secker and Knopf shared some of Lawrence's more open doubts about the novel: about its public reception and its saleability, but they agreed to publish it in any event because of the great importance that Lawrence attached to it. They finally set up a tight production schedule for the English and American editions, and Lawrence went along with their plans. In the end he had to settle for a hurried though intense revision of the galleys, making not a great many but nevertheless radical changes, largely in the final chapters.[5] Even so, Lawrence was not fully content with what he had done. According to Frieda, he regretted not giving the novel a different ending, already having made significant revisions here at every stage of composition (Frieda Lawrence 149). Unfortunately, no hint remains of what he had in mind for yet another change in the novel's conclusion.

With all this evidence of a novel growing but never maturing to the author's satisfaction, we might even conclude that the statement in the Cambridge "Note on the text" reverses what actually took place in the editing: that in fact the editor worked backward from the published text to the beginnings. But no, I am not reviving my original thought of making *E1* a base-text. What I am suggesting is that there was no necessity for specifying a base-text: that our having done so was little more than bowing to a perhaps milder form of tyranny than that which Greg pointed out, but tyranny nevertheless. I found support for my opinion in an unexpected quarter: from a staunch defender of the CEAA editions, Thomas Tanselle, who writes: "If one has a rational basis for selecting one reading over another at all points of variation, there is no need for one text to be designated as 'copy-text' at all" (Tanselle, "Classical" 63).

This is precisely the situation with *The Plumed Serpent*. The unknowns that inspired Greg's theory of copy-text are known quantities here. With all texts in his possession, the editor has no need to adopt a procedure whose theoretical justification and its vesting of overriding authority in a single text is dependent on conjecture stemming from an entirely different set of conditions. What is best applied here, recalling

Greg's phrase, is "the general theory of textual criticism." It was in accordance with this supposition that I undertook the following restoration of what appeared to me a superior text of *The Plumed Serpent*.

The most pondered decision of the whole task was what criteria to follow in choosing between *MS* and *TSR* variants. The common practice—which in itself denies the primary authority to the author's manuscript that the term "base-text" implies—is to adopt a straightforward chronology of intention: that is, to accept an author's later revisions as superseding earlier readings. I decided against a strict adherence to this practice. Following his usual custom, Lawrence read the typescript without referring to the manuscript, even though he had *MS* at hand and mistranscriptions in *TS* are rife. In a great many instances, he missed them altogether. When he did happen to notice a typist's misreading that was coherent but did not appeal to him, or when his attention was caught by one that was incoherent, his way was to repair the mistake by revising straight out of his head, ignoring *MS*. Disagreement with what I did in dealing with these "constrained revisions" will not be far to seek, I am sure. I simply found these *TSR* changes to be in the main hasty and ill thought-out: to be inferior, in short, to text produced in *MS* in a blaze of creativity. In nearly all cases I restored the earlier readings, not only for the mistranscriptions that Lawrence failed to catch but also for the constrained revisions. These ranged from one word to phrases of some length. At 240:17 in the Cambridge edition, a line in one of the hymns, the typist pecked out "truins" for *MS* "ruins." Since "railways" occurs in the same line, Lawrence by association changed the word in *TSR* to "trains," which makes sense in the context but loses the contrast between ancient and modern that the original line carried. So I restored "ruins." In another chant—at 176:2—the loss of poetic tone was even greater. In *MS* Lawrence imagined "The Snake of the coiled cosmos" as "heaving its plasm." The *TS* typist saw "heaving" as "hearing," which Lawrence in *TSR* then replaced with "wearing," producing a much less effective image. So I restored "heaving." For a longer example, at 26:4, Owen Rhys says in *MS*, speaking of how the *toreros* were performing in a bull-fight, that "there was some very skillful work, very plucky." The typist misread "plucky" as "pretty," which Lawrence left intact but added "Really very plucky." The rhythm of the original phrasing seemed superior to me, therefore I restored it. However, in a few instances of this sort, *TSR* was allowed to stand. At 118:36, where Lawrence is describing one of the Quetzalcoatl emblems, it was said in *MS* to resemble the Mexican flag, with an eagle "holding in its talons a writhing snake." The typist wrote "cactus" for "talons," which makes no sense. Lawrence substituted "beak and claws" for "cactus," which was accepted because the new wording more exactly describes the actual emblem on the Mexican flag.

To judge only from what I have said thus far, it may seem reasonable to conclude that the authority accorded to *MS* by this procedure with constrained revisions would justify calling it the "base-text." But when voluntary revisions came to be considered—that is, when *MS* was correctly transcribed yet Lawrence made many limited and several sweeping revisions—I can only say what the weight of evidence again and again seems to me to support: that Lawrence's attention was more fully engaged at these points, energized into what I will call a momentum of revision that began to come into play here and was sustained in the later stages of reshaping toward full realization of the story in the published work. Two brief citations will suffice as examples: *TSR* "unabashed" for *MS* "boyish" at 393:26, and—to show a typical progression of changes through all states of the text—*MS* "moon" becoming "leopard" in *TSR* and at last "glory" in the final proofs. For more complex decisions on the same order, the reader may look at 73:13, 106:16, and at many other entries easy to locate in the "Textual apparatus."

Certainly it is going pretty far to reject forced changes and to accept voluntary revision, in the same text, on the grounds that the author appears to the editor to have expended less creative energy on the former than on the latter. In taking this step, I was guided by a criterion that some will condemn: that of selecting what to me was the *best* Lawrence. In my judgment, such a practice reflects a sound principle of textual criticism, providing the critic has an intimate acquaintance with the author's work and his habits of creation. Indeed the laborer who refuses to take such responsibility is, to me, not worthy of his hire—such hire as there is. He is shirking his scholarly responsibility or else he suffers from mistrust of his own judgment.

Another disagreement that might arise on the relationship between *MS* and *TSR,* since Lawrence ignored the first while working on the second, is whether to take *TSR* as a whole new effort at creation and thus, far from advancing *MS* as the basis for a new edition, to strip it of nearly all authority. But Lawrence did not undertake the construction of *The Plumed Serpent* in that spirit—that is, not after abandoning the Chapala version for a fresh start. His letters provide ample evidence that, not only with this novel but with others too, he thought of his work as evolving in stages, even though he was frequently too impatient—and in this instance too much under the shadow of recent illness—to make sure that all details from an earlier phase of composition were transferred to the next. It does not follow, for me, that because he allowed mistranscriptions to stand he did not care about such particulars, and that we should not either in editing his work. So goes the "passive acceptance" theory that some scholars argue for: that an author accepts by default whatever he allows to pass in proofs, and thus it becomes his forever. This position appears to me to make a virtue, again, out of dodging responsibility. Every author is subject to editorial oversight of some sort, as often as not to interference that does damage to his work, and for a number of reasons he may be unable or at the moment too preoccupied with something else to do anything about it. (I know this from years of dealing with editors of my own fiction.) If the textual critic does not know his author well enough to identify certain nuances of his work lost to careless transmission or the unwarranted assumption of authority by publishers' editors—nuances that he would probably be thankful to have rescued and restored to his text, then the critic should either pick another author or else another profession.

Bowing to "passive acceptance" in editing *The Plumed Serpent* would have meant, for one thing, the loss of one of the greatest merits of *MS*. It contains untouched Lawrence's characteristic punctuation—the whole range of accidentals, to be exact, and these are superior by far to the tangle of styles that ensued. The transmission of the novel's text in fact stands as living proof of Greg's hypothesis on the degeneration of accidentals from manuscript through later forms of the text. In *The Plumed Serpent* the deterioration began with Dorothy Brett's pecked-out transcription, then proceeded through Curtis Brown's typists, the house-styling of Martin Secker, and the habits of the compositors at Dunedin Press who set type for *E1*. All such accidentals were dismissed in the present edition in favor of those from *MS*, unless the changes were demonstrably made by Lawrence himself—or, rarely in *E1*, conjectured to be so. Those who prefer their Lawrence to be written by Lawrence, down to colons and dashes, and not by others fussing over the text, will applaud the decision.

Thus a preponderance of accidentals and a fair number of substantives were adopted from *MS*. Still, the far greater mass of Lawrence's substantive revisions in *TSR* were retained; and from *TSR* on, the chronology of his intentions was generally adhered to: through *E1,* the last authoritative text, seeing that *A1* was set from a copy of the final *E1* proofs supplied to

Knopf by Secker, and Lawrence had no hand in the preparation of it. The overwhelming bulk of the Cambridge text, then, is already present in *E1*: which is not to minimize the importance of those elements recovered from earlier states of the text. Indeed, what I have to add now may constitute an argument to anyone fond of numbers that we may still refer to *MS* as a "base-text." We should keep in mind, though, that numbers alone can be misleading. The Cambridge text includes about thirty-five hundred changes from the published versions of *The Plumed Serpent* formerly available. Some seventeen hundred of these—about thirteen hundred accidentals and four hundred brief substantives—were adopted from *MS*. But if *MS* contributes about as many alterations as *TSR* and *G* combined, the adoptions from *TSR* and *G* loom much larger in volume and significance. When all of this is taken into account, the Cambridge text of *The Plumed Serpent* is an eclectic text based not on *MS* but on what appeared preferable to informed critical judgment from the whole assemblage of the extant texts.

Obviously my editing approach sets aside the fact that Lawrence could have done everything I did in establishing a text for *The Plumed Serpent* and yet chose not to take that opportunity. I think of what I did, and for the reasons set down above, as serving his work better than he chose to serve it himself, on the assumption that such proceeding lies within the province—and indeed constitutes the duty—of the textual critic.

Now I do not wish to leave the impression that I put one over on the Cambridge Board in the editing pattern described. They inspected and approved the entire text. For all our other differences, our opposed conceptions of the nature of the endeavor we were engaged in were never a serious impediment. —Of course, the Board never knew what my conception was.

To sum up what I have said with particular reference to other current controversies on the nature of textual criticism, first of all I disagree with the hypothesis that each time an author revises the latest state of his text in the ongoing process of composition, he has in effect created a new work, and so advances by a series of "synchronic" texts. The only two forms of *The Plumed Serpent* conceivable as "synchronic" are the rejected first *Quetzalcoatl* and *E1*. In my opinion, *MS, TS, TSR* and *G* must be viewed as Lawrence saw them: as imperfect drafts of the eventual work of art that he pursued from the time of setting forth, as stages in a "diachronic" process. I am aware that here we enter the treacherous ground of defining what this "eventual work of art" may be, this "ideal text" whose very existence may in fact be questioned. To speak from the standpoint of common sense and the demonstrable experience of many authors—Lawrence emphatically among them, this perfected form of course does not exist, not even in the only place where it could: in the imagination of the author. After all, as stated above, Lawrence is reported to have been unhappy with the ending of *The Plumed Serpent* that he had already altered three or four times. An "ideal text," assuredly in this case and I believe in any other, is thus a mere abstraction that it is pointless to discuss.

This line of reasoning may appear to lead, once again, to the adoption of *E1* as the culminating form of Lawrence's artistic endeavor, assuming as I do that the evolution of the novel was diachronic. But here another consideration came into play. Too much went into the making of *E1* from sources other than the author. Choosing it as the dominant text would have entailed acceptance of the theory of a "sociological text"—in which the author is almost as dead as God is said to be. To paraphrase one critic, he is a mere "organism" funneling the streams of his culture through to those who make their own essential contributions to the text: editors, compositors, anyone who touches it, even anyone who reads it after publication![6] This theory holds that the "text" is never finished, that a new text springs into being under each eye that falls on it, that no "authority" can ever be asserted for any specific text—and so on. Of course one might pause to consider here that this continuum of transformation goes on by definition after the death of the author—I mean after his literal death, not the socially determined state of lifelessness the poor sap was in when he thought he was writing a book. The later scholarly editor then has a perfect right to enter the continuum himself and to establish a text as he sees fit: which would seem to argue for almost any kind of *Plumed Serpent* text I might have desired. Short of that extreme, and with a reordering of some of the premises behind the theory, there is yet a modicum of good sense in it. To repeat, I believe Lawrence to have been striving all the while toward an unattainable ideal text—a "diachronic" intention. He may have classified the final stage of this creation—briefly—as his greatest work to date, but other evidence points to his discontent with any state of the text. What better argument could there be for the textual editor to seek a solution to the contradiction by reinstating what is, in his judgment after long study, the best of Lawrence's creative intentions—and thus the nearest to what would have pleased him?

In the hope of avoiding misinterpretation, even yet, of what I have said here, I had better add a final word of explanation. For in spite of my efforts to specify how an editorial method understood in certain terms by the general editors and in others by the volume editor can still lead to a defensible text, some readers may yet conclude that my remarks call into questions the value of my edition: whether I intend them to or not, even whether I realize they do or not. I can only appeal to such readers to exercise a sense of discrimination that I can best illustrate by a sort of fable:

A traveler looking for a certain village stopped two men on the road to ask directions. The first man he met gave him a map showing the road system, the location and course of streams, the distribution of wooded and open land, topographical contour lines, and so on. The second man he met described the landscape ahead: hills, trees, streams, a curious rock formation, the color and size and grouping of houses, and other observable characteristics.

A little later another traveler in search of this village came along, inquired the way of the same two men and received the same answers. The first traveler went by the map, the second by the description of the countryside.

They both arrived at the same village.

NOTES

1. Tanselle offers a thoroughgoing history of the controversy in *Textual Criticism*.
2. ". . . the copy-text, by which, here as throughout the book, I mean the text used in each particular case as the basis for mine. . ." (McKerrow xi).
3. As a title for his novel, Lawrence chose *Quetzalcoatl*, the name of a major Aztec god, of whom Don Ramón Carrasco is the fictional incarnation. The change of title to *The Plumed Serpent* was made at the insistence of Alfred Knopf, over Lawrence's protest that it sounded "a bit silly" (*Letters V* 263). The Chapala version, under the original title, was published in 1994 by Black Swan Books, edited with an introduction by Louis Martz.
4. The argument advanced in the remainder of this paragraph is based on a close inspection of evidence gathered from the following pages of *Letters V:* 260, 264, 267, 268, 270–71, 272, 286n1, 287, 291, 297n2, 314, 320, 323, 332, 342, 370, 373, 374, 375, 387, 402.
5. For particulars of Lawrence's last revisions and the publishers' scheduling, see my "Introduction" to *The Plumed Serpent*, xxxv–xxxviii.
6. For a good example of this kind of argument, see Peckham.

WORKS CITED

Brett, Dorothy. *Lawrence and Brett: A Friendship*. Philadelphia: Lippincott, 1933.

Clark, L. D. "Introduction" to D. H. Lawrence, *The Plumed Serpent*. xix–xlvii.

Greg, W. W. "The Rationale of Copy-Text." *Studies in Bibliography* 3 (1950–51): 19–36.

Lawrence, Frieda. *"Not I, But the Wind. . . "*. New York: Viking, 1934.

McKerrow, R. B. "Note on the Treatment of the Text Adopted in This Edition." In *Works of Thomas Nashe*, Vol. I. Ed. R. B. McKerrow. London: Sidgwick, 1904.

Peckham, Morse. "Reflections on the Foundations of Modern Textual Editing." *Proof* 1 (1971): 122–55.

Tanselle, G. Thomas. "Classical, Biblical, and Medieval Textual Criticism and Modern Editing." *Studies in Bibliography* 36 (1983): 21–68.

———. *Textual Criticism since Greg: A Chronicle, 1959–1985*. Charlottesville: U of Virginia P, 1987.

Editing the Cambridge *Lady Chatterley:* Collaboration and Compromise

Michael Squires

To say that *Lady Chatterley's Lover* proved a complex text to edit masks the truth, for not only did editing the novel pose surprising challenges, but (even more surprising) the internal process of collaboration and compromise between editor and Editorial Board yielded its own set of challenges. L. D. Clark's essay in this volume shows how such a dual challenge invited problems of copy-text and coordination. Since the editorial work on *Lady Chatterley's Lover* required fifteen years to complete, it may be useful to explain—from my perspective as editor—how various forms of negotiation delayed, but often strengthened, the edition that resulted. Inside the editorial process, the pattern I discovered was one of *recursive accommodation:* hypotheses were proposed, challenged, modified, then refitted against the evidence of the surviving prepublication artifacts. This extended process, although it operated imperfectly, much improved the reliability of the newly edited *Lady Chatterley's Lover.*[1] To assess the way in which recursive accommodation worked, I start with a narrative; discuss examples of negotiation and compromise; then ponder the politics of scholarly editions and the theoretical model governing the Cambridge Lawrence.

I

Approached in 1975 by Michael Black, publisher of the Cambridge University Press, I prepared a detailed proposal outlining strategies for editing the novel and in April 1976 was given a contract. As I explain more fully in the volume's introduction, I proposed in essence to use as base-text the holograph manuscript (*MS*) located at the University of

Texas at Austin, and to emend it with authorial variants from the sole surviving typescript that Lawrence corrected and expurgated (hereafter called *TSR,* or "type script revised") as well as from the Florence edition Lawrence published privately in 1928 (hereafter *F*). I began recording variants from the manuscript. By the time I had reached chapter 6, I noticed that peculiar patterns of variation in *TSR,* such as ellipses replacing Lawrence's periods, suddenly disappeared, to be followed in chapters 6–12 by a great many changes in Lawrence's manuscript wording, which had not been evident up to that point. The troubling question was, what could account for this strange sequence of textual differences? Clearly, some hypothesis was needed to explain how the text was transmitted. Did several typists transcribe—inaccurately—Lawrence's handwritten manuscript? Had Lawrence revised an intermediate typescript, now lost? Could his wife Frieda or his Italian publisher Pino Orioli, or Orioli's novelist-friend Norman Douglas, have made corrections on a lost document?

After much deliberation, I proposed that Lawrence's typists *had* interfered with his text, mangling his punctuation and his words, forcing a responsible editor to rely heavily on the manuscript for accepted readings. But with many documents missing—two of the three copies of the typescript, as well as the proofs—how could we be sure? I presented this hypothesis at the 1979 D. H. Lawrence Conference in Carbondale, Illinois. Here is part of what I wrote:

> As best I can determine, chapters 6 through 12 were typed by several typists; one, whom I call the London typist, made all three copies of chapters 6 through 8 and part of 12, and it is obvious from examining chapter 6 alone that she frequently altered Lawrence's substantives— though why she presumed to alter them is unclear.[2]

She had, for example, altered "father" to "Daddy," "smudge of blacklead" to "black smudge," "child" to "little girl," and "slender" to "slim."

The Editorial Board was naturally cautious. Michael Black wrote in November 1979: "Carl [Baron, a Board member] and Lin Vasey and I are all in some degree uneasy about the hypothesis that the typist/typists were so high handed. . . . One begins to cast around for an alternative explanation." In December 1979 Lindeth Vasey, an American textual scholar hired by the Press to assist with the Lawrence Edition, wrote that she had been selected to visit me in Blacksburg, Virginia. "Should be a lovely chance to marshal all our arguments and evidence," she wrote in the following month. Collaboration had begun. We worked in my office one whole February day, trying out possible counterarguments: *Could* the patterns of corruption be characteristic of Lawrence himself? *Could* an (as yet) unidentified friend, perhaps named in an unpublished letter, have served as copy editor? *Could* the Italian compositors, though they spoke no English, have altered his text? Before Lin Vasey departed, she felt "inclined" to agree with my hypothesis about how the text was transmitted. A few days later she wrote, "I must admit the theory is tempting."

As I expected, the Editorial Board preferred inferences drawn from hard evidence such as Lawrence's unpublished letters, which were being collected at the University of Tulsa and then later at the University of Texas. By 9 May she voiced again the familiar worry: "Carl . . . and one or two other members of the Editorial Board are not [yet] convinced. . . ." Perhaps—we agreed—another examination of the original documents would yield a more persuasive hypothesis. In June 1980 I returned to the Humanities Research Center (HRC) at the University of Texas at Austin, to recheck both manuscript and surviving typescript, to consult the file of Lawrence's letters that the Center had recently acquired, and to fashion somehow an alternative hypothesis. Warren Roberts, Lawrence's bibliographer—then still active on the Editorial Board—listened most sympathetically, then told me that he doubted Catherine Carswell, one of Lawrence's typists and a steadfast friend, would intentionally have altered a syllable of the master's prose. Nor, he thought, would she have recruited typists from among her friends who would alter his work. Thereupon I looked hard, thought long, kept asking, "What if *this* rather than *that* happened?" Speculation reigned. But when I left the Center, I wrote to the Board that I had (regrettably) "found nothing to alter my hypothesis about the typing and transmission of the text of *Lady Chatterley*." So far, negotiation had yielded no solution to the novel's textual problems.

What to do? The Board, communicating through Vasey, next proposed an outside consultant as a way of mediating these views of the text's transmission. In August she wrote: "Warren suggested having an unprejudiced outside reader look at the final introduction and text." In my uncertainty I imagined a hostile outside reader as a tool to terminate my contract and in effect to waste the time I had invested in the edition. Worse, two of my American colleagues in Lawrence studies had just been refused contracts to edit, respectively, *The Rainbow* and *"The Prussian Officer" and Other Stories*.

I was perplexed about how to proceed. In November 1980 Vasey reassured me "that we find your editorial work satisfactory and . . . that the outside reader would only be evaluating the introduction. . . ." The following April, Michael Black also wrote reassuringly: "I feel confident you can produce a reasoned statement on the [limited] evidence you now have." This reasoned statement is what I attempted when I began slowly to rewrite the Introduction. Vasey's optimism ("the end is . . . in sight") proved premature, for a year later, in May 1982, Michael Black wrote me again:

> We have just been having a meeting of the Editorial Board of the DHL Edition. . . . You are engaged on one of the most difficult and problematic texts. We believe you have correctly identified the *nature* of the problem, but handling it poses other problems. For instance, we believe that doubtful cases must all be settled *one way*. . . .

The Board and I still needed to agree on several matters: (1) how to identify the several typists who had been engaged to prepare the typescript; (2) how to treat those revisions in Lawrence's hand that appeared in the revised typescript but not in the Florence edition; and (3) how to treat variants that appeared only in the Florence edition.

In November 1983 the Editorial Board was reconstituted: Vasey and John Worthen joined Black and James T. Boulton as active members, Roberts and Baron serving now as advisors. Soon thereafter, Worthen, wholly unfamiliar with the problems of the *Lady Chatterley* edition, was asked in effect to serve as the long-awaited consultant; he had already edited the Cambridge edition of Lawrence's *The Lost Girl* and knew Lawrence's work intimately. I first heard from him in June 1984: "First thing to say: what a monster of a problem!" He largely concurred with my assumptions about how the text of *Lady Chatterley* was transmitted, and soon emerged, along with Vasey, as a vital collaborator.

We agreed that chapters 1–5 were at first typed in duplicate, another copy being made later, in London, not from the manuscript (as one might have expected) but from one of the typed copies, this *retyped* copy then serving as printer's copy. We also agreed that chapters 6–12 were typed by a series of amateur typists, on different typewriters, on different sorts of paper, with different spacings and margins. And we agreed—at last—that these amateurs very often interfered to "improve" Lawrence's style. Here are five examples from among hundreds that could be adduced:

Lawrence wrote: "Connie pondered this" (chap. 6).
His typist typed: "Connie considered this."

Lawrence wrote: "He opened the door with curious quickness" (chap. 6).
His typist typed: "He opened the door quickly."

Lawrence wrote: "In a question of the masters and the men. . ." (chap. 7).
His typist typed: "In a dispute between masters and men. . . ."

Lawrence wrote: "dipping silent" (chap. 8).
His typist typed: "dipping silently."

Lawrence wrote: "sitting at table" (chap. 12).
His typist typed: "sitting at the table."

The problem of the multiple typists having been resolved, Worthen focused attention on a different problem—how to regard the corrected and expurgated typescript which Lawrence had sent to his American publisher, Alfred Knopf. Earlier I had argued that in this typescript (the only one that survives) Lawrence's corrections, as distinguished from his expurgations, ought to be included in the newly edited text. I reasoned that we can see on the corrected page how Lawrence wanted his text revised, and that if Knopf had published the novel (as Lawrence hoped when he sent the typescript to New York), then the corrected text is what, for decades, Americans would have read. Worthen countered with his persuasive "cul-de-sac" argument:

> . . . you might consider whether *TS* represents anything except a cul-de-sac, so far as textual emendation goes. Should one even *try* to make use of it? . . . [Lawrence] chose which text to use as setting-copy. . . .

And that text was not, he argued, the typescript that survives. Lawrence, for instance, wrote in the manuscript: "He [Mellors] sat there in the hut, his face pulled to mocking irony" (217:30), but in the Knopf typescript (though not in the Florence edition) Lawrence revised *irony* to *bitterness*— a reading that we ultimately rejected from the Cambridge edition. A few pages earlier Lawrence wrote in the manuscript: ". . . she [Bertha Coutts] was with that fellow at Stacks Gate" (202:31), then added, "It's a bit degenerate" to the Knopf typescript, an addition not found in the Florence edition (and eventually rejected from Cambridge).

Although I understood the principle Worthen urged—that in expurgating a typescript Lawrence's intention had presumably changed—it is also arguable that an author can simultaneously have mixed intentions: can want to expurgate but can also want to improve his text. Splitting expurgation from improvement would in some cases require editorial judgment. But (I reasoned) if I could establish that Lawrence's typescript corrections were made later than his expurgations—and hence that he may have gone over the revised typescript again to improve rather than expurgate—then the revised text would embody Lawrence's *latest* thoughts and hence provide a strong claim as a source of emendation. Collaboration again proved decisive. I remember sitting with Vasey in the conference room at the Humanities Research Center, both of us gravely disappointed that the typing paper had so yellowed and cracked, and that Lawrence's ink had so faded and changed color, that we could draw no convincing conclusions. Even now, I suspect that Lawrence probably corrected and expurgated this typescript *after* he sent the setting-copy typescript to his Florentine printer: but a compelling case cannot now be made. Negotiation reduced editorial risk.

About a year later, in May 1985, Worthen wrote: "My sense is that the textual argument is now right, in most respects. . . ." In July he and I met for the first time in Bristol, England, at the 1985 Lawrence Centenary Conference, held at a restored Victorian mansion ominously near the "suicide bridge" to Clifton, and tried to determine how best to present the various kinds of evidence that had accumulated. The Board wanted the introduction to be no longer than twenty thousand words. I have a keen recollection of a high-ceilinged room overlooking a terraced lawn, and a long, animated discussion of where in the introduction I should discuss the third version of the novel in the context of the first two versions, and where—in an appendix?—I should differentiate the typing characteristics of the four amateur typists. My journal entry for 20 July reads as follows:

Yesterday I spent 2½ hours with John Worthen going over my Introduction. The session was useful. He said the Introduction was "very good" but warned me that "the hardest part is yet to come," meaning that Jim Boulton and Michael Black are likely, still, to rewrite and restructure what I've written.

II

Examples of negotiation and compromise will reveal how the process of recursive accommodation worked. Having taken a general editorial stance of eliminating as much interference as possible from the text of *Lady Chatterley's Lover*, I confronted more than a few cases that demanded editorial judgment.

As we collectively mulled over the difficult cases, there was rarely any question about whether a spurious reading was aesthetically better than an authorial reading: our principle was to choose a manuscript (base-text) reading whenever we suspected interference. The difficulty of course was to know when suspicion was strong enough to urge rejection of a later, authorial reading—and that is where collaboration proved ultimately most valuable. For instance, in chapter 7 the reading "wisps of smoke" (75:30) appeared in *MS* and *TSR*, "men of smoke" appeared in *F*. Although I favored "wisps of smoke," Vasey countered: "(1) This is a substantive change and not likely to have been the [Italian] typesetter. (2) It is not an interfering typist. Therefore, on principle we should accept *F*." To this argument I responded: "I see your point but think that the printer must have introduced an error here, which [Lawrence], ill, miscorrected. I still favor *MS*." The rebuttal: "Explanation sounds ingenious to me." I answered at length:

No, to me there is no question about this one! Lawrence's narrative method is to employ *incremental summary* in his dialogue:

75:6   floated like tobacco-smoke [says Connie].

75:9   bridge across the chasm will be the phallus [says Dukes].

75:16   Connie says people like wisps of smoke, and Olive says . . . babies in bottles, and Dukes says the phallus is the bridge to what comes next [says Clifford].

75:23   might even be real men [says Dukes].

75:28   a civilisation of genuine men and women . . . would be even more amazing than (wisps *or* men) of smoke or babies in bottles [says Dukes].

Tommy Dukes summarizes both Connie's and Olive's statements: he understands that Connie is *responding* to Lady Bennerley's "help us forget our bodies," which "wisps of smoke" would accomplish: against which Dukes pits his "genuine men and women" who are *bodied*. To print "men of smoke" would blur the contrast Lawrence urges between bodiless and bodied, between "genuine" and "wisps" in his text. We choose *F* substantives *unless we suspect compositorial error*. We cannot know all the sources of possible error, but we can protect Lawrence's text from *likely* interference. Therefore I say *MS*. We *know* Lawrence wrote it, and we can defend it. We cannot defend "men of smoke." The printer might have set "wips" or "wiss" and Lawrence, not immediately recognizing the word, might have altered it. We must remember that, according to both Lawrence and Frieda, the proofs were thick with error.

Worthen gracefully accommodated my intransigence: "I *don't* agree, but think this is important to [Squires] and he must decide." So "wisps of smoke" it was.

Other troublesome cases required that we decide whether or not a typist's corruption had stirred Lawrence to make revisions in his text that, presumably, he would not otherwise have made. For instance, in chapter 2 Lawrence had written in his manuscript book:

> Connie had been now nearly two years at Wragby, living this vague life of absorption in Clifford and his needing her, and his work, especially his work. (18:21–23)

Perhaps because the typist changed "this vague life" to "their vague life," the reading of the Florence edition differs significantly, having a plural subject and a condensed predicate:

> Connie and Clifford had been now nearly two years at Wragby, living their vague life of absorption in Clifford and his work.

We never asked, "Is this an aesthetically better reading?" or "Is this reading creatively outdated?" but instead applied an editorial principle that we would accept *F*'s substantives unless, as in this instance, we suspected interference.

In chapter 10, in a passage about Mellors and Connie, we again had to decide whether or not the typist's corruption likely caused Lawrence to revise *TSR*. Set in its narrative context, the manuscript reading follows, with the crucial variant underlined:

. . . he subsided too, and lay utterly still, unknowing, while her grip on him slowly relaxed, and she lay inert.

And they lay, and knew nothing of *time or* even of each other, both lost. (*MS* 329)

The typist, perhaps wrongly thinking that *nothing . . . nor* formed correlatives, produced this revision of the critical sentence:

And they lay and knew nothing of *time, nor* even of each other, both lost. (*TS* 195)

The underlined words below show Lawrence's handwritten revision:

And they lay, and knew *nothing, not* even of each other, both lost. (*TSR* 134:13)

Since the *TSR* reading also occurs in *F,* Lawrence must have copied it into the setting-copy *TS* (now missing) used by the Florentine printer.

The delicate issue was to determine whether Lawrence, seeing the words *time, nor,* would probably have revised: whether the typist's corruption gave him an opportunity to condense and therefore sharpen his sentence: or whether the typist's jarring corruption stimulated him to amend his sentence *in ways that corruption dictated.* Although a case can be made for either *MS* or *TSR* readings, we were guided here as elsewhere by editorial principle: we adopted *F* substantives unless we suspected a compositor's interference, and agreed finally that the argument that corruption had instigated revision was not strong enough to compel us to choose the *MS* reading. We chose *F.*

Similar cases occurred in the last portion of the novel, chapters 13–19, which Maria Huxley typed in Switzerland. In chapter 17, I would have accepted Lawrence's *TSR* revision if Vasey, while checking the original documents at the HRC, had not detected the typist's underlying corruption. Here, with key variants labeled, is the sentence in which Connie Chatterley, on holiday in Venice, recognizes that she is pregnant:

So the stupor of sunlight and lagoon salt and (*MS*: sea-baths) (*TS:* sea-bathe) (*TSR:* sea-bathing) and lying on shingle and finding shells and drifting away, away in a gondola was completed by the pregnancy inside her, another fulness of health, satisfying and stupefying. (*MS* 656–57; *TS* 370; *CUP* 261:19–22)

Surely, since the typist's *sea-bathe* almost certainly provoked Lawrence's *sea-bathing*, we must on principle revert to the *MS* reading. *MS sea-baths* is also, as it happens, aesthetically superior: three alliterative nouns (*sunlight, salt, sea-baths*) are followed by three parallel gerunds (*lying, finding, drifting*).

For a long time the issue of how much to regularize proved equally vexing. Early I inclined toward polishing the text of the novel, standardizing inconsistencies and irregularities. Eventually I came to see that many of Lawrence's apparent inconsistencies may be *meaning-bearing* and contribute subtleties that might well be significant to the novel's readers and critics. As Michael Black says in his essay for this volume, "If an unlikely reading can make sense, even a strange sense, it is much more likely to be what the author wrote than any more commonplace idea one can come up with oneself."

But certainly Lawrence would have expected *some* inconsistencies to be corrected. While I was collating manuscript, typescript, and Florence edition, I recognized that Lawrence was consistent in his use of a great many accidentals. Finally we decided that we would not attempt to regularize inconsistencies except where they fell within a page or so of one another: hence we printed "forget-me-nots" at 184:8 but, five lines later, added hyphens to Lawrence's "forgetmenots." I worried that readers would be distracted by inconsistencies, wondering if we had been inattentive to detail and allowed an error to creep into the text.

One area of potential regularization proved more difficult: what to do with Lawrence's inconsistencies in capitalizing "lady" and "ladyship." For years I had hoped that some principle would emerge from a study of the prepublication documents, and finally I thought I saw a beacon in the mist and, though it was later rejected, wrote this sentence for the volume's Introduction: "Since Lawrence when expurgating *TS* frequently capitalized these words in passages of direct address (e.g., *TS* 124, 174, 185, 199, 200, 328), his preference is here adopted as a consistent emendation." Later, when Vasey isolated all of them in her final round of editing, and we could see them whole, it became clear that Lawrence may have embarked on a program of regularizing *TS because* his typists had capitalized many of them: he may have been trying to edit his text to accord with a typist's preference.

As late as 1990 I wrote: "I worry now that Lawrence's rather sporadic attempts at regularizing his own typescript were stimulated at least partly by *TS* corruption." Indeed, as I saw it, Lawrence may have intended some capitalized forms to be ironic, a means of creating emotional distance, as when Mellors, after a pleasurable afternoon, parts from Connie: "'Goodnight, your Ladyship,' came his voice" (128:4), jarring Connie, and eliciting her surprised return, "'Why did you say that?'" (128:7). Altogether it seemed better *not* to try to regularize these variants and instead to preserve distinctions that Lawrence may have intended. Hence we print "my Lady" on 112:27 but also "my lady" on 215:8, "your Ladyship" on 149:5 but also "your ladyship" on 120:37. Finally, no acceptable compromise seemed possible.

Lawrence's eloquent essay *A Propos of "Lady Chatterley's Lover,"* also part of the volume, posed a different set of problems. What, for instance, were we to do with the variants that were uncovered by a collation of two central documents: first, "My Skirmish with Jolly Roger," Lawrence's preface to the Paris edition of *Lady Chatterley's Lover;* and second, the Mandrake Press edition of *A Propos,* which was published soon after Lawrence died in 1930? Were variants such as

It is owing to (*MS*)   Owing to (Mandrake)
Parisian bookshop (*MS*)   Paris form of booksellers (Mandrake)

possibly—or probably—Lawrence's? The full textual history cannot be recounted here, but the issue hinged on whether or not Lawrence was *likely* to have made such changes. I remained skeptical of them. In March 1989 Worthen commented:

It seems to me incontrovertible that DHL probably had some kind of a hand in at least some of these [changes]. . . . And . . . you accept the fact that somehow DHL managed to supply the title [*A Propos*]; that it was his handwriting, or words inscribed by [his publisher P. R.] Stephensen but dictated (or at least supplied) by DHL. . . . If you accept THAT: that DHL gave Stephensen the title, probably in person, probably in January 1930: then is it sensible to refuse to accept the other changes which Mandrake introduced to update the essay? . . . If some of the changes of substantives in *E1* [Mandrake Press edition] are DHL—and I mean by that probably DHL's ink from DHL's pen, in the hand of DHL, on the page of *P1* [Paris edition of *Lady Chatterley*] supplied by DHL, though *perhaps* only DHL's voice in the ear of an amanuensis—then I think you have to take all of 'em.

I responded:

> Yes, only now have I recognized that the essay's title may *not* be DHL's! But if we choose that title (*A Propos of "Lady Chatterley's Lover"*) in the same way that *Study of Thomas Hardy* was chosen over *Le Gai Savaire,* as the title by which the work has been known since its publication, then I believe that your argument, "if you take the title, you have to take everything else in Mandrake," loses its force. . . .
>
> Moreover, I think it entirely possible that DHL, in conversation with P. R. Stephensen, might have acceded to—or even supplied— the *A Propos* title *without having therefore approved all of the other changes in question.* So—in response to your query, "is it sensible to refuse to accept the other changes which Mandrake introduced to update the essay?"—yes, perhaps so.
>
> But the critical phrase is "introduced to update the essay": that leaves many alterations unaccounted for. . . . I find your argument— that "DHL had the opportunity" to revise, therefore he must have made these revisions: and further, that the stylistic tightening of *It is owing* to *Owing* is a change that Stephensen is "unlikely" to have made—unpersuasive. Look at all the substantive revisions we're re-jecting from *Lady Chatterley's Lover:* the Board originally thought that DHL was responsible for them. He wasn't—demonstrably. And to say that Stephensen wouldn't have interfered is as risky as saying that the London typists of *Lady Chatterley's Lover* wouldn't have inter-fered. How do you *know* he wouldn't? and even if DHL were cavalier and (exhausted) cried, "Do as you like with the essay!" we still shouldn't want such revisions in a critical text.
>
> In sum: the arguments you adduce—however intelligent and well-intentioned—seem to me so risky and so circumstantial that we're in danger of printing words that DHL never penned, or never ap-proved, or never even saw or heard.
>
> I wonder now in closing: Could we choose *only* the title and the substantives that "update" the earlier form of the essay—they are, I think, *probably* DHL's—and reject both the other substantives and all of the accidental variants, which are only, I think, *possibly* DHL's?

Obviously with a view toward compromise, Worthen replied in May 1989:

It is possible to divide up the alterations in *E1* into (I think) three categories. . . .

A: those relating to the fact of 1930 publication, not 1929. I am prepared to accept that A is more of a publisher's concern than an author's: so that, although I feel fairly sure that DHL made them (in particular 6:1, which you also feel "Sounds like DHL's revision"), I'm prepared to be advised by your proper caution and let drop.

A	1:3	I brought out in 1929 *instead of* I now bring out
A	2:7	1928 *instead of* last year
A	6:1	I managed to get published the *instead of* So here is this

B: those altering wording, such as might be introduced by a fussy printer or publisher. The alteration at 14:9 I can only view as a printer's error, if it is not DHL: but the fact that it is on its own, so far away from the others, counts against it being DHL's. And as an error it is *weird*. But I am prepared to accept that B may be Mandrake—publisher or printer.

B	1:2	Owing *instead of* It is owing
B	4:14	the *instead of* an (authorized edition)
B	11:16	[young] *omitted from* all young girls
B	14:9	stale grey *instead of* stock old (puritan) [(Squires): "an odd revision"]

C: those which (to my mind) can only be authorial.

C	1:1	*A Propos of "Lady Chatterley's Lover" instead of* Introd. to Lady C.
C	1:5	hoping at least to *instead of* which should surely [(Squires): "Could be DHL revision"]
C	1:6	certainly *added before* prompt and busy [(Squires): "Could be DHL revision"]
C	2:2	or Philadelphia *added after* New York [(Squires): "Sounds like DHL addition"]
C	2:8	from Florence *added after* that I put out [(Squires): "Sounds like DHL addition"]

I suggest that we adopt category C, and consider adopting category A.

Sensitive to the merits of compromise, I soon replied:

> I think that we disagree about the procedures for gauging an author's intention. Nonetheless, I'm prepared to compromise and to accept the eight variants in your categories A and C, and to reject all of the others. Given the scanty textual and biographical evidence that exists, I think that's the best we can do.

I will give Worthen the final word. He concluded two weeks later:

> I'm sure that's right, to adopt those emendations. I'd never have been happy if we'd gone to press, and those DHLish things had been left out: they would have remained a nagging worry. It's the right compromise.

III

I want now to offer some remarks on the Edition as a whole and on the politics of editing. In spite of enormous merits, such scholarly enterprises as the Cambridge Edition of Lawrence encounter a variety of risks, as power flows from central Board to isolated editor.

In any such comprehensive edition, all assumptions about textual theory are best made explicit to volume editors. When Hans Gabler and John Kidd can disagree so vigorously about the text of *Ulysses;* when Fredson Bowers and James Thorpe can reach such different conclusions about authorial intention; when Jerome McGann, Hershel Parker, and Thomas Tanselle can challenge so differently the issues involved in creating a scholarly text, then assumptions about base-text, authorial intention, and forms of textual apparatus need to be clearly defined. If Lawrence's manuscripts have paramount authority (as they seem to), that assumption needs to be argued. If a volume's "Textual apparatus" will not permit an interested reader easily to reconstruct Lawrence's revisions or expurgations in a given passage,[3] that decision needs to be defended. Early, a critical rather than a descriptive statement of the Edition's principles might usefully have been circulated and then published. Recently, Michael Black has composed an admirably valuable statement (in his essay published in this volume):

The editor producing a reading text is therefore obliged to be eclectic. . . . For matters of punctuation, only an early stage can be authoritative, most often manuscript. For the words themselves, one has to pick one's way through the sequence, discriminating between intention and interference. The frequent absence of proofs in Lawrence's case means that late changes of substance have to be weighed for authority, and one is often forced to judge by probability: Is this likely to be a proof-correction by Lawrence himself, and in that case was it a willing change or one imposed on him? Or did the publisher just intervene himself? Here is an element of judgment. . . . The argument has to be based on a firm grasp of the chronological sequence, which determines that a carefully chosen state of the text is used as the base, and is emended in the light of earlier or later states according to an argued principle.

One can agree wholly with the precision of this summary editorial statement, especially its insistence on discriminating between intention and interference, and still wonder how, in gray areas, emendation "according to an argued principle" is accomplished—and still wonder, also, whether such principles emerge as cleanly as this statement implies (that they did not in the *Lady Chatterley* volume is evident) or whether, instead, the processes by which principles emerge may themselves beg critical examination. As the preceding pages have illustrated, the *mechanism* for establishing principles is itself complex, is founded on elitist attitudes, and depends on the working of power relations that are rarely acknowledged. To say so is not to imply fault but rather to gain understanding of the way in which human and institutional factors vitally shape textual decisions. Recursive accommodation came to include political accommodation. About the edition as a whole, Michael Black says elsewhere in this collection, "our only principle was that the materials themselves must dictate how they were handled." Well, *is* that statement disingenuous? The process by which materials "dictated" editorial decision also (perhaps inevitably) results from a bureaucratic construct. That construct allows an Editorial Board—empowered to award or deny contracts, to accept or reject editorial positions, to modify them at critical junctures, to rewrite or restructure introductions—to draw upon its institutionalized perquisites in order to effect its will.

Although I greatly admire the insight and intelligence that have informed the Cambridge Lawrence Edition, although I laud the meticulous care lavished on the text and apparatus of *Lady Chatterley's Lover,* I also perceive that the Editorial Board has from the start functioned as an impersonal abstraction. The Board's power is hierarchical and seemingly unassailable. Each stage of textual work is "approved" first by Lin Vasey, then (in my case) by John Worthen, then by the rest of the Board. Its commentary "revises" assumptions, "corrects" mistakes, "improves" style, "fixes" proportions, adds "necessary" detail, removes "unnecessary" detail. Further, the Board, which consists of busy professionals, must often make editors wait several months for its responses, thereby diluting an editor's potential resistance to criticism; inadvertently, an editor's submission may be encouraged. These uses of power are worth recognizing for their effects on individual volumes. It is easier to say "we aren't persuaded" than it is to marshal fresh counterarguments. It can be difficult for an editor to remember his or her precise frame of mind three years ago, even ten years ago, in order to justify a statement later questioned, as when Vasey posed the following query in 1986: "Do we have two interfering typists? I don't credit that." Only by returning to an earlier critical frame can one respond to such lingering reservations. My point is not that editors should not receive criticism (they *must*) but that an Editorial Board incurs a serious risk—the risk that editors may not resist criticism vigorously enough to articulate what they perceive as Truth: and that authority structures may, inadvertently, reduce differences of opinion, stifle disagreement, urge compliance, to the possible detriment of establishing a sound text.

In October 1989, for example, a Board member, having read carefully through Lawrence's 1926–28 correspondence, wished to alter my discussion of the composition of version 3—this time to expand it. A revision was proposed. Here is a piece of it:

> There is surprising[ly] little in the surviving correspondence about the writing of this version. Perhaps because it was a *re*writing, Lawrence did not feel so deeply involved in it, but also in the few comments he does make, he stresses its improperness and that it is "shocking" which would limit the persons he might feel inclined to tell.

Lawrence *not* feel deeply involved in his rewriting of the novel? My considered view differed: Lawrence was *deeply* involved, he rarely discussed the composition of the novels he published in the 1920s, and so his correspondence poorly gauges the depth of his involvement. I insisted on striking those sentences. Although the Editorial Board entertained compromises of strategy and phrase, an editor must indeed make such efforts, often sustained efforts. Of course that is what good editors are expected to do: to protect their volume from *any* kind of error. But over a period of fifteen years, a grave risk exists, I would argue, that the effort may *not* be made, especially when other professional commitments or simple weariness intervenes. Even now, I occasionally worry that, in the early years especially, I may not have resisted firmly enough the attempts to revise my work.

For such a major Edition to succeed, it may be that the amount of supervisory work demands a hierarchical power structure, but I suspect that the Board's assumptions about its authority were never seriously questioned and that alternative models were never seriously explored by the Press. In closing, I would propose some revisions of the model that the Cambridge Lawrence has adopted.

Rather than asking editors for a formal proposal describing how they would edit a text, then accepting or rejecting that proposal, the Board might find an alternate approach more useful and efficient. Prospective editors might be asked not only to identify what textual authority each document such as manuscript, typescript, proof, and printed text might have: editors might also be asked how other scholarly editors have approached similar evidence in related texts written by roughly contemporary writers—Stephen Crane, Joseph Conrad, William Dean Howells. This groundwork would ensure a context informed by the problems that related texts pose and would help to clarify assumptions about textual theory.

Funded by advances on royalties or contributions from the D. H. Lawrence Estate, discussions at an early stage might be organized between prospective editors and the Editorial Board. Occurring well before a final proposal is submitted, these meetings would be opportunities to stress *cooperation* in finding solutions to the most difficult textual problems; they would also be opportunities to stress the critical importance of *accuracy*. Most scholars not trained in textual editing are unaware of the immense resources of Error to undermine sustained editorial work. For example, even though my collations were carefully checked three times, Vasey succeeded in identifying a few variants that had slipped by unrecorded.

Audiotapes of the discussions of the Editorial Board's meetings in Cambridge might be mailed to volume editors in order strongly to reinforce the message that a collaborative process is valued more highly than a verdict on a sheet of paper. Sharing "rough drafts" of the stages of the Editorial Board's thinking would help to avoid resistance, to elicit cooperation, and to make more democratic the hierarchical model on which the Edition is based.

In order to offset the additional cost of these procedures, inexpensive student editions of all widely used texts should be produced as soon as possible after clothbound publication. I understand that if libraries anticipate a paperback reprint, they may not order an expensive clothbound book. Still, scholarship of this magnitude cannot adequately be subsidized by library sales of clothbound books and must be assisted by the sale of student editions. Since among the volumes of the Cambridge Lawrence apparently only *Mr Noon* has sold in toto more than 2,500 copies, a student paperback can help to support a revised model on which the Edition as a whole may proceed.

These suggestions apart, I happily conclude that much about the Edition has proved satisfying and successful: most notably, the steady production of distinguished volumes. And what Lawrence scholar would wish to quote—or wish students to quote—any texts other than the Cambridge editions? Lawrence has been well served by honorable people who demand the finest texts for future generations and who are fully committed to collaboration with volume editors in order to achieve a high textual standard. Because of this collaboration with intelligent, persevering colleagues, the *Lady Chatterley's Lover* volume has a different, often-stronger shape than otherwise it might. The contours of the Introduction, the accuracy of the text, the application of editorial principles, the precision of the apparatus, the completion of numerous notes, and the inclusion of an appendix and a dialect glossary—all depended upon collaboration between the Editorial Board and the volume editor. Although my name appears alone on the title page, my collaborators deserve much of the credit for whatever success the volume enjoys.

NOTES

1. D. H. Lawrence, *Lady Chatterley's Lover / A Propos of "Lady Chatterley's Lover,"* ed. Michael Squires (Cambridge: Cambridge UP, 1993). Page:line references to this edition are cited parenthetically in the text.
2. "Editing *Lady Chatterley's Lover*," in *D. H. Lawrence: The Man Who Lived*, ed. Robert B. Partlow Jr. and Harry T. Moore (Carbondale and Edwardsville: Southern Illinois UP, 1980), 64.
3. See, e.g., the "Textual apparatus" entries on 175:13 and 201:40.

Text and Intertexts, Authorship and Culture: Annotating Lawrence's *Twilight in Italy*

Paul Eggert

The postmodern erosion of traditional distinctions between fiction and fact, or fiction and objective knowledge, and their common conversion into forms of textuality, have left traditional understanding of the genre of travel writing in difficulty. It has been traditionally assumed that travel writing emanates from the author's visit to a foreign place, that it should not be just armchair opinionating or library research: we have expected the writer at least to have traveled and then to have distilled the experience for us. The interest does not lie, as in earlier travel literature, in tales of the marvellous, or in unknown places "discovered"—whether along the Amazon or in the Dark Continent. Rather the interest lies in the writer's responses to a foreign culture with which we as readers are already partly familiar. Additionally, as one commentator put it: "The touch of intimacy is required. The reader, to know what a place is really like, needs to know its effects on someone he knows, someone whose character, preferences and values he understands . . . it is the projected personality of the author that is the interpretative gauge" (Murphy 7). That comment, written twenty-five years ago, articulates nicely the shift from Enlightenment to Romantic attitudes about the travel book which give authority to individual response to place but yet leave the "place as in itself it really is," to adapt Matthew Arnold's phrase, essentially intact. On the one hand a relativity, both personal to the author and cultural, is sanctioned: we, the audience, wish to know what this particular writer feels the place is *like*—an expectation that locks the account into our shared cultural experience. But, on the other hand, the objectivity of the place itself is not questioned.

This traditional understanding has always consigned the travel book to a different category than the novel: even if, for instance, very strong evidence were adduced to challenge received notions of Jessie Chambers's attitude to sexuality, it would not necessarily invalidate the account in *Sons and Lovers* of Miriam Leivers's timidities being the partial cause of Paul Morel's inhibitions. But in *Twilight in Italy* we would have expected Lawrence to be writing about Italy; and indeed in a letter to Cynthia Asquith in 1915, Lawrence, hard at work on the book (it would be published in 1916), reported: "I am writing a book of sketches, or preparing a book of sketches, about the nations, Italian German and English, full of philosophizing and struggling to show things real" (*Letters II* 386). He is not claiming a photographic realism; indeed, he is characteristically not making *any* claims about technique, for after *Sons and Lovers* he would acknowledge no gap between a strong perception of truth and its depiction in art. (In his essay on Cézanne, "Introduction to These Paintings," he is not at all interested in the painter's medium; and elsewhere he even denies that Verga was a realist because to him this was a misleading emphasis.[1]) Nevertheless, with *Twilight in Italy* Lawrence believed his struggle was to show things "real" about the nations. His nations are not mythical ones or fictional ones but the nations themselves.

However, the implicit separation of subject and object—the writer writing and the nations written about—ignores the tissue of cultural assumption that joins and supports subject and object, and runs together the apparently "natural" distinction between them. Lawrence was of course a great and invigorating iconoclast, so that it may sound perverse to emphasize the cultural supportedness of his travel writings. Indeed, if one compares say, Samuel Butler's *Alps and Sanctuaries* of 1881 or R. L. Stevenson's *Travels With a Donkey in the Cévennes* of 1879 or, much more clearly, a host of lesser travel books of the late nineteenth and early twentieth centuries, the writers' carrying their culture about with them is so blatant that one wonders sometimes who is holding the pen. How else does one account for the numberless encomiums on natural beauty, especially mountain scenery, facilitating a rush of religiose emotion and an exercise of the writer's "sensibility": "At rare intervals—but very rare— . . . the setting sun would gild and flush and glorify this mighty expanse of scenery with a bewildering pomp of color that held the eye like a spell and moved the spirit like music." Even the irreverent Mark Twain—this is his—was not immune (276). In writing such as this, it would seem that intertexts are virtually producing the text, that the individualizing voice has gone mute.[2]

Although I used to think that it was sufficient to reverse this equation if one wanted to describe Lawrence's travel writing in *Twilight in Italy,* the more I think about it, the more intertwined with other texts his book becomes, the less distinct the separation between subject and object even with him. My thoughts have not led me to put more obviously culture-bound writings on a par with Lawrence's—by no means. But I have come to read *Twilight in Italy* as more of a symphonic conducting—a virtuoso gathering and adaptation—of a multitude of voices than an author's un-mediated solo about the object of his interest: Italy, or the Italian nation. This awareness cannot but affect how one comes to think of the jobs that critical editions should be doing, of the relative importance of the elements of the edition, and of the manner in which those elements are supposed to relate to one another. Let me say at once that I have abandoned the assumption that I brought to critical editing that explanatory notes are of strictly secondary importance or are just peripheral to the reading text.

The early versions of the first four essays in *Twilight in Italy* ("Christs in the Tirol" and "Italian Studies"), dating from 1912–13, were written on the spot, but the later versions were written more than two years later, in wartime England, and in response to the earlier versions themselves—which collation shows he must have had open in front of him. He had also his very efficient memory to go on, and of course, feeding that memory, his legendary quickness of registration of what he had seen, read, and done. For the remaining six essays in the book, that is probably all he had to go on: despite Keith Sagar's statements in his *Calendar* (38, 44) that early versions of the remainder of *Twilight in Italy* were written in 1913, no extant manuscript or letter confirms the speculation. Indeed, the very absence of obviously interpolated material in the essays from "San Gaudenzio" to the end of the volume argue that this long section—more than half of the book—was first written in 1915.

The freshness of immediate experience of the Lake Garda region and Lawrence's walk through Switzerland into Italy in 1913 (the subject of the last two essays) had inevitably, by 1915, been blended with a wider range of influences. This is to phrase the situation in a way—the traditional way—that preserves the distinction between the work and the influences on it. By "influences" one would mean what Lawrence had read in the intervening period, what he had written in letters, poems, and prose works, what he had done, where he had been, whom he had met etc., etc. Through a process of sifting, one might then be in position to refer "factually" to the influences on the 1915 writing that were not in operation in 1913.

But such a separation of influence from authorial work would be just letting in by the back door the subject/object distinction I am contesting. As Robert Scholes remarks: "We are always outside any particular text we may attempt to read. This is why interpretation is a problem for us. But we are never outside the whole web of textuality in which we hold our cultural being and in which every text awakens echoes and harmonies. Every text that comes to us comes from before our moment in time, but each text can be read only by connecting it to the unfinished work of textuality" (6). This situation puts a special responsibility on the editor-as-annotator that finally makes him (in my case) question whether "annotation" of a fixed text is in fact what he is doing.

Certainly the job of annotating the Cambridge University Press edition of *Twilight in Italy* has made me reconsider the role of explanatory notes in the critical edition. (I do not here refer to the defenses of preferred readings which are also placed among the notes in the Cambridge volumes.) One finds that, surrounding the reading text, invading it, arguing with it, confirming it, competing with it, are a host of alternative partial texts, many known directly to Lawrence, some indirectly, and some possibly not at all. But they *are* known now, which is the same moment in which, as we read it, *Twilight in Italy* is known. We do have knowledge of earlier readings of the work, including our own, but we have this knowledge in the present.

In thus forcing the past and present together, I am nevertheless acceding to the traditional assumption that annotation, although operating in the present, is necessarily concerned with the specifically delimited past of the author's writing. There *is* an alternative view, which Scholes's observation may seem to be countenancing. It would be perfectly possible to annotate on the principle that whatever helped illuminate the annotator's present reading of the text ought to be included, from whatsoever period or source it came. However the primary value of such annotation would be the insights it gave into the reading habits of the annotator. Readers would be triangulating author (as best they could, unassisted) against annotator (amply documented) in their own reading of the text. Would this situation be extraordinary? There is, after all, a longstanding interest in marginalia. If Lawrence had not only written his *Study of Thomas Hardy* but also annotated his reading of Hardy's novels, his notes—even if unfair, wayward, chronologically impossible—would be worth the reading for he was such a *strong* reader. However, if he had not been a novelist and written nothing but the annotations, would we be interested any longer? Then he would have been forced to share the fate of most modern annotators who have accepted the boundary lines of chronology, availability, probability, economy of expression on the grounds that these desiderata, if observed, would be more useful to the numerous readers interested in locating the author's writing in the context of his or her contemporaneous culture. Even a deconstructive reader depends on a prior interpretation, an intended or historically located meaning, to read *against*.

In an essay of 1981 that usefully brought together and analyzed preexisting understandings of the role of annotation, Martin Battestin defined its aim as "to clarify the author's specific meaning and intention."[3] The twist I am seeking to give this generally accepted approach benefits from the changed understandings of authorship and text over the last ten or twenty years, in particular the widespread loss of confidence in notions of authorial autonomy in the origination of text. To think of the author instead as participator in the textual meaning, the indispensable agent of its gathering and organization, is to think of annotation as naming and therefore potentially reinvoking the cultural voices or intertexts which the author tangentially drew upon or directly borrowed, implicitly answered, or merely drew sustenance from. The historical aim is not resigned, but the notes take on an importance in one's understanding of the overall task of the critical edition which they had hitherto lacked.

As far as *Twilight in Italy* is concerned, the alternative or intersecting that which the explanatory notes point to in the reading present include: newspaper reports of the same events as Lawrence describes, histories of the Lake Garda area, contemporary Baedeker travel guides, Antonia Cyriax's book about San Gaudenzio in 1913, Lawrence's descriptions in his letters of events in *Twilight in Italy,* recorded interviews from the 1970s with the actual people or the relatives of people Lawrence gave accounts of in *Twilight in Italy,* and photographic versions (visual "texts") of the same people. Textual mediation seems inescapable. Photographs I have of Paolo and Maria of San Gaudenzio are of large professional drawings of them, said to be "good likenesses." That is, they are photos of pictorial interpretations open now for further interpretation. The interviews are verbal equivalents but complicated by being bi-vocal: my questions and the answers of the interviewees, a son and daughter of Paolo and Maria, and the daughter of the man whom Lawrence said would never marry, Il Duro. I also have a photo of him as paterfamilias in a family group-shot.[4] Frederick Owen met Il Duro in 1971, and in his thesis he gave an account of the meeting, but unfortunately Owen spoke no Italian. The transmissional interference in their communication is only a pronounced case of the problem of all the partial texts that surround and beg questions of *Twilight in Italy:* none of those texts has a limpid and unambiguous meaning; each requires interpretation, and each interpretation will have inevitably its own social and historical location.

If all this sounds like a dilemma, a recipe for obfuscation or despair, then I have to say it does not appear that way to me. In preparing the annotations for the Cambridge edition of *The Boy in the Bush,* I began to be aware how fully that initially collaborative novel was an interfusing and enfolding of voices—Mollie Skinner's and Lawrence's obviously—but also other voices: the *Western Australian Year-Book for 1902–03,* which the novel both quotes and echoes, Skinner family memories, Lawrence's reading and Mollie Skinner's, ideas from *Kangaroo* and "Quetzalcoatl." The notes to the edition of *The Boy in the Bush* unfold the text into what might be called a continuum of intertextuality. Indeed one way to understand the text of a Lawrence work is to think of it as the authorially focussed intersection of such surround- and inter-texts, but recognizing that only some of them, despite one's best efforts, are accessible. If reading involves not just the reading of the text but also in some sense the reading of the contexts it initially inhabited, then the explanatory notes in a critical edition are arguably part of the larger text of the author's communication. To my mind, one of the best decisions the Cambridge series of Lawrence's *Works* made was the one to include explanatory notes: such annotation is not routinely included in critical editions, thus reinforcing the assumption that literary works can be thought of more or less as Verbal Icons—self-sufficient textual objects emanating unproblematically from an authorial source.

Even the provision of birth and death dates for people described in *Twilight in Italy* challenges this assumption. Lawrence and Frieda's landlord at Lake Garda, called Signor di P. in the early version of "The Lemon Gardens" and Signor di Paoli in *Twilight in Italy* was in fact Pietro De Paoli, 1845–1917. He died a year after the book was published. His wife, called Signora Gemma in the essay, whom Lawrence sees avidly kissing her baby nephew, was Silvia Comboni De Paoli, 1868–1931. The De Paolis have apparently died out, but the Combonis have not, so perhaps there are still people around Gargnano who remember her. For me, she lives as a part of Lawrence's text, as a partial text I found on a headstone in the Gargnano cemetery, and on an official document from the Comune di Gargnano attesting her dates of birth and death. Yet she lived before the text of Lawrence's essay came into existence, and she lived on after its publication. She happened to cross Lawrence's path and the "text" of her life as *she* knew it was momentarily appropriated: "I could see she wanted to go away with the child, to enjoy him alone, with palpitating, pained enjoyment. It was her brother's boy. And the old padrone was as if nullified by her ecstasy over the baby" (77). This is the comment of the 1915 Lawrence, the Lawrence who had written *The Rainbow*. In 1913 there had been no "palpitating, pained enjoyment" and the Signore had been "insulted" (215) rather than "nullified"; and what Signora Gemma said to Lawrence was slightly different from what she is reported to have said in the 1913 version. But Silvia Comboni De Paoli had not uttered another word to him.

In both 1913 and 1915 there was another intertext in operation: the Bible. Lawrence refers in the 1913 version to the "men of the Old Testament. It was as though [Signor di P.'s] manliness were not proven till he had a child" (215). In *The Study of Thomas Hardy* of 1914, recalling the third and fifth books of the Patriarch, Moses, Lawrence comments: "but before the Father a eunuch is blemished, even a childless man is without honour" (82; the references are to Deuteronomy xxiii 1 and Leviticus xxi 16–23). Thus by the 1915 version of "The Lemon Gardens," Lawrence was able to go further than he had in 1913: "It was as if his [di Paoli's] *raison d'être* had been to have a son. And he had no children. Therefore he had no *raison d'être*. He was nothing. . . . This, then, is the secret of Italy's attraction for us, this phallic worship. To the Italian the phallus is the symbol of individual creative immortality, to each man his own Godhead. The child is but the evidence of the Godhead" (78). Meanwhile, between the two publications, Pietro De Paoli had said nothing more in Lawrence's hearing, and he had only two more years to live. Lawrence's 1915 text is obviously getting its inspiration elsewhere, filtering and growing from other textual sources. These the annotator must try to identify, bearing in mind the crucial fact that because, in 1915, Lawrence was responding more immediately to a literary text (his own version of 1913) than to a situation in which he was a participant, he had an added freedom to cast his intertextual net wide.

In this case, his text could be netting E. M. Forster's understanding of

Italian life in *Where Angels Fear to Tread*. Forster visited the Lawrences in February 1915, some months before Lawrence turned to prepare *Twilight in Italy*, and they corresponded for most of that year. But I have found no evidence in Lawrence's letters that he read Forster's *Where Angels Fear to Tread*. He *may* have, nevertheless (it was published in 1905), and there were in any case other opportunities for Lawrence to have picked up Forster's ideas about the child in Italian life. In Forster's novel, Miss Abbott, an Englishwoman, watches the Italian, Gino, wake his baby son and fall "suddenly musing, filled with the desire that his son should be like him, and should have sons like him, to people the earth. It is the strongest desire that can come to a man—if it comes at all—stronger even than love or the desire for personal immortality" (153). As Gino bathes and kisses the baby, Miss Abbott feels he "was majestic; he was a part of Nature" (155). It may be that Forster helped Lawrence to see the "Italian Godhead in the flesh" (*Twilight* 78) more generously in 1915 than he had in 1913. Then he had been more fumbling and halfhearted, commenting: "the Italian feels, no matter what he believes, that he is made in the image of God, and in this image is his godliness, and with its defacement and crumbling, crumbles himself. Which is why he often gives one the feeling that he has nothing inside him" (215).

If Forster was an influence, he cannot have been the only one. No English or German traveler in 1912 can have gone to Italy without myths and visions of Italy, without culturally reinforced longings for a land of sunshine, grapes, and sensuous abandon. And spending the following winter of 1913–14 in Italy, at Fiascherino, would have allowed Lawrence to deepen his impressions and digest an increasingly wider range of textual feeders—his letters show it happening—in a way that would inevitably tell in his 1915 rewritings of the Lake Garda sketches.

I am not here trying to reduce *Twilight in Italy* into a mere example of intertextuality. To do that would be to ignore the energetic, alert, and risk-taking authorial focusing of the surround- and inter-texts I have been describing. But I am trying to portray Lawrence's travel essays as, in a sense, temporary authorial fixings of a swirl of textual influences that would go on beyond *Twilight in Italy* and would take other forms in his subsequent writings. Annotating a Lawrence volume brings this sense forcibly before one's mind. Although annotation is aimed at serving the reading text in a critical edition and thus serves to reinforce its status as the single representation of the work, annotation also, subversively, shoots the text through at a hundred points with other texts that, if pursued, continuously unfold it into their multiple histories. If this is true of Lawrence's travel writing—where the process is peculiarly open to inspection, and where traditional expectations about the genre facilitate the opening-up—then it is also true of his other writings. Indeed the gradual weakening over the last twenty years of the traditional distinction between fact and fiction, and of the polarity of subject and object, into different forms of textuality has been tending to shift his travel writing into the same category as his prose fiction. And to the extent that revelation of the surround- and inter-texts of his travel essays questions the textually self-sufficient status of their reading texts, so too does such a revelation question the status of the reading texts of *all* his works. "Annotation," newly understood, lays down this gauntlet for literary critics, editors, and other readers who continue to entertain a more or less traditional understanding of critical editions.

My second example concerns the essay "The Theatre" with its account of an obscure company of actors visiting Gargnano and led by the man who plays Hamlet so revealingly: Enrico Persevalli. There was, I found, no local newspaper in Gargnano or indeed anywhere on the western side of Lake Garda in 1912–13, and the theatre critics of the main Brescian newspapers of the day, *La Sentinella Bresciana* and *La Provincia di Brescia* seemed interested only in the well-known professional companies that visited Brescia and in the theatrical life of Milan and Rome. However, a section of both papers was regularly devoted to Brescian provincial news, though the bulk of it had precious little to do with theatre and Gargnano only occasionally got a mention. But eventually I did find a reference to Gargnano's *Festa del Fiore,* a patriotic organization raising funds through festivals for the Italian Red Cross during the Libyan War. Coinciding with the festival, a theatrical company owned by Adelia Di Giacomo Tadini would mount several performances at Gargnano (*La Sentinella* 16 Jan. 1913). In other issues of both newspapers there appeared announcements and reviews of the performances Lawrence attended and described in the two versions of "The Theatre." Competing texts had suddenly risen into view. And for me, Enrico Persevalli had taken on a new and alternative textual existence. No longer was he Lawrence's creation only.

But there was a problem. The man who had played the parts Lawrence described was indeed called Enrico, but Enrico *Marconi* rather than Persevalli. I could not see how Lawrence could have forgotten or why he would have changed a name that must have been all about the town in

January 1913. He did alter the name of the owner of the company, whose first name was Adelia, into "Adelaida," without mentioning her surname. The "aida" in "Adelaida" had some appropriate operatic echoes for the woman whose voice Lawrence describes mock-heroically as "plashing like violin music, at my ruthless, masculine cruelty. Dear heart, how she sighed to rest on my sheltering bosom!"[5] Adelia Di Giacomo Tadini seems to have been the principal attraction for the audiences. She is referred to as "la squisita prima attrice" (the exquisite principal actress), and Marconi, who played the leading male roles, as "un giovane attore pieno di volontà e di studio" (a young actor, very determined and well prepared) (*La Provincia* 16 Jan. 1913).

The reviews and news items about the company were not written by staff journalists on the Brescian papers but by correspondents from Gargnano. They have the character of enthusiastic announcements of that night's performance or of congratulatory reviews. Unlike the mainstream reviews, they are never critical. The newspapers' policy seems to have been to give the readership of the whole Brescia region a sense of participation in the papers. If self-celebration was what the locals wanted, then so be it. Nevertheless, amidst the superlatives, the language of the correspondents hints at differences in the actors' reputation and performance. Three members of the company had their Evening of Honour just as Lawrence says, but the price for the leading lady's could safely be increased apparently (*Twilight* 112) and with less journalistic puff, whereas for Enrico Marconi's playing Hamlet, considerably more effort was evidently felt to be necessary. *Provincia di Brescia* predicted that the audience would give Marconi "giusto incorragiamento" (proper encouragement) (16 Jan. 1913) and *La Sentinella* predicted that Marconi, "un protagonista fine ed intelligente . . . porterà con tutto il senso della sua arte completa, una creazione così personale" (Marconi, a refined and intelligent leading actor . . . will create, with all the feeling of his perfect art, a quite personal interpretation) (16 Jan. 1913). Although Marconi had played at Gargnano previously—in the winter carnival of 1908–9 (*La Provincia* 9 Jan. 1913), he evidently lacked the established following among the local audience that Adelia possessed. Marconi, the company's director, seems to have had a taste for the more intellectual kind of play. But the company's owner was Adelia and she, if less "refined and intelligent," seems to have known the nearer way to the audiences' hearts.

The reports in the Brescian newspapers, textually encoded amid their superlatives with the niceties and only half-suppressed anxieties of small-town politics, offer a countertext to Lawrence's. For the most part, that text wings along beside his account, amplifying rather than challenging it. Nevertheless, the very existence of this competing and differently motivated version of the same events is a reminder that both the newspaper reports and Lawrence's version of 1913 are drawn from a tangled and interlocking web of texts. The very act of retrieving some of those skeins—what I have called the surround- and inter-texts—underlines, for the editor-annotator, the historical locatedness of Lawrence's writing. In this frame of mind, it becomes difficult to imagine how editions that have been taken seriously as historical enterprises could ever have been thought capable of functioning without them.

But the fragmented, selective, and specifically motivated newspaper narrative of Enrico Marconi also stresses the different acts of selection and emphasis—the fictionality—of Lawrence's account. His alteration of Marconi's surname demonstrates this nicely. The name "Persevalli" first appears in the 1913 version, but I doubt that Lawrence was worried that Marconi would be likely to read the *English Review* and object to the portrayal. However, all of Lawrence's readers would have known of Guglielmo Marconi, inventor of wireless telegraphy in 1895. In 1896 he took out an English patent on his discovery, set up a company to market it in 1897, and in 1909 received a Nobel prize for physics. But in 1911 there was a scandal involving the letting of a Government tender for a chain of Imperial wireless stations to the Marconi company, and another in 1912 involving a secret Government purchase of silver. This became known as "the little Marconi case." The participation of Jewish politicians in both scandals led to allegations of a Jewish plot. It may be that Lawrence felt merely that the use of the actor's real name would introduce irrelevant associations for his readers.

Why did he hit on the name "Persevalli" for the 1913 version and retain it for the 1915? Lawrence's interest in Richard Wagner in his Croydon period, 1908–12, is well-known. Although his surviving letters of the period do not indicate that he saw Wagner's opera *Parsifal,* he would undoubtedly have known of it. The story concerns Parsifal's search for the Holy Grail—in Arthurian legend, a symbol of perfection, also identified as the cup of the Last Supper in which Joseph of Arimathea caught the blood of the crucified Christ. Tennyson's version ("The Holy Grail") of 1869 uses the name "Percivale"; in Sir Thomas Malory's *The Tale of the Sankgreal,* the name is "Perceval." Lawrence's spelling is simply an Italianizing of the name.

It may be that the similarities between Parsifal and Hamlet struck Lawrence when watching Marconi in the latter role, thus suggesting the sobriquet. Certainly the stories have striking similarities. The succession both at Montsalvat and Elsinor has been compromised by sin (Amfortas with Kundry, Claudius with Gertrude); the two innocent protagonists, Parsifal and Hamlet, do not understand what has happened but learn through supernatural means (Klingsor, the Ghost) that it is given to them to set all to rights and cleanse the state of sin; both are tempted from their task by the consolation of love (Kundry, Ophelia) but refuse it; and both finally succeed in their task.[6]

In the 1913 version of "The Theatre," Lawrence seems simply to be having a bit of mock-heroic fun at Marconi's expense. His name is first mentioned in this way: "During the week we moved in a storm of little coloured bills, 'Great Evening of Honour of Enrico Persevalli.' Now this is the actor-manager. The title of the play was kept dark. . . . Not for worlds would I have disappointed Signor Enrico Persevalli" (227). Throughout the 1913 essay, there is a touch of condescension for Persevalli, for the pretensions of his troupe of peasant actors, for the behavior of the audience, and for their preferences for the sentimental and the violent over Ibsen and Shakespeare. Lawrence does not look down his nose exactly, but he cannot have been unaware that a gently ironic outlook would gratify his English audience: he was in great need of money at this time when he was having to prove to himself and to Frieda that he had a future as a professional writer.

He had written a succession of travel essays after leaving England in May 1912, leading up to his writing, in 1913, the Lake Garda essays, "Italian Studies," for the *English Review*.[7] In the essays of 1912, a distancing, self-conscious wittiness and rather weak comedy is attempted. It is as if Lawrence were searching for an equivalent in the travel sketch for the impersonality he was striving for in *Sons and Lovers*. In the 1913 essays, his liberal use of the first person brings only a superficial personalizing which his audience would have recognized as appropriate to the travel sketch. We watch the author's reflecting, wryly detached mind rather than being drawn into the movement of it.

But by 1915 Lawrence had written *The Rainbow* and was a changed man. There is a new determination to get to the bottom of his 1913 impressions. The name "Persevalli," probably a mere whimsy then, now gathers into itself deep significances from its context in the rewritten essay. Lawrence's remembered response to Marconi's acting of the Hamlet role is interrogated by the North/South polarity which he sets up in the 1915 essays. In 1913 Lawrence commented: "When a decent Italian, Enrico Persevalli, put himself through the creepings and twistings of the unwholesome Dane [Hamlet], I disliked it" (229). By 1915 he has realized why:

> There is, I think, this strain of cold dislike, or self-dislike, through much of the Renaissance art, and through all the later Shakespeare. In Shakespeare it is a kind of corruption in the flesh and a conscious revolt from this. A sense of corruption in the flesh makes Hamlet frenzied, for he will never admit that it is his own flesh. Leonardo da Vinci is the same. . . . But that is all four hundred years ago. Enrico Persevalli has just reached the position. He *is* Hamlet . . . the modern Italian, suspicious, isolated, self-nauseated, labouring in a sense of physical corruption. But he will not admit it is in himself. . . . Of all the unclean ones, Hamlet was the uncleanest. But he accused only the others. . . . The play is the statement of the most significant philosophic position of the Renaissance. (122–23)

Lawrence slides between commenting on the actor and the role, the character and the author, the play and history. Marconi's acting has become the initiator of one of Lawrence's boldest pieces of literary criticism; and in 1915 Marconi's Holy Grail, which despite his efforts he cannot reach, is recognized as Northern self-consciousness. Feeling the lack of it, and thus in this in advance of his countrymen, this Italian Parsifal is doomed to "self-dislike and a spirit of disintegration" (122).

Throughout *Twilight in Italy* one finds Lawrence in one way or another putting people on stage or stopping life in moments that beg for an epiphany. His breathtaking sweeps away from the originating event, sculpture, or person into the history of European civilization feed off the conventional expectation that he should offer an exegesis of the moment's or work of art's significance. As readers we respond, I believe, as much to the stride of the thinking—to the man-in-thought—as to the thought itself. By 1915 Lawrence has found the confidence and the way to usher us into the process of his thinking rather than presenting us, as in 1913, with the thoughts themselves, neatly encapsulated and wittily distanced. He is creating an attunement in his audience rather than appealing to a preestablished one. The particular is no longer of interest for itself—for its ironies, drollness, or picturesqueness; it is important, now, for its ability to reveal the general. With the change has come an amplitude and urgency of thinking lacking in the 1913 version.

In terms of my argument about surround- and inter-texts, a remarkable thing has happened by 1915. In using Marconi's acting as a focus for meditation, Lawrence has gathered a peculiarly dense intertextuality into the notion of an Italian Persevalli—an Italian striver after a Northern consciousness. Lawrence signals it quite plainly; he knows what he is doing. In the quoted passage, he joins Leonardo's and Michelangelo's spiritual conditions to Persevalli's; and as the meditation proceeds over the next few pages, his mind ranges daringly over the spiritual condition of Orestes, Agamemnon, and Clytemnestra. Thus do the polarities of Self and Not Self gain momentum and definition, allowing Lawrence to go further: to Macbeth, Jesus, David, and then to plot the turning point in the history of his polarities at the Renaissance. And so English history is brought into it: Henry VIII, Cromwell, Godwin, Shelley. Lawrence relocates history in the force-field of his polarities. Those intertexts are momentarily drawn into his text, and others he does not mention are also silently gathered: his "Foreword" to *Sons and Lovers,* his "Study of Thomas Hardy," some of his letters. Although we may revel in the sheer energy of the gathering, the skeptic in us begins to mutter that there are other more likely interpretations. And as our sense of the competing histories of those intertexts dawns in us, the intertexts threaten to turn perfidious to Lawrence's purpose. His intellectual daring continually courts its own undoing.

What, then, is "the text itself" in all of this? It seems only as stable as an Aeolian harp. The winds that blow through it in 1913 are intertextual zephyrs, but by 1915 they are hurricanes, and Lawrence has learned how to ride them in wide-ranging meditations that grow from rather than conceal their personal centers. Thus intertextuality does not deny personal agency but confirms it. Authorship can be seen, in Lawrence's case, not as an act of pure origination but of garnering, reshaping, and of daring extension. In this situation, the editor-annotator recognizes the hopelessness of the task. The object of attention, the reading text, will not stay in place, pulled this way and that on its intertextual web. But the recognition itself is healthy—for editor and readers. Given a dominant convention that explanatory notes are not a place for literary critical interpretation and that they must be scholarly in address, impersonal in tone and economic in expression, the best the editor can do is refer to many strands of that web, thus inviting readers to perform their own, newly sensitized spidering.[8]

NOTES

1. Cf. "[T]he Frenchy idea of self-effacement . . . didn't go very deep, as Verga was too much of a true southerner to know quite what it meant" (Lawrence, "Preface" 249).
2. In Twain's case, it could be plausibly argued that the writing is ventriloquial, that Twain is mischievously donning yet another mask. But at the local level at least, one cannot tell it from the real thing.
3. Battestin 16. Articles on the general principles of annotation are uncommon: Battestin discusses an essay of 1942, the last before his; and an essay by Small has since appeared. It deals with the difficulties inherent in the annotator's postulation of an original readership which may have been as splintered in its understandings and responses as today's. He worries that annotation may be "indistinguishable from criticism" (292). In its capacity to rule out certain interpretations (say, on chronological grounds) and to open up a range of others for the reader by bringing other texts into collision with the reading text, annotation, Small argues, is inevitably interpretative in its consequences. I do not see this as a problem.
4. For photographs and interviews, see Eggert, "Subjective Art" 293–328 and *passim*.
5. *Twilight* 117. A more likely influence than the opera is Beethoven's setting of the song "Adelaide" (pronounced in German as Lawrence writes it); it was a very popular salon piece for piano and high voice, and Lawrence could scarcely have helped hearing it in his childhood. It is lightly sentimental in character.
6. I wish to thank Keith Sagar for suggestions that helped fill out the comparison between Parsifal and Hamlet.
7. "French Sons of Germany," "Hail in the Rhineland," "A Chapel Across the Mountains," "A Hay-Hut Across the Mountains," and "Christs in the Tirol" precede his writing of the Lake Garda essays. All will be published in the forthcoming Cambridge edition of *Twilight in Italy* as well as two other, recently discovered travel essays of the same period and an early version of "Christs in the Tirol."
8. Cf. Hans Walter Gabler's plea for a "New Commentary" in critical editions that would interrelate "the acts and impulses of the writing" and thus correspond to the "writing process as both a scribal and a mental activity" (15). For a description of the "rhetoric" of explanatory notes, see Eggert, "Textual Product or Process" 26.

WORKS CITED

Baedeker, Karl. *The Eastern Alps.* . . . 12th ed. Leipzig: Baedeker, 1911.
———. *Northern Italy.* . . . 14th ed. Leipzig: Baedeker, 1913.
———. *Switzerland.* . . . 24th ed. Leipzig: Baedeker, 1911.
Battestin, Martin. "A Rationale of Literary Annotation: The Example of Fielding's Novels." *Studies in Bibliography* 34 (1981): 1–22.

Butler, Samuel. *Alps and Sanctuaries of Piedmont and the Canton Ticino.* 1st ed. 1881. Rev. ed. London: Fifield, 1913.

"Corriere delle Provincie. Gargnano." *La Provincia di Brescia* 9 Jan. 1913: [p. 5, col. 2].

"Corriere delle Provincie. Gargnano." *La Provincia di Brescia* 16 Jan. 1913: [p. 5, cols. 3–4].

"Cronaca della Regione. Da Gargnano. La festa del fiore per la Croce Rossa— Trattenimenti drammatici." *La Sentinella Bresciana* 16 Jan. 1913: [p. 3, col. 2].

Cyriax, Antonia. *Among Italian Peasants.* London: Collins, 1919.

Eggert, Paul. "The Subjective Art of D. H. Lawrence: *Twilight in Italy.*" Diss. U of Kent at Canterbury, 1981.

———. "Textual Product or Textual Process: Procedures and Assumptions of Critical Editing." In Eggert, *Editing in Australia.* 19–40.

———, ed. *Editing in Australia.* English Dept., University College ADFA, Canberra, Australia. Distrib. New South Wales UP, 1990.

Forster, E. M. *Where Angels Fear to Tread.* London: Edward Arnold, 1947.

Gabler, Hans Walter. "Textual Studies and Criticism." In Eggert, *Editing in Australia.* 1–17.

Lawrence, D. H. "A Chapel Across the Mountains." In Lawrence, *Love Among the Haystacks.* 57–70.

———. "Christs in the Tirol." *Westminster Gazette* 22 Mar. 1913: 2.

———. "Foreword to *Sons and Lovers.*" In *The Letters of D. H. Lawrence.* Ed. Aldous Huxley. London: Heinemann, 1932. 95–102. Rpt. in *Sons and Lovers.* Ed. Helen Baron and Carl Baron. Cambridge: Cambridge UP, 1992. 465–73.

———. "German Impressions: I. French Sons of Germany." *Saturday Westminster Gazette* 3 Aug. 1912: 9.

———. "German Impressions: II. Hail in the Rhineland." *Saturday Westminster Gazette* 10 Aug. 1912: 5.

———. "A Hay-Hut Across the Mountains." In Lawrence, *Love Among the Haystacks.* 71–82.

———. "Introduction to These Paintings." In Lawrence, *Phoenix.* 551–84.

———. "Italian Studies: By the Lago di Garda. I. The Spinner and the Monks. II. The Lemon Gardens of the Signor di P. III. The Theatre." *English Review* 15 (Sept. 1913): 202–34.

———. *Kangaroo.* London: Secker, 1922.

———. *Love Among the Haystacks.* Ed. David Garnett. London: Nonesuch P, 1930.

———. *Phoenix: The Posthumous Papers of D. H. Lawrence.* Ed. Edward D. McDonald. New York: Viking, 1936.

———. "Preface" to *Cavalleria Rusticana* by Giovanni Verga. In Lawrence, *Phoenix.* 240–50.

———. "Quetzalcoatl." MS early version of *The Plumed Serpent.* Harry Ransom Humanities Research Center, University of Texas, Austin.

———. *Twilight in Italy.* London: Duckworth, 1916.

Malory, Thomas. *The Tale of the Sankgreal.* . . . In *The Works of Sir Thomas Malory.* Ed. Eugène Vinaver. 2d ed. Vol. 2. Oxford: Clarendon P, 1973, 3 vols.

Murphy, Richard M. "The Structures of Authorial Control in the Travel Books of D. H. Lawrence." Diss. University of Texas, Austin, 1970.

Owen, Frederick I. "Laurentian Places: An Investigation of Imagination and Accuracy in D. H. Lawrence's Travel Writings." M. A. thesis. U College of Swansea, 1977.

Sagar, Keith. *D. H. Lawrence: A Calendar of His Works*. Manchester: Manchester UP, 1979.

Scholes, Robert. *Protocols of Reading*. New Haven: Yale UP, 1989.

Small, Ian. "Annotating 'Hard' Nineteenth Century Novels." *Essays in Criticism* 36 (1986): 281–93.

Stevenson, R. L. *Travels With a Donkey in the Cévennes*. London: Chatto, 1919.

Tennyson, Alfred. *Idylls of the King*. In *The Poems of Tennyson*. Ed. Christopher Ricks. 2d ed. Vol. 3. London: Longman, 1987.

Twain, Mark. *Roughing It*. In *The Works of Mark Twain*. Ed. Franklin R. Rogers and Paul Baender. Vol. 2. Berkeley: U of California P, 1972.

Western Australian Year-Book (Thirteenth Edition) For 1902–1904. Ed. Malcolm A. C. Fraser. Perth: Government Printer, 1906.

Cough-Prints and Other Intimacies: Considerations in Editing Lawrence's Later Verse

Christopher Pollnitz

Finished painting tends to cover its traces. Whereas drawing, in its apparent impulsiveness, seems more open: scanning it, you can guess at the sequence of the network of marks (however partially) and enter the story of its construction. A finished painting may not tell you how it was finished; a drawing nearly always will. This is why drawing seems, though it may not actually be, a more "intimate" medium than painting. It offers a narrative of perception. . . .

—Robert Hughes, "Frank Auerbach"

During the year in which Lawrence composed his later verse, between November 1928 and November 1929, he wrote almost half of what has been regarded as his collected poetry.[1] He was to see proofs for two volumes of the verse written in this year, *Pansies* and *Nettles*, and Richard Aldington would edit from manuscript two posthumous collections, *More Pansies* and *Last Poems*, published under the single title *Last Poems*. The bulk of the verse from this year Lawrence himself assembled in three notebooks.[2] Listed in the manuscripts section of Warren Roberts's *Bibliography* as E302d, E192a[1] and E192a[2], these repositories of the later verse will be referred to, respectively, as the *Pansies* notebook, the *Nettles* notebook (though *More Pansies* was also extracted from this notebook), and the *Last Poems* notebook. The three notebooks are the focus of my concern, as an editor collaborating with Carole Ferrier on a variorum *Poems* for the Cambridge Edition of Lawrence's *Works*.

Since Aldington's publication of the greater part of the manuscript verse in *Last Poems*, and his description of the *Nettles* and *Last Poems* notebooks (in his "Introduction"), the verse from the notebooks has received increasing critical attention and a quota of textual discussion. E. W. Tedlock described the *Pansies* notebook (104–12); Vivian de Sola Pinto and Warren Roberts printed a number of poems Lawrence did not use from the *Pansies* notebook (Lawrence, *Complete Poems* 828–45); and T. A. Smailes published texts for six poems Aldington omitted from the *Nettles* notebook. Aldington has been belabored for his sins of commission as well as omission. Recent commentators have argued against Aldington's separation of the meditative *Last Poems* from the satirical verse that preceded it. A critical consensus has emerged that Lawrence's later verse should be considered as a whole, a gradual elaboration of his initial concept of poetic *pensées*.[3] Keith Sagar has proved erroneous Aldington's assumption that the *Nettles* and *Last Poems* notebooks were used contemporaneously, the one serving as "a first jotting-book" from which Lawrence redrafted certain poems into the other. Sagar shows the two notebooks were used sequentially: when the *Nettles* notebook was filled, Lawrence went on to the *Last Poems* notebook, which he left unfilled, and unfinished, at his death (Sagar, "Genesis" 47–53).

Aldington's own correspondence demonstrates that he compiled *Last Poems* without extravagant editorial ambitions: "Huxley is wrong in saying L. never corrected but re-wrote. He did re-write, but that *MS* vol of *Last Poems* I edited was so corrected and crossed out and interpolated I had great trouble finding the real text" (Aldington, *Literary Lifelines* 16). Given the rise in critical interest in Lawrence's poetry, surprisingly few inquiries have been made into Aldington's editorial assumptions about the later verse, and these have been, at best, piecemeal. Even de Sola Pinto and Roberts, in the *Complete Poems,* while correcting numbers of Aldington's lapses, did not attempt to show Lawrence's practice as a reviser of verse, and seem to have based their editing, in part, on photocopies of the notebooks.[4] These procedures call into question the accuracy of their final reading text for the manuscript verse. More telling is their failure to challenge Aldington's editorial presumptions about the status of Lawrence's notebooks. No wholesale effort to re-edit the three notebooks has been undertaken since 1932.

The thousands of new letters assembled for the Cambridge Edition of Lawrence's *Letters* provide a fund of new information for contemporary editors of his work. Collated with other biographical information and the sequence in which poems have been entered into the three notebooks, the letters make it possible to date the composition of Lawrence's later verse with a new precision. Chronology is not beside the point when evaluating the current preference for reading all Lawrence's late verse as a form of *pensée*. The scrutiny of Lawrence's practice as a reviser of his own verse is not only of value in preparing a variorum edition. It uncovers previously unpublished specimens of Lawrence's poetry and gives reason for emending the texts of familiar poems. It underlines basic procedures for editing holograph manuscripts, among them an editor's need to access the manuscripts themselves, not only photocopies or facsimiles. Finally, the case of Lawrence's later poetry offers the opportunity and creates the need for devising new means of representing holograph poems that have undergone multiple revision. *Pace* Aldington, it is not only the thicket-like appearance of some of Lawrence's manuscript pages that makes for difficulties determining a "real" or reading text of his verse. The very coherence of his redraftings points towards new editorial procedures.

Sagar has remarked of these notebooks, used in the final eighteen months of Lawrence's life, "There are no bloodstains on the manuscript" (Sagar, "Genesis" 47). While the deromanticizing asperity is welcome— bloodstains there are none—moving signs remain of what Lawrence was able to achieve during a year of rapidly ebbing health. Not browns or reds, but a fine blue ink-drizzle coats some notebook pages. A reader finds himself in touch with the dying poet's cough-print, doubled, it seems, like a Rorschach blot, as Lawrence snapped the notebook to. For this editor, at least, opening these notebooks stirs a sense of privileged intimacy with the processes of a sudden late flowering.

Reading the late notebooks is also an "intimate" experience in the sense in which Robert Hughes refers to a viewing of Auerbach's heavily reworked drawings as intimate. As part of the pleasure of looking at a drawing may come through a speculative awareness of the stages by which it reached its exhibited form, so a multiply revised Lawrence poem allows a reader of the original manuscript to reconstruct the stages of its composition, and to read the stages as completed drafts. An internal consistency is maintained, not only in a version on a given notebook page, but at each level of revision, or in each version, of the poem on that page. A variorum edition should aim at reproducing the experience of polysemy that comes with reading manuscript verse, of an enriching competition of alternative revisions. A variorum edition of Lawrence's verse should also aim at reproducing the clarity with which Lawrence evolved versions of poems, intact and entire, even when successive versions were drafted, one over the other, on a single, heavily revised page.

Deletions and blackings-out, as well as differences in lineation and ink-color, are usually sufficient to distinguish the various levels of revision of a Lawrence manuscript poem. In addition, a reader's critical sense can act as an alarm, a warning that an apparent version is lacking in characteristic consistency. Although the final determination of a text should be based on bibliographical or textual grounds alone, the critical sense may come into play in the initial stages of distinguishing an internally consistent version. The few examples I discuss should make clear the limited degree to which I have found such aesthetic considerations useful in arriving at texts of the notebook verse.

Taken together, all three notebooks allow a tracing of three waves of Lawrence's poetic activity during a remarkable, if not miraculous year, November 1928 to November 1929. It should be noted the three waves do not wholly coincide with—they loosely correspond to but are not contained within the dikes of—the notebooks' six boards. It should also be appreciated that the rising of the first wave, or the sequence in which Lawrence began composition of his *pensées,* is obscured by the present ordering of the *Pansies* notebook. As well as the 164 *pensées,* the notebook contains an earlier poem, two prose fragments, a draft introduction to *Pansies,* and a draft contents list.[5] What remains in the notebook is entered in reversed order: Lawrence has turned the notebook over, signed the back endpaper, and entered all the prose and poetry the notebook still contains from back to front. Like other Lawrence workbooks, the *Pansies* notebook has had leaves torn from it. More than a signature of leaves was torn from the original front of the book, for instance, suggesting why it was reversed. Leaves conjugate with those removed are sometimes loose; some have been reinserted. One has been restored to its original position—one of the "two pages" Lawrence sent to a Philadelphia collector, David V. Lederhandler, on 25 May 1929 (*Letters VII* 306). (Inspection of the signature at this reinsertion shows a second leaf still missing: Lawrence's "two pages" meant two leaves.) Three further loose leaves have no self-evident place in the notebook. Tedlock relegated them to the end of his listing of the notebook's contents because they did "not seem to be in proper position" (111). They have since been wrongly inserted between the leaf bearing the first 18 lines of "The Young Want to be Just" and that bearing lines 19 to 29 of that poem. At some time after Tedlock described the notebook and before the Humanities Research Center acquired it, the notebook was defaced by an inaccurate page-numbering in pencil, a numbering that corresponds to the inaccurate reinsertion of the three leaves.[6]

The three leaves are of particular interest because there are indicators that they hold some of the first *pensées* Lawrence composed and entered in the *Pansies* notebook. Although some notebook leaves with early *pensées* may now be lost, it is possible to order those that remain.

Publication dates of the first three items in the notebook as reversed establish that these items must have been drafted in the notebook before Lawrence began composing *pensées*. The first *pensée* in the notebook appears to be the untitled "I know a noble Englishman," which Lawrence has interleaved with the third of the three earlier items, a half-page fragment of the essay "Sex Locked Out." There are two reasons for associating this first *pensée* with two others that are found on one of the three misplaced leaves, the *pensées* "How beastly the bourgeois is!" and "If you live among the middle classes." The three poems are all untitled and are written in a black ink now discolored brown. The three *pensées* on the two remaining misplaced leaves, "Natural Complexion," "The English Voice," and "The Gentleman," are written in a gray-blue shade of ink, except for the last fifteen lines of "The Gentleman," written after a refilling of the fountain pen in the same decidedly blue ink as "What Matters." Taking into account ink-color and the stubs of torn-out pages, I should propose the following as the correct sequence for the first nine *pensées* that Lawrence entered in the *Pansies* notebook (always admitting some pages may have been lost):[7]

[1] [*untitled*] I know a noble Englishman (The noble Englishman)
[2] [*untitled*] How beastly the bourgeois is!
[3] [*untitled*] If you live among the middle classes (Worm either way)
[4] Natural Complexion
[5] The English Voice (The Oxford Voice.)
[6] The Gentleman.*
[7] What Matters.
[8] The Young Are not Mean in Material Things (A played-out game—; The combative spirit)
[9] The Young Want to be Just. (A played-out game—; The combative spirit)

The order confirms Sagar's suggestion that the spur that started Lawrence on his later poetry was Richard Aldington, as a type of the

English bourgeois gentleman, though it was Aldington as editor who would later describe these satires as the work of "the Lawrence of off days, the Lawrence one could most easily do without" ("Introduction" 11).

From Christmas 1928 to 11 February 1929, Lawrence prepared two separate typescripts of *Pansies*. The ribbon and carbon copies of the first typescript (see Roberts E302f), posted to Lawrence's London agent on 7 January 1929 (*Letters VII* 122), were the registered letters seized by the Postmaster-General, acting for the Home Secretary, Sir William Joynson-Hicks (Nehls III, 308–12). Lawrence heard of the seizure on 21 January (*Letters VII* 147); he had begun work on a second typescript by 27 January (*Letters VII* 157); and he completed this typescript (Roberts E302g) by 11 February (*Letters VII* 173). Both first and second typescripts contain *pensées* not found in either the *Pansies* notebook or the *Nettles* notebook.[8] The notebooks are not a complete record of Lawrence's late verse, but their very incompleteness suggests that Lawrence continued to compose poems while he was busy revising and typing them for *Pansies*.

Although it is difficult to fix a *terminus a quo*, it is likely Lawrence began composing the second wave of *pensées* in the *Nettles* notebook in May 1929, after a break of about three months. During March 1929, he travelled to Paris, to make arrangements for a cheap edition of *Lady Chatterley's Lover*. It was not until April that he journeyed south again, arriving at Palma de Mallorca around 14 April. He stayed on Mallorca until 18 June 1929.

While there, Lawrence received from John Middleton Murry a letter lamenting the failure of their friendship, to which he responded on 20 May (*Letters VII* 294). The letter was the stimulus for the mordant "Correspondence in After Years"—the sixth newly entered *pensée* in the *Nettles* notebook.[9] Lawrence's letter quotes from Murry's: "I know too well that we 'missed it,' as you put it." "Correspondence in After Years" begins: "A man wrote to me: We missed it, you and I." The fourth, fifth, and sixth newly entered *pensées*, "To a Certain Friend," "The Emotional Friend," and "Correspondence in After Years," all refer to Murry's letter, but all appear in the *Nettles* notebook as pencil revisions of a single draft in ink, "Love," which has no reference to the letter. The thirteenth newly entered *pensée*, "Andraitx.—Pomegranate Flowers" does, however, tend to confirm the impression that Lawrence began composing the new *pensées* in the *Nettles* notebook on Mallorca. Andraitx is on the island's western side, and Lawrence's letters mention no excursions from Palma de Mallorca before May (*Letters VII* 275). It would be nice to be able to conclude that, as

Aldington goaded Lawrence into the composition of the first wave of *pensées*, so Murry did the second; but, alas, the manuscript record is more dubious than that—not so neat, but not therefore less intriguing.

The text of the ink *pensée* underlying those provoked by Murry's letter is:

Love.

I shall never love you unless you are beyond me
unless your aloneness is intact
and I cannot touch it.

In all the intimacy
in all the contact
in all the interpenetration
I shall never love you, unless beyond me
your aloneness is ⟨like a star⟩ absolute

I want to hold you in my arms
But I want to see, beyond me, the star of your aloneness
in the night.

The texts of the three *pensées* Lawrence penciled over the top of "Love" are:

To a Certain Friend

You are so interested in yourself
that you bore me
thoroughly, I am unable to feel any interest in your
interesting self.

* * *

⟨Trust⟩ The Emotional Friend.

He said to me: You don't trust me!
I said: Oh yes I do!
I know you won't pick my pocket,
I know you'll be very kind to me.
But it was not enough, he looked at me almost with hate.
And I failed entirely to see what ⟨further trust⟩ he meant
Since there was no circumstance requiring trust between us.

* * *

Correspondence in After Years

A man wrote to me: We missed it, you and I.
We were meant to mean a great deal to one another,
but we missed it.—
And I could only reply:
A miss is as good as a mile
Mister![10]

My critical judgment tells me the three *pensées*, with their pounce and dispatch, are more worth preserving than the text they seem to supersede, but I am not unimpressed by "Love." Although one has met with star-equilibrium before, in *Women in Love* or *Mr Noon*, the original *pensée* treats the symbolism with a muted lyricism which makes it by no means the most negligible item in Lawrence's canon. Yet, to my knowledge, no editor has yet suggested "Love" is an unpublished Lawrence poem, presumably because it has been regarded as an "early version" of the three *pensées* written over it.

Reading in this way is like an archaeological dig exposing levels of a city in different centuries of its existence, or, to take a less grandiose analogy, like peeling away transparencies showing two-dimensional cross sections of a three-dimensional anatomy. "Love" is not an isolated instance: other manuscript verse revised for publication in *Pansies* and *Nettles* differs as radically from its published versions as "Love" does from the poems interpolated through and over it. It is in this sense that Lawrence's three notebooks still contain hitherto unpublished verse.

Other considerations apply in the case of a single, heavily revised text. Embedded among the satirical *pensées* Lawrence selected for *Nettles,* though it did not appear in that edition, "Emasculation" is one of the poems that gave Aldington "trouble finding the real text"—so much so he did not include it in his *More Pansies.* This was a pity, because "Emasculation" is a good specimen of mature Lawrencean wit, a melding of the tokens of high and low popular culture to produce a discomforting paradox. Fortunately, de Sola Pinto and Roberts provide a text, on the grounds that the *pensée* was "not crossed out" in the notebook (*Complete Poems* 658–59, 1032):[11]

Emasculation

When Mercury and Love and Death
and even the grand horse of Physical Energy

have all, by Mr. Watts and the Victorians, been
                        carefully emasculated—

so that all our Daddies were quite British "pure,"
they never did anything—
all dear Daddy-do-nothings!
Hypocrites and eunuchs,
eunuchs and hypocrites!

What are we, O what are we
immaculately conceived
Daddyless
children of Daddy-do-nothing?

Little boy blue
come blow up your horn—

The holograph text of "Emasculation" in the *Pansies* notebook has
three unrevised opening lines, followed by multiple revisions—a tangle of
interlineations, ink-shades, and marginalia. The multiple revisions cannot
be represented clearly by means of traditional lemmata. Even an attempt to
represent the manuscript poem in print laid out as a black-and-white
quasi-facsimile would be misleading, because such a text would not allow a
reader to reconstruct each successive stage of revision of "Emasculation."
The reader would be able to see the range of revisions but would lack
information regarding their sequence.[12]
       With the *Nettles* notebook in front of him, a reader of the multiply
revised "Emasculation" can inspect not only penciled insertions but
changing ink-shades, both insertions between the notebook's ruled lines
and marginal additions, and thereby separate the levels of composition in
this quasi-palimpsest. Further, the analogies that have been drawn, to the
levels of a palimpsest or archaeological excavation, suggest a means of
repeating, in print, the intimate experience of notebook reading: represent
the stages of composition of heavily revised poems as separate versions.
The printed page will bear little visual resemblance to the holograph
manuscript, but the editor can dispense with a cumbersome apparatus and
offer the reader ease of access to the poem at each stage of its revision.
       There are three stages of composition in the notebook text of "Emas-
culation." The first version reads:

When Mercury and Love and Death
and even the grand horse of Physical Energy

> have all, by Mr. Watts and the Victorians, been
> carefully emasculated—
>
> What can you expect, in the third and fourth generation
> but a race of hypocrites and eunuchs?
>
> The Englishman of today is
> the hypocrite and the eunuch,
> the eunuch and the hypocrite.

To arrive at the second stage, Lawrence made a number of minor revisions and replaced "The Englishman of today is" with a rhetorical question. With the first three lines omitted (they are unchanged throughout the poem's development), the second version reads:

> What can you expect, in the third and fourth generation
> but hypocrites and eunuchs?
>
> Oh England, where every horse, dog, cat is gelded
> what sort of people are you full of?
> Hypocrites and Eunuchs,
> eunuchs and hypocrites!

In the third stage, Lawrence revised all the lines inserted at stage two, and added a new conclusion. After the unaltered first three lines, the third version reads:

> So that all our Daddies were quite British "pure,"
> they never did anything—
> all dear Daddy-do-nothings!
> What are we, O what are we
> immaculately conceived
> Daddyless
> children of Daddy-do-nothing
>
> *Little boy blue*
> *come blow up your horn*—

The last six lines of the third version are written in a notional right-hand margin or column, alongside the last five lines of the second version. Three of the second version's last five lines have been cancelled; the concluding two have not. Throughout his manuscript verse, Lawrence is usually scrupulous about cancelling superseded phrasing and ensuring that new versions appear in their exact syntactical relations. He is not an Emily Dickinson or Dylan Thomas, leaving a page littered with alternatives. Hence, de Sola Pinto and Roberts follow what could be elevated into a rule for editing Lawrence's manuscript verse, when they retain the two lines "Hypocrites and Eunuchs, / eunuchs and hypocrites!" The lines are construed as filling out the left-hand column, before the concluding six lines in the right-hand column. Reconstructing the order of composition of the versions, however, establishes that these two uncancelled lines belong to the second version of the poem. The last six lines of the third version begin higher on the page and end lower than the two uncancelled second-version lines. For this reason, they are more adjacent to the preceding line of the third version than are the concluding two lines of the second version. It is possible to read the third version as requiring a visual sidestepping after "all dear Daddy-do-nothings!", rather than as requiring a visual completion of one column before starting on another.

As a matter of aesthetic preference, I should like to omit the couplet "Hypocrites and Eunuchs, / eunuchs and hypocrites!" It seems to belong tonally to the earlier, more strident versions, to be otiose in the final version. This consideration alerted me to the possibility that Lawrence himself, in preparing the final notebook version, may have overlooked deletion of the couplet. We are left with this finely poised question: Is the critical judgment that the couplet is extraneous to the version's internal consistency—in combination with the textual observation that the disposition of the manuscript on the page is ambiguous—*sufficient* to allow an editorial verdict in favor of omission? I believe they *do* give warrant for omitting the couplet. Though omission creates an exception to the rule that Lawrence cancels discarded verbiage from an earlier version, it maintains the principle underlying the rule, that Lawrence revises until a new version attains a new coherence.

A critical judgment about the coherence of a Lawrence poem, though insufficient warrant in itself for emending it, can help isolate a textual crux. It precedes if it does not predicate emendation. After I had decided narrowly against the couplet from "Emasculation," I came across a letter Lawrence wrote to Charles Lahr on 23 August 1929 (*Letters VII* 441–44). Enclosed in the letter is a five-page holograph manuscript of six poems (Roberts E266b), including a version of "Emasculation" under a new title, "Never had a Daddy." A fair copy of the third notebook version

incorporating all the revisions, "Never had a Daddy" omits the two uncan-
celed lines. It is likely Lawrence redrafted "Emasculation" on the day he
wrote to Lahr, and left the third notebook draft in an uncharacteristically
ambiguous form.

Unlike the *Pansies* notebook, the *Nettles* notebook has been all but
filled, and filled with poetry. Sixty-nine of its seventy leaves are used for
drafts of poems. There is also a back endpaper, but at some time a number
of leaves and the front endpaper have been removed or lost. Aldington
reports that "The inner cover is inscribed: 'D. H. Lawrence, Bandol, Var,
France, 23rd Nov. 1928'" ("Introduction" 5). Since no inscription can
now be found, it may be, as Sagar has suggested, that the dating was on
the now-lost front endpaper (*Life into Art* 359). The missing date probably reflects the date of purchase, shortly after which Lawrence seems to
have begun entering the first *pensées* in the notebook. The chronology of
the notebook's use can be outlined with the help of the biographical
record.

Remarks in Lawrence's letters and his peregrinations are recapitulated
in a number of *pensées*—"Lucifer" and "Forte dei Marmi," "13 Pictures,"
and "Storm in the Black Forest" among them—and make it possible to
match his progress in the notebook with his wanderings through Italy and
Germany in summer 1929. The bulk of the poems must have been written
in July and August, while he was staying at the Kurhaus Plattig, bei Bühl,
or below, in Lichtenthal, Baden-Baden. Three short satires, the untitled "I
heard a little chicken chirp," "'Gross, coarse, hideous',," and the untitled
"Dearly-beloved Mr Squire," are the 236th to 238th *pensées* in the *Nettles*
notebook, and mark an end to these summer poems. The first two poems
relate to the exhibition of Lawrence's paintings at the Warren Gallery,
which was raided by the police. On 24 August Lawrence wrote to Rhys
Davies that his "idea of the lily-white policemen of London fainting with
shock at the sight of one of my nudes would make an A.1. squib" (*Letters
VII* 448); "'Gross, coarse, hideous'" puts the idea in a quatrain. Also on
24 August Lawrence received a copy of the *New Statesman* with T. W.
Earp's critique of the Warren Gallery exhibition. His two-quatrain response, "I heard a little chicken chirp," was dispatched to Charles Lahr on
the same day (*Letters VII* 447). And in the same letter he advised Lahr he
was leaving next day for three to four weeks before returning to Bandol.
After the three short satires, there remain nine mythopoeic poems in the
Nettles notebook, in mood and subject closer to the *Last Poems* notebook.
Indeed, four of the nine poems are redrafted in the *Last Poems* notebook.

The transition, from the scurrilous squibs of summer to the elevated autumnal mood of the nine poems that conclude the *Nettles* notebook, is as sudden as any to be found in the notebooks. For Sagar, the move from Lichtenthal and Lawrence's ill health in Rottach are sufficient to account for this change. Pointing out that Rottach furnished the images for such poems from the end of the notebook as "Glory of Darkness" and the early "Ship of Death" (*Calendar* 187), Sagar concludes that Lawrence finished the *Nettles* notebook there ("Genesis" 48). There is a neatness in having Lawrence fill the remaining pages of the *Nettles* notebook in Bavaria, then begin the *Last Poems* notebook in Bandol, but internal evidence, from the nine poems that close the *Nettles* notebook, casts doubt on this dating. "Let there be Light!", the first of the nine, might be a psalm to the Mediterranean light Lawrence praises in several letters after returning to Bandol (*Collected Letters* 1200, 1203). Ink-color also groups the nine poems with the *Last Poems* notebook. "Let there be Light!" is the first poem in the *Nettles* notebook to be wholly penned in a blue-black ink, the same ink used for the first 24 poems in the *Last Poems* notebook. But Catherine Henderson, checking letters held at the Harry Ransom Humanities Research Center, tells me that the change in ink-colors is found, for example, between the letters Lawrence wrote to Frederick Carter, on 23 and 30 August 1929 (*Letters VII* 444–45, 455–56). Although Lawrence continued to use the same ink after moving from Rottach to Bandol, the evidence tends to confirm that the last nine poems in the *Nettles* notebook were, as Sagar suggests, written or at least begun in Rottach, and that Lawrence began work on the *Last Poems* notebook after the move to Bandol. It also illustrates how much more compelling are bibliographical data, like ink-color, than evidence drawn from the content of the poems.

Though not conclusive, the evidence indicates that the third wave of Lawrence's verse, 1928–29, took rise in Rottach. There, in early September, Lawrence took to his bed, weakened as much by an arsenic and phosphorus treatment of his tuberculosis as by tuberculosis. Possibly the new mythopoeic poems started to flow from his pen once he had completed his "Pornography and Obscenity" essay and taken himself off the poisonous diet, on 13 Sept. 1929 (*Letters VII* 470, 477). Having left Rottach around 18 September and reached Bandol on 23 Sept. 1929, Lawrence may have begun composing and entering poems in the *Last Poems* notebook with only a brief delay. Early in October 1929, the preoccupations in Lawrence's letters—with the Mediterranean as Homeric or as a specific against the ills of the modern world, and with lunar and solar astrology—become those of the first poems in the *Last Poems* notebook, "The Greeks are Coming!", "The Argonauts," and "Middle of the World." Astrology is still prominent in "Invocation to the Moon," the fifteenth entry in the notebook. The sixteenth entry, the *Last Poems* version of "Butterfly," marvels "Already it is October." But the seventeenth and eighteenth entries turn back the calendar to the "soft September" of "Bavarian Gentians." Circumspection is called for with internal references. A more convincing date for the *Last Poems* notebook is provided by the powerful sea invoked in the thirtieth entry, "Mana of the Sea." On 27 October Lawrence described to Max Mohr the storms at Bandol, and on 29 October wrote to Frederick Carter about the concept of *mana* (*Letters VII* 543, 545). In his letters Lawrence only once alludes to what might be his work in this third notebook, confiding to Maria Huxley on 10 October that he was "writing a few poems" (*Letters VII* 523). To Achsah Brewster he read some poems he described as *Dead Nettles,* presumably poems from the *Nettles* notebook not selected for the volume *Nettles,* and mentioned having written some other "verses about death" which he found himself unable to read (Brewster 308–09). The Brewsters arrived in Bandol around 18 October (*Letters VII* 532). It may be surmised that Lawrence, having begun composition in the *Last Poems* notebook in late September, had written about thirty of its sixty-eight poems by the end of October.

A *terminus ad quem* for the *Last Poems* notebook is also elusive. "All Souls Day" and "After All Saints Day" make up the fifty-third and fifty-sixth entries in the *Last Poems* notebook. If the thirtieth entry, "Mana of the Sea," was composed at the end of October, "All Souls Day" and "After All Saints Day" were probably written some time after November 1 and 2. "Beware the unhappy dead," which comes between them, first sets itself in October, "now as November draws near," then in November, "on this day of the dead." "Shadows," the third-last in the *Last Poems* notebook, speaks of the season's moving "on, on to the solstice." On 28 December, Lawrence wrote to Emil Krug thanking him for the gift of a fountain pen and mentioning that his old pen had given up the ghost (*Letters VII* 610). My notes record no sign of Lawrence's fountain pen breaking down in the *Last Poems* notebook. Hardly enough evidence presents itself to speak of a balance of probabilities. On 20 November he reported Frederick Carter's arrival in Bandol, and Carter, before his departure on 30 November, recalled Lawrence as already having "written nearly twenty thousand words of introduction" for *The Dragon of Revelation* (Lawrence, *Apocalypse* 18; Nehls III, 417). In the absence of other information, it might be hypothesized that, in mid-November 1929, Lawrence turned from the composition of his *Last Poems* to take up his last prose volume, *Apocalypse*.

To sum up: Lawrence began composing *pensées* in the *Pansies* notebook around 17 November 1928, and finished using the notebook for that purpose around 20 December. He entered the first nineteen poems in the *Nettles* notebook early in December 1928; in May 1929 he resumed using that notebook, writing 229 *pensées* and "nettles" before the end of August, and completing the remaining nine mythopoeic poems in September. The entries in the *Last Poems* notebook were made between late September and mid-November 1929. There can be no certainties, but there are indications that the verse Lawrence wrote during the twelve months from mid-November 1928 to mid-November 1929 may itself be broken into three lesser periods that correspond roughly to Lawrence's and Aldington's volume-divisions: *Pansies* first; then *Nettles* and *More Pansies;* then *Last Poems*.

Though Lawrence reversed the *Last Poems* notebook to enter the sixty-eight poems it contains, the notebook presents few of the difficulties encountered in the other notebooks in establishing a reading text or a sequence of entry. It is still possible, nevertheless, to misconstrue the manuscript verse, if care is not taken to reconstruct the sequence of revision. Much of the revision undertaken in the notebook centers on two long poems, originally titled "Demiurge" and "When Satan Fell," which have been broken up into two sequences consisting of five and six shorter poems.[13] A reconstruction of the two stages of composition of the sequence will result in emended reading texts for some poems from these sequences. As was the case with "Emasculation," the general principle applies: to establish a reading text for a poem, it is necessary to reconstruct the stages of its composition. To this editor, there is further critical interest in discovering that "The Ship of Death" is not the only long poem to be found among the stages of revision of the *Last Poems* notebook. For the poet Lawrence, the last things included the problem of evil and the question of the soul's disembodiment or embodiment, as well as the journey into death and a possible afterlife.

Preparation of the Cambridge edition of Lawrence's *Poems* is both yielding some new reading texts and suggesting some new, Lawrence-specific strategies for editing manuscript verse. Not all of Lawrence's revisions require the reconstruction or reproduction of early versions to the extent "Emasculation" does. Lawrence was capable of minor revisions. In this sense Aldington was right to dispute Huxley's view that Lawrence "was incapable of correcting," that he always "rewrote" (Huxley xvii). But if one refines Huxley's observation about Lawrence, if one says that Lawrence rewrote, not to improve the word or the line, but with the internal consistency of an entire poem before him, the observation is borne out in version after version of his later poetry. For the present editor, Huxley's insight has a prescience about it; it shows an intimacy with Lawrence's working methods.

ACKNOWLEDGMENTS

The three notebooks examined are part of the Lawrence holdings in the Harry Ransom Humanities Research Center of the University of Texas at Austin. Quotations from Lawrence's poetry are made with the consent of the Harry Ransom Humanities Research Center, and with the permission of Cambridge University Press, Laurence Pollinger Ltd., and the Estate of Mrs. Frieda Lawrence Ravagli.

NOTES

1. A page count based on Vivian de Sola Pinto and Warren Roberts's *Complete Poems* shows the verse from *Collected Poems* occupying 364 pages. The verse from the last four collections takes up 299 pages, or 45 percent of the total collected verse.
2. On a count based on titles, the three notebooks contain at least one version of at least 80 percent of the later poems.
3. The principal contributors to this consensus have been Ross C. Murfin, Gail Porter Mandell, M. J. Lockwood, David Ellis, and Howard Mills (see Works Cited).
4. De Sola Pinto describes the text in *Complete Poems* as "corrected from photostats of the notebooks" (1027). Warren Roberts has pointed out to me that, for his part, he certainly did work from the original notebooks. It is less certain how far the text in *Complete Poems* incorporates Roberts's work with the notebooks.
5. The present contents of the *Pansies* notebook are: an early version of a poem, "The Old Orchard," published in the *Calendar of Modern Letters* in April 1928 (Roberts C153); a fragment of a review of works by Robert Byron and others, published in *Vogue* on 20 July 1928 (C172); a fragment, "Sex Appeal," of an essay published in the *Sunday Dispatch* on 25 Nov. 1928 under the title "Sex Locked Out" (C179); 164 *pensées,* eleven in Rhys Davies's hand; a first draft of an introduction to *Pansies;* and a contents list comprising 197 titles. For a

further fragment from the draft contents list for *Pansies* (Roberts E302c), see Tedlock 71. The seven-page manuscript draft of "The Blue Moccasins" (Roberts E50a), with the list fragment on the back of its last page, was presumably torn from the *Pansies* notebook at some time after Lawrence had completed entering the *pensées* and compiling the list. For other writings formerly contained in the notebook, see Note 10.

6. As well as wrongly reinserting the three leaves, the numbering faces the torn edges of two leaves outwards from the spine, and places the leaf bearing lines 19 to 29 of "The English Voice" before that bearing the first 18 lines.

7. I have assigned the numbers to the *pensées* and designated untitled poems by first lines. The title of a *pensée*, as it appears in revised form in the unexpurgated edition of *Pansies* (Roberts A47c), is shown in brackets after the notebook title, if the title differs in more than punctuation and capitalization. A title followed by an asterisk indicates a *pensée* not revised for publication in any form in *Pansies*. See Tedlock 105–11, items 6–159, for a listing of the other *pensées* in the *Pansies* notebook. (Tedlock's item 160 is simply the conclusion of item 159.) Since examining the notebook and arriving at this order for the first nine *pensées*, I have found it confirmed in a description of the notebook prepared by D. J. Wells and H. K. Wells after an exhibition at Harvard of Frieda Lawrence's manuscript collection (Squires 262–63). The Wellses indicated that, in January 1937, the notebook held holograph manuscripts of the following additional items: "The Flying Fish"; the review for *Vogue;* and the essays "Sex Appeal" and "Do Women Change?" (the last three items not being described as incomplete). In the descriptive catalogue prepared by Lawrence Clark Powell in June 1937, "The Flying Fish" and a second holograph version of the review for *Vogue* appear as separate catalogue items (Squires 277, 290). Detaching "The Flying Fish" presumably caused the pages bearing the early *pensées* to come loose from their signature.

8. The unexpurgated edition of *Pansies*, set from a carbon of the second typescript that Rhys Davies took to Charles Lahr (*Letters VII* 233), includes eighty-six titles not found in any version in the surviving leaves of the *Pansies* notebook. Perhaps thirty of these poems had already been written by Christmas 1928; the draft contents list includes over thirty titles of *pensées* not found in the notebook.

9. This is the twenty-fifth poem in the notebook, the sixth after the nineteen poems entered in December 1928.

10. There are no substantive differences between these texts and those in *Complete Poems* (602–3), but there are numerous rectifications in capitalization and punctuation.

11. The semiotic possibilities of such cancellations—whether they indicate a poem has been rejected or completed, has been selected for publication or revised in another manuscript—are not canvassed by de Sola Pinto and Roberts, though the cancellations are used to exclude some manuscript verse from the *Complete Poems*.

12. For an illustration of the confusions that can be created by quasi-facsimile representations of multiply revised poems, see Gail Porter Mandell's editing of

the manuscript pages on which Lawrence reworked "Glory of Darkness," until eventually arriving at the second version of "Bavarian Gentians" (Mandell 228–31). Mandell's printed reproductions of two versions of "Glory of Darkness" do not accurately separate the four stages of composition of this *pensée;* nor does her printing of the first version of "Bavarian Gentians" show the three stages of composition of that poem. The final version of "Bavarian Gentians" is not the result of four levels of revision, as Mandell's layouts suggest, but of nine.

13. The long version of "Demiurge" was divided into: the shorter version of "Demiurge"; "The Work of Creation"; "Red Geranium and Godly Mignonette"; "Bodiless God" (originally titled "Likeness of God"); and "The Body of God." The long version of "When Satan Fell" was divided into: the shorter version of "When Satan Fell"; "Doors" (originally titled "What is Evil"); "Evil is Homeless"; "What then is Evil?"; "The Evil World-Soul"; "The Wandering Cosmos"; and "Death is not Evil, Evil is Mechanical" (originally titled "Death is not Evil, Evil is not Death").

WORKS CITED

Aldington, Richard. "Introduction." In Lawrence, *Last Poems* xi–xxii.

————, and Lawrence Durrell. *Literary Lifelines: The Richard Aldington— Lawrence Durrell Correspondence.* Ed. Ian S. MacNiven and Harry T. Moore. London: Faber, 1981.

Brewster, Earl and Achsah. *D. H. Lawrence: Reminiscences and Correspondence.* London: Secker, 1934.

Ellis, David, and Howard Mills. *D. H. Lawrence's Non-Fiction.* Cambridge: Cambridge UP, 1988.

Hughes, Robert. "Frank Auerbach." *Scripsi* 6.1 (1990): 1–32.

Huxley, Aldous. "Introduction." In *The Letters of D. H. Lawrence.* Ed. Aldous Huxley. London: Heinemann, 1932. ix–xxxiv.

Lawrence, D. H. *The Collected Letters of D. H. Lawrence.* 2 vols. Ed. Harry T. Moore. New York: Viking, 1962.

————. *The Complete Poems of D. H. Lawrence.* 2 vols. Ed. Vivian de Sola Pinto and F. Warren Roberts. 2d rpt. London: Heinemann, 1972.

————. *Last Poems.* Ed. Richard Aldington. London: Secker, 1933.

————. *Pansies.* London: Privately printed, 1929.

Lockwood, M. J. *A Study of the Poems of D. H. Lawrence.* London: Macmillan, 1987.

Mandell, Gail Porter. *The Phoenix Paradox: A Study of Renewal through Change in the "Collected Poems" and "Last Poems" of D. H. Lawrence.* Carbondale and Edwardsville: Southern Illinois UP, 1984.

Murfin, Ross C. *The Poetry of D. H. Lawrence: Texts and Contexts.* Lincoln: U of Nebraska P, 1983.

Nehls, Edward, ed. *D. H. Lawrence: A Composite Biography: Volume Three: 1925–1930*. Madison: U of Wisconsin P, 1959.

Roberts, Warren. *A Bibliography of D. H. Lawrence*. 2d ed. Cambridge: Cambridge UP, 1982.

Sagar, Keith. *D. H. Lawrence: A Calendar of His Works*. Manchester: Manchester UP, 1979.

———. *D. H. Lawrence: Life into Art*. Harmondsworth: Viking, 1985.

———. "The Genesis of 'Bavarian Gentians.'" *The D. H. Lawrence Review* 8.1 (1975): 47–53.

Smailes, T. A. "D. H. Lawrence: Seven Hitherto Unpublished Poems." *The D. H. Lawrence Review* 3.1 (1970): 42–46.

Squires, Michael, ed. *D. H. Lawrence's Manuscripts: The Correspondence of Frieda Lawrence, Jake Zeitlin and Others*. London: Macmillan, 1991.

Tedlock, E. W., Jr. *The Frieda Lawrence Collection of D. H. Lawrence's Manuscripts: A Descriptive Bibliography*. Albuquerque: U of New Mexico P, 1948.

"Giving Your Self Away": Lawrence's *Letters* in Context

Paul Delany

The letters of the great English modernists provide an extraordinary resource for biography, literary theory, social history, and the study of literary institutions. In no other period of English literature have letters been of such a consistently high standard, or so rich and varied in their interest. The editing of modernist letters is therefore an important branch of literary studies. It is also one with a distinct set of textual problems, arising from the differences of production and reception between a letter and a literary work.

No edition of an author's letters can be truly complete, because many of his or her letters are sure to have been lost or destroyed before editors begin their work of assembly and publication. After his mother and brother died, T. S. Eliot destroyed much of his correspondence with them, and shortly after his second marriage in 1957 he destroyed all his letters from Emily Hale (who had upset Eliot by depositing his letters to her at Princeton, to be sealed for fifty years after the death of the last survivor).[1] Jessie Chambers destroyed all of D. H. Lawrence's letters to her, and Lawrence probably destroyed his letters to his mother (one has survived).[2] The editor thus begins with a mutilated or otherwise incomplete corpus; and for the texts that are available, obstacles to publication abound. If we take the major modernists to be W. B. Yeats, James Joyce, Wyndham Lewis, Virginia Woolf, D. H. Lawrence, Ezra Pound, and T. S. Eliot, only one—Lawrence—has now had his surviving letters published in full, in the Cambridge Edition published from 1979 to 1993.[3] Woolf's letters have been published nearly complete, with excisions due to "the risk of libelling or deeply offending some living person" (Woolf, *Letters III* xi).

173

For none of the others is a complete edition likely to be published in this century, even though they died between 1939 (Yeats) and 1972 (Pound). Publication of the letters of any of these seven writers requires means, motive, and opportunity, and there is no single explanation for the degree of success in each case. Virginia Woolf's letters had the smoothest passage, thanks to the Bloomsbury boom and a cooperative literary estate: six volumes appeared in five years (1975–80) from a trade publisher, and with paperback editions following. The five authors without a complete edition have lagged for various reasons. Yeats's handwriting is so difficult to read that any edition would have thousands of errors and omissions (Yeats had trouble reading his own writings once he had put them down). The literary estate of James Joyce is unlikely to sponsor a complete edition of the letters in the near future. Lewis's letters are probably not commercially viable, and Pound's are so numerous and complex that an army of richly endowed scholars would be needed to tackle them. Valerie Eliot started editing her husband's letters in 1965; the first volume appeared in 1988, but has had no successor.

Lawrence's letters therefore stand alone in having been published complete, under the imprint of a university press and edited by a team of professional literary scholars.[4] *The Cambridge Edition of the Letters and Works of D. H. Lawrence* is a merged edition of two different kinds of writings, edited on different principles. The *Works* appear as authoritative single texts that have been refined by editorial labor from a much larger body of surviving manuscript and printed sources. With the *Letters,* however, the aim is not refinement and exclusion, but inclusiveness:

> all Lawrence's available letters—those to which he contributed as well as those originating with him—will be published in their entirety. . . . The editors have not felt it legitimate to exclude any. Nor have any been excised or bowdlerised. (*Letters I* xi)

"Print everything you can find" makes an editor's work simpler, if also more arduous. Aldous Huxley's edition of Lawrence's letters in 1932 had something under 400,000 words in one volume; Harry T. Moore's in 1962 was more than 500,000 in two volumes; Cambridge ends up in the region of two million words in seven volumes (plus an index volume). In deciding what to include, Huxley had to step very carefully to protect the sensibilities of people still alive.[5] Then, both Huxley and Moore were constrained by commercial forces to cut out letters that were "trivial," repetitive, or concerned with business. The selected editions therefore showed Lawrence as, above all, a prophet and artist: a larger-than-life character who might fit easily into one of his own novels. The Cambridge Lawrence is a more petty, irritable, everyday sort of person. When every letter is included, the writer is bound to seem more banal, since biographers always use their power of selecting evidence to make their subjects' lives more dramatic than they actually were. The Cambridge *Letters* stand as a corrective to the partial views of Lawrence given by editors and biographers.

In his introduction, and through his power of selection, Huxley presented Lawrence as a tragic and isolated genius. By excluding background information and suppressing so many names—even printing "Mrs. _____" for "Mrs. Weekley"—Huxley made Lawrence seem a solipsist, given to lyrical outbursts on the slightest excuse.[6] Moore, thirty years later, still used annotation quite sparingly; he emphasized the role of the letters as biographical evidence. The Cambridge rule of completeness means that a "selective" Lawrence is not available to its editors. Still their Lawrence is shaped by the textual company he keeps: introductions and chronologies, extensive annotations, texts from other sources, and some letters written *to* Lawrence. Beyond this, there is the contrast between Huxley's beautifully designed volume, so attractive and easy to read, and the Cambridge Lawrence whose words are tightly squeezed in and hedged around by the apparatus of literary scholarship. A necessary change of format, no doubt; but one that poignantly marks the shift from a volume that was a tribute to a recently dead friend, to an impersonal monument of erudition.

Volume One of the Cambridge *Letters* has 579 pages and ends on the publication date of *Sons and Lovers,* a suitable point to mark Lawrence's arrival as a major writer. After that, even though the volumes vary in length they do not correlate well with significant phases of Lawrence's life or literary career. Except for Volume One, therefore, there are no distinct and self-sufficient volumes.[7] The introductions to each volume more or less concede that, between such arbitrary dates of starting and ending, no unified biographical phase can be defined. The consequent running together of volumes reinforces other monolithic tendencies in the project as a whole. If each volume had its own shape, Lawrence's life would appear as a series of acts or chapters; but the Cambridge editors prefer to let the massive record of the letters unfold with only a minimal periodization imposed by editorial imagination or literary judgment. With tireless industry, they explain what has become unfamiliar and fill in what has become inaccessible; any master-interpretation of Lawrence as a letter writer they leave to the initiative of others.

How well do these editorial principles accord with the reasonable expectations of those who will be using the Cambridge Edition of the letters for decades to come? Editors for all the Cambridge volumes seem to strive to be quietly authoritative, to avoid speculating or casting too wide a net in their commentary, to eschew humor, and to keep their own personalities in the background. Since the volumes are expensive, and unlikely to be revised, the editors would not want to include material that might become obsolescent; this might be one strong reason, among others, for making only minimal reference to the secondary literature on Lawrence.

But important issues of editorial practice remain. The grand design of the overall Cambridge Edition was laid out in the mid-1970s, and seems likely to remain constant until the completion of the project more than twenty years later. That design was a somewhat uneasy hybrid of two separate tendencies in Anglo-American literary studies. One, the "New Criticism," viewed the text as a self-sufficient aesthetic object, the site of a complex interplay of meanings; the other, positivist scholarship, sought to stabilize the text by specifying its relation to surrounding historical "facts." One tendency privileged the *internal* relations of textual elements; the other, the *external* relations between literature and a knowable real world. The Cambridge Edition seeks to reconcile these perspectives by positing their convergence on a single ideal, the text that Lawrence "would have wished to see printed." But the editors recognize that such texts "will differ . . . often radically and certainly frequently, from those seen by the author himself."[8] We are left, then, with a synthetic text, validated by the supposed intentions of a unitary subject—that is, the ideal author who stands behind the ideal final text. For both the literary works and the letters, the Cambridge Edition set out to preserve Lawrence's texts in a stable and authoritative format—like some precious object in a museum cabinet.

DIALOGISM AND THE LETTERS

Just as the Cambridge Edition was established with these ambitions, Anglo-American literary studies were being invaded by Continental literary theories directed against that ideal authorial subject who supported the Edition's claim to knowledge and fixity. Prominent among these rival models of textual production were Foucault's critique of the "author-function"; Bakhtin's "dialogism"; and Kristeva's "intertextuality."9 In different ways, all these models challenged the idea of a text being made stable, knowable, and delimited by an authorial intention. Rather, these critics (along with many others) dispersed the individual *work* into a wider and more impersonal textual field, now called a *discourse*.

It could be argued that letters can stand up better to such deconstructionist forces than literary works can. Letters are tied to a specific audience, moment, context, and intention, and almost all of Lawrence's survive as single holograph manuscripts. What is left for the editor to do, beyond putting the letters in order and transcribing them accurately from manuscript?10 Nonetheless, Continental literary theory is bound to affect the way modern readers interpret these documents, and relate them to other "contiguous" texts: Lawrence's literary writings, the Cambridge annotations, Lawrence criticism, and so on in widening circles. Formally, the letters are indeed signed, private, and specific utterances, whereas the literary works are public and assignable only to an authorial *persona*. Bakhtin speaks of the novel as an "internally dialogized" genre, where the author simultaneously lets his characters speak and implies judgment on them. Letters, in contrast, may be seen as "monologic," arriving at their destination as the "direct words" of their authors (Bakhtin *Dialogic* 45–46). But the division is scarcely so simple. Letters, too, are "dialogized" in the sense of being adapted to specific recipients. Two days after he arrived to teach at Croydon, Lawrence sent Jessie Chambers a letter that was "like a howl of terror"; at the same time, he wrote to his mother that "everything was all right and he was getting on well" (*Letters I* 82). We cannot reduce the discrepancy by just saying that one letter (which?) was true and the other false; rather, Lawrence wanted different things from Jessie and from his mother, and therefore presented each woman with a different version of himself. The chronological order followed by Cambridge repeatedly shows us several different Lawrences on the same day; collections that have been made of individual correspondences, such as with Louie Burrows or S. S. Kotelansky, show a much more integrated personality.

If we give up belief in a "direct word," in the sense of a transparent and unified revelation of the self, letters become as literary as everything else Lawrence wrote. "I am English, and my Englishness is my very vision" is as much implicated in textuality as "Ours is essentially a tragic age, so we refuse to take it tragically" (*Letters II* 414; *Lady Chatterley's Lover* 5). That one statement was not intended for publication, and the other was, can scarcely make a fundamental difference to the kind of self-revelation—or self-dramatization—that they offer their readers. The Lawrencean self is something that we construct from the fiction as much as from the letters: for example, it is from the novels rather than the letters that we project Lawrence's experience of tuberculosis, anality, and impotence. The letters may be read, in the first instance, as the raw materials from which biographical narratives are worked up; statements of creative intention; communications with a special legal and conventional standing; documents deeply embedded in everyday life. But all these qualities lend themselves, in turn, to literary use—which is why the novel, from the beginning, has had a close affinity with epistolary form.[11]

Lawrence explores the conventions of letter-writing in the "Gudrun at the Pompadour" chapter of *Women in Love,* where Halliday brings out a letter Birkin wrote him and reads it aloud—to the delight of his cronies in the Café and the disgust of Gudrun and Gerald. Lawrence's actual letters to Philip Heseltine have not survived, but they may have been close enough in style to the words Halliday reads.[12] In the novel, Halliday presents Birkin's words as those of a sententious clergyman:

> "Surely," Halliday intoned, "Surely goodness and mercy hath followed me all the days of my life—" he broke off, and giggled. Then he began again, intoning like a clergyman. "Surely there will come an end in us to this desire—for the constant going apart. . . ." (*Women in Love* 384)

When Ursula criticizes Birkin for preaching, elsewhere in the novel, he takes her words to heart; but Halliday seizes on the trait out of pure malice, and violates his intimacy with Birkin by using a private letter to expose him. In Bakhtin's terms, Halliday can be seen "representing" Birkin's mode of discourse to others—even as, at the same time, the author is representing, and condemning, Halliday to the novel's readers (Bakhtin, *Dialogic* 43–45). Gudrun then asks for the letter and walks off with it; she crushes it into a ball, as if to make it literally "unreadable," and excoriates Birkin for making the scene possible: "Why is Rupert such a *fool* as to write such letters to them? *Why* does he give himself away to such canaille?" (385).

It was actually an unidentified woman, not Heseltine, who read aloud at the Café Royale; and she did not read a letter, but a published volume of Lawrence's poems.[13] Lawrence made the change, in *Women in Love,* to show that in a letter one "gives oneself away" more intimately than in a literary text. A letter also involves a literal gift—the manuscript—which can be displayed and made into an object of derision, as Halliday does in the novel. That Halliday *can* misuse Birkin's letter reveals its elusive status as a document. From the side of the writer, a letter may seem perfectly direct and "monologic," a spontaneous cry from the heart. But from the side of the recipient, the letter is dialogic. When first received, it will be read as a *response* to something in the recipient's life-situation. If the letter is then published, it is made available for interpretation by a mass audience. In the case of the Cambridge Edition, at least sixty years will have passed between a letter's being written and its being read in modern form. The immediate context of any letter will be recoverable only through an effort of historical imagination; as we move further away from Lawrence's era, editors are both more necessary, and more powerful, in representing the milieu within which a letter will be understood.

THE LETTERS AND INTERTEXTUALITY

Letters are the least autarchic of texts: each one, typically, responds to a previous text and expects a subsequent one. Ideally, an edition should print both sides of a correspondence, as in the volume of letters between Pound and Wyndham Lewis. Nigel Nicholson found room only for Woolf's letters in his edition; Cambridge prints everything by Lawrence, and a small selection of letters to him.[14] Frieda's letters are a special case, and ideally they should all be blended in with Lawrence's; Cambridge prints all jointly written letters, but none written by Frieda independently. Other letters have a strong claim for inclusion, as do closely associated literary texts: letters often provide indispensable comments on Lawrence's fiction, while the fiction often takes observations from the letters and reworks them in novelistic terms. There may be no simple rule for the inclusion of ancillary letters and other documents in the Cambridge Edition. If the problem was essentially one of space, it might have been better to include *no* outside letters, but Edward Nehls's *Composite Biography* (1957–59) assumes that intertextuality and mingling of genres are needed to do justice to Lawrence's protean career. But the richness of the *Composite biography* entails also the absence of consistent editorial principles.

For an example of the relation between Lawrence's letters and other documents, we may look at the dealings between Lawrence, his American agent Robert Mountsier, and his American publisher Thomas Seltzer, documented in volume IV of the *Letters*. Mountsier and Seltzer did not get along well. Hoping to reconcile them, Lawrence brought them together for Christmas 1922 at the Del Monte Ranch in New Mexico, along with Frieda and Seltzer's wife Adele. Tensions continued, and early in 1923 Lawrence dismissed Mountsier and affirmed his loyalty to Seltzer. Before long, Seltzer found himself in financial difficulties, and in 1925 Lawrence replaced him with Alfred A. Knopf as his principal American publisher.

Relations between Lawrence, Mountsier, and Seltzer are specially relevant to Lawrence's attitudes towards Jews. In November 1921 Lawrence wrote to S. S. Koteliansky (who was Jewish): "[Mountsier] is one of those irritating people who have generalised detestations: his particular ones being Jews, Germans, and Bolshevists. So unoriginal" (*Letters IV* 113). Two weeks later, however, he wrote to Mabel Dodge Sterne: "I don't like [Leo] Stein, a nasty, nosy, corrupt Jew" (*Letters IV* 182). In the confrontation of 1923, Lawrence sided with the Jewish Seltzers against the anti-Semitic Mountsier; though in September 1924 he told Mountsier: "We are having the struggle with Seltzer that you warned me about. You were right and I was wrong about him" (*Letters V* 127). When race or ethnicity is at issue, Lawrence (like others) usually expresses his true feelings to third parties, but conceals them from the person directly involved. In any letter he writes to a Jew, we must read between the lines, supplementing the text with letters written to gentiles.[15]

Evidence relevant to this situation would include all letters exchanged between the persons concerned, but Cambridge's handling of such letters is inconsistent. In general, few letters sent *to* Lawrence have survived, because it was his habit to destroy them soon after receipt. In the Lawrence/Mountsier/Seltzer affair, however, an unusual amount of ancillary correspondence is available and has been published. *Letters IV* prints two letters from Frieda to Adele Seltzer, one letter from Mountsier to Thomas Seltzer, one letter from Mountsier to Lawrence, and one from Seltzer to Lawrence. Gerald M. Lacy (Lawrence, *Letters to Seltzer*) adds seven other letters from Frieda to Adele; one from Frieda to Thomas; one from Adele to Lawrence; one from Thomas to Lawrence; six between the Seltzers; and twenty-one from Thomas Seltzer to Mountsier.[16] Cambridge always prints such letters if they are physically linked to Lawrence letters (e.g., Frieda begins a letter and Lawrence continues it; Lawrence writes on the back of a letter he has received and forwards it). But in the absence of a physical connection, there seems to be no clear policy on what other letters will be included.

After the Seltzers had left Del Monte at the beginning of January 1923, Frieda wrote to Adele Seltzer: "Mountsier sits in his room all day and writes another of his *beastly* European articles—I *detest* him for it—. . . . as you said his spirit is just opposed to L's! If he is *hopeless,* we wont have any more of him—" (Lawrence, *Letters to Seltzer* 57). Although this letter is not included in *Letters IV,* it is crucial to Lawrence's turn against Mountsier (and also to the mingling of Frieda's interests with Lawrence's). Mountsier's anti-German views clearly got on Frieda's nerves; Adele Seltzer, who came from a German-speaking background, had allied herself with Frieda against Mountsier.[17] When Lawrence sent Mountsier away from the ranch, he made the announcement to Adele before telling her husband—and in German!: "Der Mountsier ist heute weg— fortgegangen—etc. Gott sei dank" (*Letters IV* 373). Lawrence's letter needs Frieda's in order to be understood in its context.

ANNOTATING THE CAMBRIDGE LETTERS

It is now a general rule that modernist letters will be published with explanatory notes and commentary; but the "Preface" to volume I of the Cambridge *Letters* (which sets out editorial policy) says nothing at all about principles guiding the annotation. The economic realities of publishing (even for a university press) require that commentary must be fairly restricted, and a casual inspection of the Cambridge volumes indicates that the commentary does not exceed 10 percent of the primary text of the letters. Such a limited space should be used as concisely and effectively as possible, but the Cambridge editors could have made better use of their short rations. First, Cambridge prints a very large amount of information that its readers—predominantly scholars—either already know or can easily find in standard reference works. Rather than trudging through dozens of notes to make this point, I will examine just the notes on pages 47 to 49 of *Letters IV.* In this sample, the editors give the full names and dates of birth and death of six painters, including Dürer and Rembrandt. To understand Lawrence's letter, do we need to know that Rembrandt's middle name was Harmensz? Lawrence's reference to a "farm near Cannes" is annotated "Mougins, Alpes Maritimes, France"; why tell us the Département and country? Another five-line note quotes from Curtis Brown's archives about Jan Juta's illustrations for *Sea and Sardinia;* the English edition did not use these illustrations, and I cannot see any real use for the information supplied.

More important, however, is what the editors leave out. Lawrence's reference to "the awful Rembrandts" suggests that he disliked Rembrandt as a painter. In fact, he is criticizing a proposed *selection* of Rembrandts for a schoolbook; elsewhere, to take only one example, he speaks of the "great Rembrandt . . . I loved him intensely" (*Phoenix II* 606). Also needing explanation are Lawrence's apparently callous remarks to Mary Cannan: "No, I hadn't heard of the boy's drowning. What was he doing to get drowned? J. M. [Barrie] has a fatal touch for those he loves. They die." The note on this reads: "Michael Llewelyn Davies (1900–21) was drowned in Sandford Pool, near Oxford, in May 1921, while bathing with another undergraduate." Another note lists four friends and family of Barrie who died suddenly between 1867 and 1895; but it is unlikely that Lawrence knew of these deaths. The first note is typical of Cambridge's belt-and-suspenders style in telling us twice in one sentence that Davies died in 1921. But what, we wonder, *was* he doing to get drowned? And whose deaths did Lawrence hold Barrie responsible for?

Michael was one of five sons of the beautiful Sylvia Llewelyn Davies and her husband; Barrie, infatuated with Sylvia and her children, had become pathologically possessive towards them. The husband died young in 1907; Sylvia three years later; one of the sons, George, was killed in the war. Michael Davies's death occurred under suspicious circumstances, and may have been suicide caused by an unhappy love affair. Peter Davies, the original of Peter Pan, completed the family curse by killing himself in 1960. The story of the Davies family and Barrie is long and complex; but all Cambridge needed to do was cite the authoritative book on it, Andrew Birkin's *J. M. Barrie and the Lost Boys*. However, it is Cambridge's (silent) policy to avoid referencing secondary literature.[18] As for Lawrence's apparent over-reaction, we need to know, first, that it was more than a casually snide comment or shot in the dark: he knew Barrie's emotional history well because Mary Cannan had been married to him and Lady Cynthia Asquith was his secretary. Lawrence's comments also suggest two of his master-ideas: that possessive love is a deathly force,[19] and that "accidents" really come from a deep intentionality in both perpetrators and victims. A relevant example for the Davies case would be the drownings at the Crich water-party in *Women in Love*.

My commentary here is speculative; it suggests a biographical context for Lawrence's jeering at Barrie; it cites relevant secondary literature; and it links some casual remarks in a letter to Lawrence's fictional themes. Under the Cambridge convention of editorial self-restraint, these are all reasons for the commentary to be excluded. "Objective" annotation, such as Rembrandt's dates or mention of the place where Davies drowned, is unassailable (if correct) and will never become obsolete. "Interpretive" commentary is personal, vulnerable to challenge by critics who disagree with it or would choose a different emphasis. The "facts" are complete in themselves; whereas an interpretation might take us to fifty other texts, inside or outside Lawrence's work. Nonetheless, much of the objective annotation could have been deleted in favor of economical and suggestive references to the two major textual fields that interpenetrate the letters: Lawrence's creative works (which are, after all, the reason for the Edition's existence), and the critical literature about him.

CONCLUSION

The presence of James T. Boulton as editor or coeditor on all volumes of the *Letters* seems to have guaranteed a strictly defined and consistent policy on annotation; the alternative could be seen as a vague and variable proliferation of commentary, acting to diffuse the knowable core of Lawrence's 5,500 letters into an ocean of textual indeterminacy. What if each of the ten editors of the *Letters* were allowed to follow his or her preferences in the style and extent of annotation? Each of the seven volumes would then reflect the temperament of its editor or group of editors, and would be judged differently by reviewers and scholars. The belief in a single "right" way of editing Lawrence's letters would collapse in the face of a demonstrated relativism of editorial practices and reader responses. As it is, the spirit of the Cambridge Edition is altogether contrary to such relativism. Everything about the Edition, starting with the uniformity of its cover design and typography, proclaims that this is a monumental scholarly project, based on ideals of correctness, completeness, predictability, and fixity—a work of unimpeachable authority. Similar ideals inspired the Gabler edition of *Ulysses;* and critical response, in both cases, has included a great deal of irritable demolition work. The spirit of the age, for better or worse, is one of almost automatic resistance to the kinds of claims made by the Cambridge Edition and by Gabler; and critics have accumulated an extensive set of tools for undermining all pretensions to textual authority. Any attempt to crystallize a "final" text is bound to come under fire from those whose premises include textual dissolution and dispersal.[20]

The tension between the single authoritative text and an indeterminate textual field might be resolved in the future by new modes of computerized textuality. The Cambridge Edition began issuing volumes before the general use of word-processing and computerized typesetting, which would make it prohibitively expensive to reissue the earlier volumes in any different form. But once a book exists in the "virtual" form of a computer file, it becomes a textual resource rather than a fixed configuration of words. In principle, at least, it should be possible to print it in different formats, and to extract various kinds of information from the text-base. The obstacles to such flexible access lie mainly in commercial considerations and in the copyright laws that have led Cambridge to claim property rights in a single form of its texts.

Beyond the digitization of individual works lies the prospect of a hypermedia version of the entire Lawrence corpus. "Hypermedia" means the computerized linking, in variable structures, of blocks of text, graphics, video, and sound (Delany and Landow). Projects are already under way for such computerized archives of Yeats and Robert Graves.[21] With hypermedia, scholars can structure an author's writings in a variety of ways—in effect, creating their own custom-made "virtual" editions and indexes. The simplest kind of variation would affect order: for example, if each of Lawrence's poems was a hypermedia "block," they could be displayed in chronological order as an alternative to the division by published volumes in the Pinto and Roberts edition. The letters could be regrouped into correspondences so as to highlight Lawrence's individual relationships. More complicated reorganizations would depend on the interests and ingenuity of the individual user. For example, we could display on-screen textual continuity and divergence through every stage of a work's evolution in manuscript and print. Heyward Ehrlich has demonstrated the prototype of such a program: using various colors and screen windows, it presents graphically the differences between the Random House (1961) and Gabler editions of *Ulysses*. A computerized Lawrence resource could support massive systems of cross-reference, both within Lawrence's works and making external links to bibliographical resources, to the full texts of secondary sources, to graphics and sound. A user of the resource could move directly from a footnote citation to opening the text of the cited article on screen; every painting Lawrence mentions could be instantly displayed; every place shown on a map; every song performed.[22] Much of the criticism of Cambridge editorial policy would then become irrelevant, because users would no longer be bound by Cambridge's once-and-for-all choices. We could read the November 1912 version of *Sons and Lovers* with all Edward Garnett's cuts highlighted; see the variant endings of *The*

Rainbow side-by-side; read parallel versions of *Quetzalcoatl* and *The Plumed Serpent*. There would no longer be any question of completing a single, monumental version of the Lawrence corpus, which would gradually become obsolete in the years after its publication. The Cambridge Edition arouses resentment—legitimate or not—because of its implicit claim to canonize particular readings and, in general, have the last word on Lawrence. We know that by concluding his edition of the letters with the words "This place no good," Huxley put into circulation a stereotype of Lawrence that has persisted for decades. As our understanding of how texts do their work becomes more sophisticated, we also become more aware of how books assert themselves in the world, and how powerful editors can be. That is why *The Cambridge Edition of the Letters and Works*, almost regardless of its vices and virtues, has occupied the central place in Lawrence studies—and Lawrencean politics—over the past fifteen years.

NOTES

1. Eliot *Letters I* xv, xvi. Eliot's letters to Hale will become available in 2020.
2. Chambers published excerpts from Lawrence's letters to her in her memoir *D. H. Lawrence: A Personal Record.*
3. Seven volumes have appeared. A final index volume is still to come, containing also some letters discovered while the Edition was in progress.
4. The Woolf letters, published in England by Chatto and Windus, credit on the title page Nigel Nicholson as editor, Joanne Trautmann as assistant editor. Nicholson is a former politician, writer, and publisher, Trautmann an academic. The American Edition by Harcourt Brace Jovanovich gives equal billing to both editors.
5. This was less of a problem for Moore, but he still made silent cuts—especially in the letters to Ottoline Morrell, where he had to follow Huxley. See, for example, Lawrence/Morrell 19 April 1915 in Moore (reproducing Huxley) and Cambridge. Moore also excluded altogether the crucial Lawrence/Garnett 19 April 1915 letter, though it had already been published in part.
6. There is no mention of Frieda's first marriage in Huxley, and the name "Weekley" does not occur in the index.
7. Compare volume I of the Woolf letters, which ends with Virginia's marriage to Leonard Woolf, and of the Eliot letters, which ends with publication of *The Waste Land.*
8. "General Editors' Preface," included in each volume of the *Works.*
9. Kristeva's intertextuality was closely akin to dialogism; her concept was first voiced in the context of her close study of Bakhtin in the 1960s.

10. It goes without saying that the Cambridge Edition achieves a high standard of accuracy, though a few errors have slipped by, as, e.g., Healey and Cushman have noted (Lawrence, *Letters of Lawrence and Lowell* 16–17).

11. A continuous history could be traced, here, from Richardson's beginnings as a writer of form letters to the letter—testament, pledge, and confession of faith—that concludes *Lady Chatterley's Lover.*

12. See, for example, Lawrence's letter of 15 February 1916 to Ottoline Morrell, where Heseltine is discussed (*Letters II* 539).

13. The weight of the evidence suggests this, at least; see Delany, *Nightmare* 248.

14. Healey and Cushman were able to publish both sides of the Lawrence/Lowell correspondence while the Cambridge Edition was in progress (Lawrence, *Letters of Lawrence and Lowell*).

15. For a detailed account of Lawrence's anti-Semitism, see Ruderman.

16. Lawrence, *Letters to Seltzer.* Other letters may remain unpublished.

17. Following a declaration that Germany had defaulted on reparations, French and Belgian troops occupied the Ruhr on 11 January 1923; Mountsier presumably approved.

18. Volume II of the *Letters,* edited by George J. Zytaruk and James T. Boulton, has a more liberal policy on citing secondary sources than the other volumes.

19. Lawrence's identification with Barrie, whom he saw as a fellow victim of excessive mother-love, is discussed in Delany, "Who Was the Blind Man?"

20. The intense interest aroused by the battle of the Gabler *Ulysses* suggests a possible swing of the critical pendulum, however. Much of the criticism of Gabler, especially by John Kidd, argued that the Gabler text was *not correct enough.* Controversialists often adopted a style of archaic pedantry—which, after twenty years of deconstruction, came as a new and exciting way to read texts! (see Rossman).

21. The Yeats Hypermedia Project is sponsored by the British Academy; the Graves archive by the Graves estate and the Leverhulme Trust.

22. Design issues for such a resource for James Joyce are explored in Delany, "Scholar's Library."

WORKS CITED

Bakhtin, Mikhail. *Speech Genres and Other Late Essays.* Trans. Vern W. McGee. Ed. Caryl Emerson and Michael Holquist. Austin: U of Texas P, 1986.

———. *The Dialogic Imagination.* Ed. Michael Holquist. Austin: U of Texas P, 1981.

Birkin, Andrew. *J. M. Barrie and the Lost Boys.* London: Constable, 1979.

Chambers, Jessie ("E.T."). *D. H. Lawrence: A Personal Record.* London: Cape, 1935.

Delany, Paul. *D. H. Lawrence's Nightmare: The Writer and His Circle in the Years of the Great War.* New York: Basic, 1978.

———. "From the Scholar's Library to the Personal Docuverse." In *The Digital*

Word: Text-based Computing in the Humanities. Ed. George Landow and Paul Delany. Cambridge, MA: MIT Press, 1993. 189–99.

———. "Who Was the Blind Man?" *English Studies in Canada* 9 (1983): 92–99.

———, and George Landow, eds. *Hypermedia and Literary Studies*. Cambridge, MA: MIT Press, 1991.

Ehrlich, Heyward. "The James Joyce Text Machine: A Scholar's Work Station." Conference presentation, "Joyce in Vancouver," 11–15 June 1991.

Eliot, T. S. *The Letters of T. S. Eliot. Volume I: 1898–1922*. Ed. Valerie Eliot. London: Faber, 1988.

Foucault, Michel. "What is an Author?" Trans. J. V. Harari, 1979; first pub. in French, 1969. In *Modern Criticism and Theory: A Reader*. Ed. David Lodge. London: Longman, 1988.

Joyce, James. *Ulysses: The Corrected Text*. Ed. Hans Walter Gabler. New York: Garland, 1984.

Kristeva, Julia. "Le Mot, le Dialogue, et le Roman." In *Semeiotiké: Recherches pour une semanalyse*. Paris: Seuil, 1969. English version in *The Kristeva Reader*. Ed. Toril Moi. Oxford: Basil Blackwell, 1986.

Lawrence, D. H. *The Collected Letters of D. H. Lawrence*. 2 vols. Ed. Harry T. Moore. London: Heinemann, 1962.

———. *The Complete Poems of D. H. Lawrence*. 2 vols. Ed. Vivian de Sola Pinto and Warren Roberts. New York: Viking, 1964.

———. *Lawrence in Love: Letters to Louie Burrows*. Ed. James T. Boulton. Nottingham: U of Nottingham, 1968.

———. *The Letters of D. H. Lawrence*. Ed. Aldous Huxley. London: Heinemann, 1932.

———. *The Letters of D. H. Lawrence and Amy Lowell 1914–1925*. Ed. Claire Healey and Keith Cushman. Santa Barbara: Black Sparrow, 1985.

———. *Letters to Thomas and Adele Seltzer*. Ed. Gerald M. Lacy. Santa Barbara: Black Sparrow, 1976.

———. *Phoenix II*. Ed. Warren Roberts and Harry T. Moore. Harmondsworth: Penguin, 1978.

———. *The Quest for Rananim: D. H. Lawrence's Letters to S. S. Koteliansky 1914–1930*. Ed. George J. Zytaruk. Montreal: McGill-Queen's UP, 1970.

Nehls, Edward, ed. *D. H. Lawrence: A Composite Biography*. 3 vols. Madison: U of Wisconsin P, 1957–59.

Pound/Lewis: The Letters of Ezra Pound and Wyndham Lewis. Ed. Timothy Materer. New York: New Directions, 1985.

Rossman, Charles. "The Critical Reception of the 'Gabler *Ulysses*': Or Gabler's *Ulysses* Kidd-napped," [Part I] *Studies in the Novel* 21 (1989): 154–81; [Part II] *Studies in the Novel* 22 (1990): 323–53.

Ruderman, Judith. "D. H. Lawrence and the 'Jewish Problem': Reflections on a Self-Confessed 'Hebrophobe.'" *The D. H. Lawrence Review* 23.2–3 (1991): 99–109.

Woolf, Virginia. *The Letters of Virginia Woolf*. 6 vols. Ed. Nigel Nicholson. Asst. Ed. Joanne Trautmann. London: Chatto, 1975–80.

A Note on Nomenclature

Charles L. Ross

As Gary Taylor has observed about the rhetoric of textual criticism, "We see what we can say, and if we say things differently we will see them differently" (53). Frequently used adjectives such as *definitive, accurate, (im)perfect,* and *authoritative* beg all the interesting theoretical questions. Yet their imprecisions are pervasive, from popular anthologies to specialized studies.

The Norton Anthology, for example, states that "The definitive Cambridge Edition . . . has to date issued several meticulously edited texts of [Lawrence's] fiction" (2534). *Definitive* here seems to mean "meticulously edited," though a literary work may yield different texts, each of which may be meticulously prepared but none of which will be "definitive." *Accurate* can also be misleading. When Keith Sagar writes that "the most accurate texts available for those major works . . . which have not yet appeared in the Cambridge Edition are in the Penguin Edition" (123), for example, he overlooks the fact that a judgment about the accuracy or correctness of an edited text is largely the result of interpretation.

Authoritative, as in the Cambridge "principle that the most authoritative form of the text is to be followed," is potentially the most confusing word of all ("General Editors' Preface" viii). Does authority inhere in the words or in the choices among words made by author and editors? And how will the editors establish a text that Lawrence never saw but that he would have wished to see? The first resource is "the most authoritative form of the text," by which Cambridge means primarily a text containing more of the author's punctuation than does a house-styled edition. The word *authoritative,* however, quickly loses its etymological mooring to the author. According to Cambridge, Lawrence was often "wayward in spell-

189

ing and punctuation," or careless about correcting the errors of copyists and compositors, or unable to resist the interference of "a publisher's reader" and "frightened publishers" (vii–viii). In these instances, when Lawrence is alleged to have lost authority over his texts, Cambridge editors "recover" a more authoritative text than the author wrote or "saw." It is axiomatic, however, that in the age of mechanical reproduction an author never exercises full authority in the sense of sole control throughout the creation and publication of a work; therefore, "recover" suggests an impossible or circular goal for editors. In other words, the Cambridge Edition reasserts an authority that must have been compromised from the beginning. The same is true of all verbs of repetition, such as "reconstruct" and "restore," with which Cambridge describes its goal.

More than a quibble is involved here. Cambridge repeatedly claims to have recovered an original text or "*the* text"; to have followed "the most authoritative form of *the* text"; to have collated the "forms of *the* text published in Lawrence's lifetime," and to have provided "*the* history of composition of the text" (vii–viii, emphases added). Those definite articles create an impression that Cambridge has reached behind a text or a history to the *fons et origo* of textuality. Their rhetoric of originality, moreover, is reinforced by a uniform copyright claim in every volume: "This, the Cambridge Edition of the text of [title of work] now correctly established from the original sources and first published in [date], copyright the Estate of Frieda Lawrence Ravagli [date]" (p. iv of each volume). The Estate herein seeks to do more than authorize a new edition of a text of a work of D. H. Lawrence. Their claim that the new text has been "correctly established from original sources" is divisible into two claims of unequal plausibility. Though the Cambridge editors may have consulted original sources, they cannot have "correctly established" the text. There are always rival interpretations by which to establish a text of a work from original sources, interpretations that lead to different choices among variants from texts of a work—for example, the different editions of Shakespeare published by Cambridge.

Given this linguistic free play among editors and publishers, it is not surprising that readers and teachers become victims of corrupt texts. It is surprising, however, that many Lawrence scholars ignore the textual criticism of their chosen author. In *The Visual Arts, Pictorialism, and the Novel* (1985), for example, Mariana Torgovnick reveals misplaced faith in "best" and even "perfect" texts: "The Penguin text [of *Women in Love*] is a paperback, but is widely available and—though imperfect, like all current editions—it is the best text of the novel now available." Torgovnick here assumes that the Penguin English Library edition merely reprints a previously available text. In fact, her repeated references to "South Pacific and African statues" and to "Minette or Pussum" (23, 51) indicate that she did not read the Penguin text but relied on the corrupt Viking text. The text containing these discrepancies descends from the first English edition, in which the bohemian milieu was inconsistently bowdlerized; whereas the Penguin text descends from the American first edition, which was not subjected to censorship. Lawrence originally intended there to be only "African" statues, as in the American edition, but changed some references to "South Pacific" for the English edition, in a half-hearted attempt to avoid a libel suit by the owner of the statues. A critic discussing Lawrence's artistic response to primitive artifacts ought to know this textual history.

Victims may be more or less willing. Scholars who maintain an up-to-the-minute familiarity with criticism choose carelessly among editions or fabricate textual histories to suit their purposes. *Lawrence Among the Women: Wavering Boundaries in Women's Literary Traditions* (1991) by Carol Siegel, for example, is a learned book that nevertheless cites Lawrence's texts in corrupt editions, ignoring all the new editions published during the 1980s by both Penguin and Cambridge. In *Lawrence's Leadership Politics and the Turn Against Women* (1986), Cornelia Nixon does not quote Lawrence in either a first edition or a recent critical edition, even though she has conducted archival research and discusses revision. For *Women in Love,* Nixon relies on a notoriously corrupt reprint by Viking of the Secker English edition, a text she mistakenly believes has descended from the first edition. Her textual note alleges a history that never was: "D. H. Lawrence, *Women in Love* (1920; rpt. New York: Viking Press, 1960)" (21). In fact, the Viking edition descends from the English edition of 1921, which was censored by the author and publisher to avoid a libel prosecution. By citing a reprint that was bowdlerized (among other reasons) to blur the treatment of homoeroticism, Nixon undermines the authority of her discussion of that very theme.

More instructive than individual lapses, however, is the complicity of institutions of higher education in widespread ignorance of textual criticism among literary critics. The virtual elimination of textual criticism from graduate programs, noted recently by George Bornstein, means that scholars pursue research in texts whose reliability they cannot question (5). Both *Lawrence Among the Women* and *Lawrence's Leadership Politics* are rewritten dissertations, submitted to the University of California at Berkeley and published by the University of California Press. In response to this representative failure, *Editing D. H. Lawrence: New Versions of a Modern Author* hopes to quicken a dialogue between practitioners of textual criticism, literary theory, and history.

WORKS CITED

Abrams, M. H., et al., eds. *The Norton Anthology of English Literature,* 5th ed. 2 vols. New York: Norton, 1986.

Bornstein, George. "Introduction: Why Editing Matters." In *Representing Modernist Texts: Editing as Interpretation.* Ed. George Bornstein. Ann Arbor: U of Michigan P, 1991. 1–16.

"General Editors' Preface" to Lawrence, *The Rainbow* vii–viii.

Nixon, Cornelia. *Lawrence's Leadership Politics and the Turn Against Women.* Berkeley: U of California P, 1986.

Sagar, Keith. "Letter to the Editor ('Laurentiana')." *The D. H. Lawrence Review* 20.1 (1988): 123.

Siegel, Carol. *Lawrence Among the Women: Wavering Boundaries in Women's Literary Traditions.* Berkeley: U of California P, 1991.

Taylor, Gary. "The Rhetoric of Textual Criticism." *Text.* Vol. 4. Ed. D. C. Greetham and W. Speed Hill. New York: AMS Press, 1988. 39–57.

Torgovnick, Mariana. *The Visual Arts, Pictorialism, and the Novel.* Princeton: Princeton UP, 1985.

Commentary on *Editing D. H. Lawrence: New Versions of a Modern Author*

William E. Cain

In a recent article on literary studies, Claude Rawson reports that despite the extreme emphasis on theory, many critics, teachers, and students remain "interested in and responsive to the traditional reading experience" (13). The density and sheer number of literary theories can indeed prove as daunting as Rawson says. He names three—Marxism, deconstruction, and feminism—but there are others, including reception theory, cultural critique, and new historicism; and within each, there is ample debate and disagreement about utilizing the theory to interpret texts, recast literary history, reorganize the curriculum, and renew (or undermine) the mission of the humanities. Theory is an intricate field of its own, and it strikes many in the profession as threatening to displace, even destroy, literature itself.

But while it is tempting to invoke the "traditional reading experience" as the only right alternative to this situation, the phrase is in fact deceptive. Scholars, critics, teachers, and students have always held different notions about what the "reading experience" is. If there is a tradition, it is an evolving one marked by adjustments and, occasionally, radical breaks and departures from another tradition that preceded it. When I. A. Richards proposed reforms in English studies in the 1920s, and when the American New Critics did the same in the 1930s, they were attacking a "traditional reading experience" that they perceived as careless, error-ridden, undiscriminating. To those who are unhappy with the reign of theory, Richards and his English and American kinfolk embody a venerable tradition, but in the 1920s and 1930s these critics were labeled the enemies of tradition, subverters of basic literary values.

Richards, William Empson, and F. R. Leavis in England, and Robert

Penn Warren, Allen Tate, Cleanth Brooks, and others in the United States advanced powerful arguments for a new kind of critical approach. In many respects the changes they fought for and institutionalized were positive, and we continue to rely upon them. But they faced opposition from the traditionalists of their era; and, whatever their shared sense of a new movement, they also differed about how criticism and teaching should be conducted. In America, Warren, Tate, Brooks, John Crowe Ransom, Kenneth Burke, Yvor Winters, and R. P. Blackmur all emphasized the need for close attention to the words on the page. But the specific theories that each developed, and the analyses he offered to support them, were often only partially convincing to the others, and sometimes were not at all.

Then, too, there is the question of the literary canon, the group of texts upon which the so-called traditional reading experience should fasten. Under the leadership of T. S. Eliot, twentieth-century critics challenged the prime place that tradition had assigned to Milton and the Romantics. And they articulated a new literary history that highlighted the metaphysical poets, Pope, Hopkins, and their modernist successors. This was the goal—and the achievement—of Leavis's *New Bearings in English Poetry* (1932) and *Revaluation* (1936), Brooks's *Modern Poetry and the Tradition* (1939), and Brooks and Warren's influential textbook, *Understanding Poetry: An Anthology for College Students* (1938).

For my purposes in this commentary, however, the issue of "which texts?" should be understood in another sense. Consider the case of Walt Whitman. It is appealing, in the midst of feminist, new historicist, Marxist, deconstructionist, and gay studies' interpretations of Whitman, to get back to the "traditional reading experience" of his poetry and prose. But libraries and bookstores overflow with editions of Whitman's work, and the experience of reading Whitman thus depends—more than we like to admit—upon the specific edition that a scholar prefers and that a student purchases or consults. Another complication is that the scholar might favor one edition for his or her research yet not select it for courses for the simple reason that it is too expensive for students to purchase.

D. H. Lawrence honored—though he also quarreled with—*Leaves of Grass* and played a role in making Whitman interesting and reputable enough to merit inclusion in the American literary tradition. But what is *Leaves of Grass?*—the 1855 edition, the 1860 edition, the "deathbed" edition of 1891–92, or one of the many other editions published between 1855 and 1892? Or is it instead *all* of these editions and their manuscripts and notebooks as these are appraised in sequence? Or a massive variorum edition that opts for one arrangement of the text but lists the endless variants and revisions?

The general point here can be pressed further. The experience of reading Crane's *The Red Badge of Courage,* Dreiser's *Sister Carrie,* and Joyce's *Ulysses*—to name just three controversial examples—will be different from one reader to the next not only because readers (and critical methodologies) are different, but also because these readers may settle in with competing versions of the text.

And that is not all. Some important modernist works, such as Pound's *Cantos,* are seriously flawed in the edition and in the reprinted selections now available. One wonders therefore how much sense it makes to speak of a "traditional reading experience" of texts like the *Cantos* that carry an esteemed author's name but are textually tainted. You may be reading Pound, but not *really* reading what he wrote. Do we even know what he wrote? There will one day be corrected, authoritative editions of texts, like Pound's, that exist in disputed versions or corrupt editions. But another question then arises: once these editions appear, what will be the fate of the tradition of reading experiences, criticism, scholarship, and pedagogy built upon the old editions? Will it have to be abandoned?

Translated texts pose yet another problem. The experience of reading *The Iliad, The Brothers Karamazov,* and *À la Recherche du temps perdus* may be wonderful for readers, but it is not easy to say what the "traditional experience" of reading these texts consists of. Many foreign language texts are translated poorly and packaged in unreliable editions keyed to faulty editions of the original. Is the person who uses one of these translations reading the author's work or not? Maybe he or she is not, not really, but is having an experience that is still worthwhile and that is in some way close to the experience he or she would have enjoyed if the author's actual work had been read. But a claim like this one is critically loose and anti-intellectual. It implies that accurate texts, and reliable editions and translations, are only marginally important, and that somehow the "traditional reading experience" can be achieved even if the book in one's hand does not present what the author wrote.

Most people in literary studies dislike having to think about such issues. These guiltily bring to consciousness the articles that have been written, and the classes that have been taught, with no thought given to the edition of the text one has used. During the past decade, the arguments about *The Red Badge of Courage, Sister Carrie,* Twain's *Puddn'head Wilson,* Hemingway's *The Garden of Eden,* and, especially, *Ulysses* have circulated widely. But they affect most critics and teachers as special instances that illustrate a textual crisis from which, luckily, other authors and texts, and the persons who study and teach them, are safe.

Few texts are safe. Once one enters the domain of the editors and textual specialists, one discovers that nearly all texts are controversial and that disputes about this or that edition are everywhere, though usually hidden from common view. Textual scholars, it has to be said, are somewhat to blame for this scandal. They have failed to convey to a general readership the impact of their work and the controversies that it kindles. But the other side is that most readers refuse to read textual scholarship. They are not keen to seek mastery over a vocabulary that is arcane to them, and would as soon leave the whole affair to the experts.

"Theory" projects a glamorous appeal that textual scholarship does not. The same people who have endless patience with Derrida's, de Man's, and Lacan's labyrinthine prose balk at reading an essay about editorial decisions and dilemmas. Yet the irony is that such an essay could fundamentally alter the understanding of, for example, Dreiser or Joyce in a way that an interpretive, highly theoretical essay by Derrida or de Man or one of their followers could barely rival.

It remains to be seen whether the issues that the Cambridge Edition of D. H. Lawrence has sparked will be widely noticed. The essays gathered in *Editing D. H. Lawrence: New Versions of a Modern Author* are a step in the right direction. And they supplement and extend the lively, sometimes painfully sharp reviews and exchanges about the volumes that have already been published (Dennis Jackson traces the interesting reception history of the Cambridge volumes elsewhere in this collection). Lawrence is, arguably, the foremost modern writer in the English language, the one with the most diverse body of accomplished work in fiction and nonfiction, poetry and prose—and in his extraordinary letters as well. As the essays in this collection make clear, the difficult job of editing Lawrence's work will shape our knowledge of Lawrence, the novel, and modernism. Much is at stake.

Many readers of this collection will agree with Leavis's judgment that *The Rainbow* and *Women in Love* are "astonishing works of genius" (*Great Tradition* 26; see also *D. H. Lawrence: Novelist*). But until the full story of these two novels has been told, the complicated process of their writing and publication made known, the variant readings mobilized, and *The Sisters* published—until all of this, and more, has been done, can we presume that we really *know* these "astonishing works?" In so far as it has enabled readers to know Lawrence better, the Cambridge Edition is a major achievement. But it is an ambiguous one, and, judging from the essays in this collection, it has both enriched and bruised the lives of the people associated with it.

I wish here, however, not to dwell upon the relations between Board members and editors, and the sometimes unpleasant personal and intellectual compromises that the Cambridge project has required. Rather, I aim to consider two sources of tension that are present in all the essays. The first is a tension between the commitment to principle and the reliance on personal judgment, and the second is between the idea of a text-in-process and the need for a stabilized, orderly text for readers.

The first kind of tension is clear in Michael Black's "Text and Context: The Cambridge Edition of Lawrence Reconsidered." Black stresses that "[r]eaders have to be confident" that decisions "have been consistently made according to some stated principle, or they can have no faith in the text as a whole." These are firm words. Yet almost immediately, Black adds that "[e]ditors must apply principles, and the arguments about a text must start from the principles involved." This reminds us that editors formulate and then employ the principles: persons, not laws or rules alone, are responsible for the decisions. The reader's faith in an edition hence rests not with a "stated principle" itself but with the persons who have established and applied it.

This distinction is obvious enough, but it is more important than Black realizes. Toward the end of this essay, he notes that he and his colleagues sought freedom "from preconception." They would not adopt "textbook concepts and traditional procedures." "Apart from that," he explains, "our only principle was that the materials themselves must dictate how they were handled, and procedures had to emerge from relating the documents to each other as intelligently as we could manage." This policy sounds persuasively modest and restrained, but it cannot, I think, succeed in practice.

The materials do not "dictate" the labor performed upon them. Persons work with these materials, and decide about them based on their sense of the proper (or at least the most likely) order and arrangement. Black observes that Lawrence's "punctuation is, very often indeed, a crucial vehicle of his more subtle sense, especially his metaphorical and dramatic sense." This is an interpretation that expresses Black's notion of how Lawrence's writing should be understood. The same holds true for Black's account of the "constantly-revising author" that he links to the modern period and of the "profound unity" that he perceives in the careers of Lawrence and Eliot.

Maybe there is no unity at all, or else unity of a different sort from what Black describes, in the span of Lawrence's and Eliot's works. Leavis, for one, judged that in *The Four Quartets* Eliot retreated from the imaginative resourcefulness and confidence of his earlier poetry. It exhibits, Leavis states, an imprisoning "self-contradiction" and "acceptance of defeat" that Eliot wrongly registers as "spiritual courage" (*Living Principle* 181). One could compile a long list of critics who take issue with Black, Leavis, or both; and one could name authors before the modern period (for example, Whitman and Frederick Douglass) who "constantly revised" their texts. Interpretations of Eliot and Lawrence, of course, abound, as do examples of authors prone to constant revision.

I am not denying the interest of Black's claims about unity and revision: they are well worth heeding and arguing about. But claims like these—the clear product of interpretation—sit uncomfortably alongside others in which he affirms that editorial choices arise from what the materials mandate, as though the materials interpreted themselves.

One sees here why readers often find editors an exasperating lot. On the one hand, the editor lays claim to a principle that identifies him or her as the minion to manuscripts, texts, and related documents that signal their own best form. But, on the other hand, the editor's explanation of his or her procedures betrays the guesswork, informed speculation, surmise— in a word, the interpretations—in which the editor is enmeshed. ·

As the essays in this collection show, editors are now admitting that they are critics and interpreters and that editing, criticism, and interpretation are parts of a connected activity. They are more sensitive to the mixed nature of their work and willing to say when particular decisions derive from personal preferences and aesthetic judgments.

L. D. Clark's "Editing *The Plumed Serpent* for Cambridge" is a good example. In his edition of this novel, Clark selected what to him seemed "the *best* Lawrence," and he says, "In my judgment, such a practice reflects a sound principle of textual criticism." He rejects the "'passive acceptance' theory that some scholars argue for: that an author accepts by default whatever he allows to pass in proofs, and thus it becomes his forever." This position, Clark declares, "appears to me to make a virtue . . . out of dodging responsibility." He is not shunting principle aside, but is, instead, openly stating that one of his central principles is reliance on his own "informed critical judgment."

But surely some readers will bristle when Clark avers that he has served Lawrence's work "better than he chose to serve it himself." These words have behind them specific interpretations that Clark has made about "external" and "internal evidence," interpretations that others likely would question. *Their* sense of how best to serve Lawrence may differ from Clark's. Perhaps they will not locate defensiveness, as Clark does, in Lawrence's "magnified claims" for the greatness of *The Plumed Serpent*, or conclude that "reluctance to publish the novel at all" and "protestations that it was too good for the public" masked "uncertainties." Clark's honesty should not veil from us that he edits through a series of interpretations that some will accept and others dispute.

I prefer Clark's admission of the part played by personal judgment to Black's confidence in the dictation issued by his materials. Yet I suspect I am not alone in feeling uneasy about the prospect of reading a text that bears Lawrence's name but that is, in fact, the text that Clark judges serves Lawrence best. Does Clark know better than Lawrence? Who is the author, Lawrence or Clark? Whose name belongs in pride of place on the cover of the book?

In "Cough-Prints and Other Intimacies," Christopher Pollnitz similarly describes how he scrutinized the stages of composition of "Emasculation" and followed his "aesthetic preference" and "critical judgment" in omitting two lines of the poem. Pollnitz thus produced a third version of "Emasculation" that he believes has more "internal consistency" (he asserts that Lawrence himself, in revising, "may have overlooked deletion of the couplet"). Likewise, Michael Squires, in "Editing the Cambridge *Lady Chatterley*," tells of cases when he relied on "editorial judgment." When Squires defended his reading "*wisps* of smoke" to the Board, which leaned toward "*men* of smoke," he contended in a memo that "to me there is no question about this one! Lawrence's narrative method is to employ *incremental summary* in his dialogue." It is his sense of Lawrence's artistic methods and strategies that leads Squires to his choice. Again, as with L. D. Clark's choices, it is open to challenge by those who understand Lawrence as a writer differently.

Such moments of high confidence in an edited text make me sympathetic to the idea of multiple texts, to which Black and Pollnitz briefly refer. Black evokes the possibility of the "generation by computer-graphic means of a text-in-process that is the scholarly equivalent of Duchamp's cubist painting of the nude descending a stairway, where every position of the figure in space is represented, or the Futurist paintings by Balla or

Marinetti which also rendered motion in space and time." In a similar vein, Pollnitz, speaking of his work on Lawrence's poetry, suggests that a variorum edition

> should aim at reproducing the experience of polysemy that comes with reading manuscript verse, of an enriching competition of alternative revisions. A variorum edition of Lawrence's verse should also aim at reproducing the clarity with which Lawrence evolved versions of poems, intact and entire, even when successive versions were drafted, one over the other, on a single, heavily revised page.

Like many involved in the Cambridge Edition, Pollnitz aspires to transmit the sense of movement, development, and alteration that Black's prophecy of a computer-aided text-in-process gestures toward. He is aware of the tension between a single edited text and the range of texts from which it is drawn. John Worthen mentions this multiplicity as well, if in a more limited fashion, in "Facts in Fiction." He indicates, for example, that an editor of *Great Expectations* might restore the original ending and deposit the revised ending in an explanatory note, or possibly "print both endings side by side, giving priority to neither."

Here, however, one glimpses the difficulty of the Cambridge editors' task. They recognize the complex, multiple status of Lawrence's texts and wish to communicate to readers the *process* that the stories, novels, essays, poems, and other writings embody. Yet they must construct a text for readers. Black expresses the point succinctly: "there is, in the end, a text to be identified." How, then, to deal with the fact that editors will sort out and decide about the same materials differently and identify different texts?

Worthen suggests the texts that editors identify could be adjusted according to the demands of the market. "If Lawrence's *Movements in European History* were being produced by Cambridge University Press for use in schools, it would clearly be desirable for the historical record to be set straight and the numerous errors in the text corrected." Would, however, this policy for handling multiplicity be wise? Some schoolteachers in a history course may want the errors corrected, but others might not. Would Worthen recommend that every text by a novelist, man- or woman-of-letters, critic, or intellectual be purged of errors because these might misinform students? These texts, and those by historians, too, contain all kinds of errors that later researchers uncover, but this does not necessarily lower the texts' value or interest. Then, too, there are the problems that could arise if this particular Lawrence text were being used in literature courses, as part of a unit on Lawrence. Teachers of these courses might want students to know that Lawrence's conception of history transcends his local errors. It would be his historical vision and imaginative power that would matter most.

Worthen argues that the market would stabilize the process in which Lawrence's texts are implicated: we know that different texts are possible, that editors create versions of a text that the author only approximated, and thus we should be mindful of the specific audience for which we prepare an edition. The marketplace, though, is hard to pin down, and the decisions that an editor makes for this or that audience could prove mistaken on both intellectual and commercial grounds. Still, Worthen's position does represent an improvement upon Black's, in that Worthen recognizes the "text to be identified will never be the only one possible. The text that an editor identifies is a selection made from multiplicity."

In "Reading a Critical Edition With the Grain and Against," Paul Eggert embraces the paradox of many texts in one text to which Worthen calls attention. Eggert maintains that the Cambridge quest for a "reading text" is undercut by the evidence in the apparatus of multiple texts and by intertextuality. He urges that we read the Cambridge Edition "against the grain," "not for what editions were set up to do but what they do in spite of themselves." "[T]he need for singularity," Eggert states, "serves in the end to release multiplicity. . . . Texts—unstable in composition, revision, and production—are temporarily stabilized by the act of commercial publication or by critical editing and publication; but they resume their unstable dynamism when they are read."

Eggert backs away, though, from the dynamic textuality that he proclaims. He contends that it is only possible to read *in Women in Love,* for there is no single text of *Women in Love* that will stand still. Yet he also concedes that he cannot dispense with the "convention" that readers share a single *Women in Love* and have it as "a common point of reference from which to work." But Eggert himself shows how dubious this convention is by emphasizing that one cannot "do *other* than read *in Women in Love.*" Why not go all the way and describe "Women in Love" as the large, multiple, intertextual reality and the book *Women in Love* that we hold in our hand as merely a partial report? The first title would name the swirling textual elements from which the second is constructed—and not by Lawrence, but by his editors.

What are the consequences of Eggert's position for studying and teaching Lawrence's novels? Not all, I wager, will be happy with them. I recall my own good experience as an undergraduate when the class studied *Women in Love*. Using the Viking Compass edition, which includes Lawrence's foreword and an introduction by Richard Aldington, the professor traced the organization of Lawrence's language, explored its rhythmic patterns and imagery and metaphor, and showed the vital, if problematic, coherence of the text. Like Leavis, with whom he had studied, this professor always fastened his and our observations to the words on the page.

I came to know Lawrence through a prolonged inquiry into his language in *Women in Love*. But given the full complexity of the manuscripts and texts of *The Rainbow, Women in Love,* and *The Sisters,* and given, too, the editions of *Women in Love* that Charles Ross (Penguin, 1982) and David Farmer, Lindeth Vasey, and John Worthen (Cambridge, 1987) have done, I wonder what it was that I read. As Ross has pointed out in his monograph on *Women in Love,* Lawrence called his post-*Sons and Lovers* project "The Sisters" or a "Brangwensaga" through eight years of writing multiple versions: he perceived the novels as manifestly intertextual and hence not to be severed from one another. What, then, is the status of the conclusions about Lawrence, and about the language and artistic structure of *Women in Love,* that my classmates and I achieved? Did we gain real knowledge about Lawrence or take pleasure in a supreme fiction?

Admirers of *Sons and Lovers* may be impelled by Helen Baron's essay to ask similar questions about that novel. Baron deals cogently with the problem of whether to publish the novel as it exists in manuscripts or, as has been done for decades, to continue with the version that incorporates Edward Garnett's cuts. She especially focuses on Lawrence's punctuation and the changes in it that the compositor made, and shows that the compositor's alterations bear directly on the style and content of Lawrence's prose. Even so slight a change as the substitution of a comma for a dash "can reverse the meaning of the words" that Lawrence wrote. For Lawrence, unconventional choices of punctuation were, says Baron, intimately part of his technique as an artist.

But Baron is not comfortable with her discoveries. She stresses that punctuation is "not a trivial consideration," and, later, when noting Lawrence's reliance on commas and sparing use of colons and semicolons, she remarks that these choices reveal "a fundamental structure of his prose: that it was paratactic rather than syntactic." On the other hand, in the midst of her commentary on a passage from chapter 13, she observes that the compositor's changes do not distort "the overt meaning," as though such changes, while noteworthy, leave the overt or explicit meaning intact.

In her closing sentences, Baron claims that she has not engaged in aesthetic analysis: "[t]he case mounted here is purely bibliographical." But I think her discussion of the compositor's changes is obviously tied to her critical and aesthetic interpretation of Lawrence's characters, scenes, themes. She is not just an editor and bibliographer, but a critic, an interpreter, as well.

Indeed, Baron's critical insights lead her to say that the *Sons and Lovers* now in the public domain distorts Lawrence's meaning: "the repunctuation of Lawrence's novel was so comprehensive and drastic that in reading the printed text hitherto the general public has not had full access to Lawrence's meaning." Lawrence is not really present in that text—which Baron states is "botched, censored, and butchered." He can be found, and his meaning apprehended, in the manuscript. From this perspective, one would, I believe, have to judge the scholarly tradition of work on *Sons and Lovers* as skewed—a body of writing that should be "interred" (to borrow a word from Baron's conclusion) along with the edition that it cited. Should students who have read *Sons and Lovers* in literature courses burn their notes? Perhaps it is not surprising that Baron refrains from voicing the rather alarming implications of her argument, with its strong claim that the public has not had access to Lawrence's meaning.

Eggert does discuss some of the implications of his views in "Text and Intertexts, Authorship and Culture," as he shows how *Twilight in Italy* is entwined with other texts. But Eggert seeks to control the intertextuality that he sets in motion. He first asserts that the editor, under way in his or her annotation of *Twilight in Italy,* quickly "finds that, surrounding the reading text, invading it, arguing with it, confirming it, competing with it, are a host of alternative partial texts, many known directly to Lawrence, some indirectly, and some possibly not at all." His point is that texts draw upon other texts whatever the intentions of the author. *Twilight in Italy,* Eggert maintains, evokes *Where Angels Fear to Tread:* Forster's text is *in* Lawrence's. Even more—and here I take a step that Eggert does not— Lawrence's text is *in* Forster's. Both texts are now present to us; intertextuality is not governed by chronology any more than by authorial intention.

Eggert's theory allows for the inter-animation of texts, backwards as well as forwards. Neither chronology nor the author's intentions should matter. But in fact Eggert rests his case for intertextuality on the role of the author. It is Lawrence, he insists, who "fixes" and "focuses" surrounding texts and intertexts. As the example of Lawrence's response to Marconi's acting attests, "Lawrence signals it quite plainly; he knows what he is doing."

"Authorial focusing" is the term that Eggert deploys to limit and contain the saturation of one text by others. But can we know with certainty when an author is "focusing" text and intertext? Is it legitimate to invoke the author as a principle of coherence when the text that we are reading is one that editors, not the author, have constructed? You cannot have it both ways: you cannot dramatize the intertextuality of texts and speak of reading *in* a text rather than reading *a text,* and then seize on authorial control to keep some intertexts out and let others in.

Intertextuality is unstoppable: that is the point of the postmodern, poststructuralist theories of literature and language that Jacques Derrida and Paul de Man espouse. More than any of the others in this collection, Eggert subscribes to these theories, but he both accepts and sharply qualifies them. He cannot abide the company of Derrida and de Man for long, for they emphasize the impossibility of the author-based project he undertakes.

But just because a project is impossible does not mean that it must be given up. Both Derrida and de Man acknowledge that persons make choices and arrive at decisions about the texts that they read and interpret and the lives that they lead. They are not pure nihilists. They want to instruct us about the fragility of the choices, the arbitrariness of the decisions, that we make, so that we are not deceived about the status of our beliefs and actions. Arbitrary decisions can still seem reasonable and can be defended. There are, after all, many ways to read, interpret, and edit texts, as the historical record testifies and as the future of criticism and pedagogy will doubtless reveal as well. The proper course is to be relentlessly self-critical when editing and interpreting texts (and editing *is* interpreting)— aware that other possibilities exist and that these cannot be declared abnormal, unnatural, flatly wrong.

This explains why I find the claims for an exclusive copyright for the Cambridge Edition unfortunate. I would propose that scholars be allowed to edit texts in the form that seems most acceptable to them, and, if I had my way, I would not want copyright to protect one edition from others. *No* edition is immune to criticism, for *every* edition is the result of many complex acts of interpretation. Other editors might construe the Lawrence materials differently, and hence would profess that they have understood the evidence rightly and at last seen through to the facts that earlier editors have missed or undervalued. Ideally, one would like a variety of editions competing for attention. Let each editor make the case for why his or her text of *Sons and Lovers* or *Women in Love* is better than others. Editing is an act of persuasion as well as interpretation, and it would be regrettable if readers were prevented from hearing a range of voices making their arguments for a range of texts.

Paul Delany in "'Giving Your Self Away'" observes that, just as the Cambridge Edition was setting out to "preserve Lawrence's texts in a stable and authoritative format," Anglo-American literary studies were "being invaded by Continental literary theories [e.g., those of Foucault, Bakhtin, Kristeva] directed against that ideal authorial subject who supported the Edition's claim to knowledge and fixity." Today, an increasing number of editors and textual scholars concede they are not able to tender claims for the *truth* of what they have done, but, instead, can only maintain that they have presented the best story, made the best text, that they can.

It seems that such editorial text-makers have embraced the program that the literary theorist Stanley Fish announced in the 1970s: "Rather than restoring or recovering texts, I am in the business of making texts and of teaching others to make them by adding to their repertoire of strategies." In response to the "real" one, Fish stated: "[This] will be felt as a criticism only if the alternative to different reading is right reading and if the alternative to the texts created by different reading is the real text." Fish added that his vision of reading and text-making "relieves me of the obligation to be right (a standard that simply drops out) and demands only that I be interesting (a standard that can be met without any reference at all to an illusory objectivity)" (180).

Fish later remarked that this was the "most unfortunate sentence" he ever wrote, because of the relativism that it implied, with each critic shunning any standard of "right" and "wrong" altogether. But his theory has nonetheless proven influential. Textual scholars who abide by Fish's position are able to show how other scholars have made narrow judgments and prescriptive choices, have subscribed to highly questionable rules for emendation, and have been blind to their status as *interpreters*. But then again, if everyone is an interpreter, who can presume to pass sentence of judgment upon others?

Delany detects when editors have interpreted badly or have not recognized that they are engaged in interpretation in the first place. But he is an interpreter himself, and can be exposed as one just as he exposes others. At one point Delany observes that the volumes of the *Letters* "do not correlate well with significant phases of Lawrence's life or literary career." True enough. But critics agree, if they agree, about the phases of Lawrence's life and career only in very general terms. One consequence of the Cambridge Edition (and the responses to and rebuttals of it, *and* the biographies in progress that stem from it) is that Lawrence's life, writings, canon, and career have become hotly contested subjects. Old assumptions are being dismantled, revised, thrown overboard.

In a sense it has always been that way. Leavis gave one report on his sense of the "phases" of Lawrence's career in *For Continuity* (1933), another in *The Great Tradition* (1948) and *D. H. Lawrence: Novelist* (1955), and a third in *Thought, Words and Creativity: Art and Thought in Lawrence* (1976). By this last book, Leavis was so intensely conscious of "the embracing organic totality of Lawrence's thought" that he said he found it difficult even to make choices about which texts to single out for examination (9). All the phases had cohered into one. And the point that Leavis's example illustrates is even more true (and more complicatedly so) today, as scholarly production has accelerated beyond anything that Leavis imagined: the "significant phases" of a writer's life and career are constantly being refocused, modified, altered.

It is striking how few sentences can be uttered safely, even one that appears fairly innocuous, like Delany's about Lawrence's significant phases. Later, Delany mentions that "objective" annotation is unassailable, because it is tied to "facts," whereas "interpretive" commentary is personal, "vulnerable to challenge by critics who disagree with it or would choose a different emphasis." This seems a good, workable distinction. But does it hold up? Does it declare a distinction that all would endorse? T. S. Eliot claimed that "a critic must have a very highly developed sense of fact," by which he meant nothing as crude as names, dates, and events, but, rather, perceptions into technique and feeling in poetry that commanded assent because of their precision and accuracy. Critics should aim for facts and know when they had encountered "impostures," when "instead of insight, you get a fiction" (31–32). For Eliot, a fact in criticism emerges from objective commentary that isolated a piece of authentic knowledge about a text. It would not be a fact as Delany means the word, for it would come from the personal impression of the critic; but it would be impersonal, incontrovertible, in its authority—a fact.

Possibly the complexities and dilemmas that I have surveyed explain why Delany, somewhat like Michael Black, beckons toward the era when we will possess "a hypermedia version of the entire Lawrence corpus." Then we will have the computer-enhanced capacity to "structure [Lawrence's] writings in a variety of ways." I agree with Delany that this will be exciting, fascinating, fun. The attractive feature of such a "version" of the corpus is, as Delany suggests, that scholars could enter at any point and navigate it in any way.

Such a prospect would ease the weight of judgment about which text is right or best or most appropriate: all judgments would be tentative, impermanent. But when the program was written and the textual "web" designed, someone would have to decide when and where to stop. If Lawrence's letters are included, as it would seem they should be, should only *his* letters be included and not those written to him? Delany states that Frieda's letters surely should be "blended in" with Lawrence's, but that other letters, too, could claim inclusion as biographical documents, as documents connected to literary texts, or as links in a "dialogic" chain of letters sent to Lawrence and to which he replied. Lots of choices to be made here, and plenty for other Lawrence scholars to interrogate.

After all, once you begin to think in terms of a "dialogic" chain, you can keep adding links interminably. Think for a moment of Melville, about whom Lawrence wrote memorably. If one were constructing the hypermedia version of the Melville corpus, one would doubtless include Melville's passionate, probing "Hawthorne and His Mosses" (1850), one of the most renowned essays in American literary history. Should the Hawthorne text about which Melville is writing, *Mosses from an Old Manse*, be included as well? And what about the texts of the Shakespeare plays—and which versions of them—to which Melville connects, compares, and contrasts Hawthorne's stories? Melville's letters to Hawthorne would also have to be part of the computerized corpus, especially the letter of November 1851 in which Melville replied to Hawthorne's letter to him about *Moby-Dick*. Hawthorne's letter itself has unfortunately been lost, a missing link in the chain that somehow must be registered, perhaps by a blank field on the computer screen. But Hawthorne did write about Melville in his Journal in 1856, and his wife Sophia and son Julian described the Hawthorne/Melville relationship, too. There are good reasons for ruling out this material, and equally good reasons for including it.

It would be hard to know when no more links should be added to the Melville chain, and the same will hold true for scholars brave enough to design one for Lawrence. It is pleasing to know that we might enter the corpus at any point, but someone will first have to establish and identify the points themselves and the paths to which they lead. Yes, it *would* be nice to have some Lawrence and some Melville texts in one another's hypertext. How do you decide how many and which ones?

The point I have highlighted about the impossibility of, and necessity for, judgment also pertains to Charles L. Ross's "Editing as Interpretation," an essay in which Ross draws upon Stanley Fish's theory of interpretation at several key junctures. Ross's inquiry into the acts of choice-making by the Cambridge editors is stimulating, yet it runs into the same problems that Delany's essay does.

Notice, for example, Ross's discussion of the scene in "Anna Victrix" where the pregnant Anna dances naked in her room. Ross disagrees with the Cambridge editor's choices in *The Rainbow*:

> [He] ascribes Anna's impulse to a mere "youthful 'crush' or an erotic memory of David dancing naked" that Lawrence probably thought better of. This interpretation justifying inaction, however, seems less than fully persuasive. "Crush" hardly describes the feelings of a married and pregnant woman in a chapter titled "Anna Victrix."

It would be intriguing to know the Cambridge editor's reply to this. Ross's forceful phrasing ("'Crush' hardly describes . . .") suggests that he deems his own interpretation of the scene to be correct—or, at least, clearly preferable. But if things were so plain, then it is difficult to imagine why the Cambridge editor made the decision that he did, and why the Board concurred with it.

It is one thing to contend that Ross is persuasive in his criticisms—to me, he is—and another to say that he is right. Fish's theory places the premium on persuasion, rather than on rightness, because it is Fish's belief that no set of independent facts can be brought to bear upon an interpretation to prove whether it is right or not. The facts, Fish has insisted, are the product of interpretation, so they have the same status as any interpretation that they are invoked to measure. Ross's language intimates his belief that he is right, obviously so. But the Cambridge editor might well continue to differ with him, and where would that leave us? Maybe no one is wrong, just unpersuadable.

It is liberating to conclude that all persons are interpreters. No one is in possession of the truth. Everything is an interpretation. Everything is debatable. A new Edition of Lawrence appears, and it generates lots of interpretation, lots of "talk about Lawrence" and efforts at persuasion. The community of Lawrence scholars discusses, criticizes, and keeps busy. It is a lively conversation, and one feels grateful to be part of it. But Lawrence's work itself is fierce, uncompromising, dedicated to exploring and struggling to lay hold of truth. Lawrence would say that he wanted to discover truth *and* compel readers to see that *that* is what he had found. This is why his writing has unsettled, uplifted, and angered generations of readers. It is troubling, even appalling, to realize that in saying these words, I am giving just another interpretation.

WORKS CITED

Eliot. T. S. *Selected Essays, 1917–1932*. London: Faber, 1932.
Fish, Stanley. *Is There a Text in This Class?* Cambridge: Harvard UP, 1980.
Leavis, F. R. *D. H. Lawrence: Novelist*. New York: Simon, 1969.
———. *The Great Tradition*. New York: New York UP, 1969.
———. *The Living Principle: "English" as a Discipline of Thought*. London: Chatto, 1975.
———. *Thought, Words and Creativity: Art and Thought in Lawrence*. London: Chatto, 1976.
Rawson, Claude. "Old Literature and Its Enemies." *London Review of Books* 25 April 1991: 11–15.
Ross, Charles L. *"Women in Love": A Novel of Mythic Realism*. Boston: Twayne, 1991.

"At last, the real D. H. Lawrence"?—
The Author and The Editors:
A Reception History, 1975–93

Dennis Jackson

Lawrence's difficulties with editors, publishers, and the "censor-morons" who delayed publication or forced him to censor his own works have become the stuff of legend. Lawrence distinguished sharply between his "voice" and the "marketable chunk of published volume."[1] Books were "incorporate things, voices in the air." Reflecting in 1925, with the suppression of *Lady Chatterley's Lover* still to come, he claimed that "since *The Rainbow*, one submits to the process of publication as to a necessary evil." It followed that he had little sympathy with bibliographers: "First editions or forty-first are only the husks" of creativity. On the other hand, he had learned, through a lifetime of barely earning a living by his pen, to be a canny self-promoter. His correspondence contains a surprising number of business letters, involving complex negotiations with publishers on both sides of the Atlantic. Though he did not live long enough to oversee a complete edition, he did prepare a two-volume *Collected Poems*. As the editorial work of the past fifteen years has revealed, Lawrence cared a great deal about the "miserable tome" that carried his voice to the world.

Though editors and publishers such as Edward Garnett, B. W. Huebsch, Thomas Seltzer, and Martin Secker, in both England and America, helped more than hindered the marketing of that voice, the serious consideration of Lawrence's texts—their genesis and transmission—did not start until decades after his death. A Romantic myth of creativity, used both to praise and denigrate his prolific output, was the chief reason for this neglect. Answering charges that Lawrence was an obscene writer who neglected his craft, defenders like Huxley and Leavis praised his "daimon" and his creative "elan," both of which compensated for local failures of craftsmanship. During the 1960s and 1970s, scholars using manuscript archives discovered that Lawrence had been, in fact, a pertinacious and inventive craftsman, willing to rewrite repeatedly in the interests of a work's inner meaning.[2] The works were also discovered to exist in many different, heavily revised drafts or versions. Spurred by this new scholarship and the approaching end of copyright, publishers took renewed interest in editing Lawrence's notoriously corrupt texts.

Those texts had suffered many indignities. Some had been altered to placate timorous publishers and to appease censors; others had been tailored by editors expressing varying degrees of sympathy toward Lawrence's innovative style and structure; still others had been reduced by Lawrence or editors to meet space limitations; and finally, most had been revised thoroughly and repeatedly in manuscript, typescript, proof, and published form(s).

In the early 1970s, Lawrence scholars moved beyond simply bemoaning the corrupt state of his texts to calling for new editions. Lawrence biographer Harry T. Moore, for example, published a letter in *The D. H. Lawrence Review* in 1973 calling for "a crusade for reliable texts of Lawrence's prose works" (231). Moore joined Warren Roberts, the Director of the Humanities Research Center, which housed the largest cache of Lawrence's manuscripts and first editions, in urging Cambridge University Press to undertake an authoritative new Edition of the *Works*. Cambridge had already committed to publishing a seven-volume Edition of Lawrence's *Letters,* so the Press was receptive; and Gerald Pollinger, the literary agent for the Lawrence Estate, warmly welcomed the proposal.

By 1975, Michael Black, the Press's University Publisher, was announcing in the *DHLR* plans for the publication of the whole canon of Lawrence's works, "critically edited on modern principles," a "landmark" Edition that "could be the first of a series in which other major authors of the century are given the same kind of scholarly care as their classical predecessors." Three years later, in a *Times Higher Education Supplement* article titled "At last, the real D. H. Lawrence," Black reported that preliminary editorial work suggested that the total effect on Lawrence's texts would be "very considerable," and that the project would "restore Lawrence's greatest and most popular works to their intended form for the first time." Cambridge, he declared, would produce the "first real publication of Lawrence."

Although more than two years were to pass before the publication of the Edition's first volume—*Apocalypse and the Writings on Revelation* (1980), CUP advocates were not alone in insisting that the "real Lawrence" was forthcoming shortly. Fueled by CUP press releases, journalists in England and America joined the excitement. In *The Guardian* of 19 Sept. 1978, for instance, Hugh Hebert reported that "at last . . . the real Lawrence is being recovered for the coming definitive Cambridge edition." Five weeks later, *The Guardian* again demonstrated the reverence already being accorded this "coming definitive" series as John Cunningham reported how the Humanities Research Center at the University of Texas had acquired a "short pencil . . . used by Dr. Mara Kalnins when she consulted the original manuscript of *Apocalypse* in preparing the definitive edition of Lawrence's last work." Attached to this "collector's item" was a note explaining the pencil's place in the history of the CUP Edition.

An aura of monumentality seems inevitably to surround the production of any such "critical" Edition. In remarks titled "Penetrating the Monumentality of the Cambridge Editions," Charles Rossman at the 1990 Lawrence International Conference in Montpellier, France, pointed out extensive parallels between Gabler's *Ulysses* and the Lawrence Edition, each "sponsored or endorsed by powerful institutional forces" and each "formidably privileged and . . . commandingly packaged." Another scholar, Vicki Mahaffey, writing recently about Gabler's *Ulysses,* described what she called "the monumental view of editing": "One formulation of the editor's task is to restore the now-dead author's literary *product,* stripping it of the grime of history, the 'impurities' occasioned by multiple transmissions. Conceived this way, editing seeks to produce a kind of literary monument."[3] This monumental view sounds clearly in the "General Editors' Preface" to each CUP Lawrence volume, where it is declared that the Edition "aims to provide texts which are as close as can now be determined to those [Lawrence] would have wished to see printed."

In numerous theoretical essays, CUP editors have equated their work on Lawrence's writings to "the process of restoring an old or damaged painting" by stripping layers of varnish and smoke discoloration to reveal "the detail of what the painter painted" (the phrasing is John Worthen's, but precisely the same image of "restoring" a painting has been used in essays by other CUP editors as they described their work[4]). The metaphor has not gone unchallenged, however. Charles Ross, a Lawrence editor outside the Cambridge fold, argued at the Montpellier Conference that "restoring" gives a mistaken idea of what editing accomplishes: "Literature exists in time, not space. Instead of cleaning or repairing a physical object like a painting or sculpture, editors of critical editions 're-create' or bring into existence one among many possible texts, none of which Lawrence 'saw' as a painter or sculptor sees the unique, finished work" ("Ethics").

Appearing in fall 1979, the first volume of CUP *Letters* was commandingly presented in both scholarly and physical ways. Reviewer John Gross observed that, while earlier editions of Lawrence's letters were books "to be bought and read through, with the Cambridge edition we are in the presence of a Project" (17). A stoutly bound red book of 620 pages, *Letters I* was wrapped in a glossy jacket, all sumptuously black and white and red around a haunting, soft-focus portrait of a red-bearded young Lawrence. A year later came the first of the *Works: Apocalypse* also sported a handsome black jacket, this time with Lawrence's signature phoenix (very stylized, in white) leaping from red flames. As in all *Works* to follow, the pages of *Apocalypse* are clear and free of footnotes, the text marked only by line-numbering (every five lines) and hollow asterisks pointing the reader to Notes at the back of the book.

Like other CUP *Works*, too, Kalnins's *Apocalypse* included: (1) the "General Editors' Preface"; (2) a chronology of Lawrence's life; (3) an introduction placing the work in a biographical context; tracing the history of its composition and availability of *MSS, TSS,* and proofs; and recounting the work's publication and early critical reception; (4) the text(s), which in this case included *Apocalypse* and several related works; (5) appendixes, including a wealth of previously unpublished draft manuscripts and/or other associated unpublished materials; (6) explanatory notes at the back of the book which are keyed to pages/lines in the text; (7) and textual apparatus noting variant readings among documents of transmission and first editions.

"Lawrence Enters the Pantheon," declared the title of one early review (Kuczkowski 159), and, indeed, from the first appearance of Cambridge's imposingly packaged *Letters I* and *Apocalypse,* it became clear that the Edition—which will eventually feature more than 40 titles—aims to complete the transformation of Lawrence from the status of an eccentric artist (a genius, but . . .) into a central canonical figure in English literature.

Reviewers of the 28 CUP volumes issued through 1993 complained often that the cost of the books seemed prohibitive to all but large libraries and the most devoted Lawrence specialists. The first seven volumes of *Letters* were listed in *Books in Print: 1993–94* with an average cost of more than $90 per book. *The Rainbow, Women in Love,* and *The Plumed Serpent* were listed at an average cost of $107, with *Sketches of Etruscan Places*

(1992) being the highest-priced volume—at $125—published in the Edition through 1993. Viking Penguin in America and Penguin Books in England meanwhile continued selling inexpensive paperbacks of nearly the entire Lawrencean canon in "the corrupt old texts" that Black in his 1978 essay ("At last") had hoped would "drop from sight."

In England, Penguin decided to bring out its own newly edited mass-market versions of Lawrence's major works of fiction, a project that ironically involved several scholars also engaged in the CUP Edition. Between 1981 and 1983, seven Lawrence editions were published in "The Penguin English Library" series: *Sons and Lovers* (ed. Keith Sagar); *The Rainbow* (ed. John Worthen); *Women in Love* (ed. Charles L. Ross); *The Plumed Serpent* (ed. Ronald G. Walker); *The White Peacock* (ed. Alan Newton); *Selected Short Stories* (ed. Brian Finney); and *The Complete Short Novels* (ed. Keith Sagar and Melissa Partridge). Each edition included a chronology of Lawrence's life; a critical-biographical introduction; notes (ranging up to 21 pages) explaining allusions and biographical connections; a glossary of regional and dialect words; and a bibliography. But no textual apparatus was included, and the Penguin paperbacks were clearly not as ambitious in a scholarly way as Cambridge's critical editions were.

All those Penguin editors were constrained by copyright law to use as copy-text either the first English or the first American edition of Lawrence's work. Editors of two Penguin novels claimed to have chosen "a text of historical importance," and coeditors of another text claimed it "represents Lawrence's latest intentions." Distinctly bolder claims were made by Charles Ross for his performance in preparing the first critical edition of *Women in Love* (claims that would later draw a fusillade of criticism from Cambridge editors seeking to discredit his Penguin edition). Ross declared:

This edition corrects all major substantive errors in Seltzer [American first edition]. As a result it has the double distinction of being the most accurate text yet published and the text that has been least impeded in its transmission to the public by the non-aesthetic demands of the marketplace. It is the text as Lawrence completed it after many years of labour and before he began tinkering with later editions at the behest of Secker [the English publisher]. Surely this product of the unconstrained authorial will has pre-eminent claim on our aesthetic judgement. ("Introduction" 47–48)

Despite such assertions, this and the other newly edited Lawrence texts in the Penguin English Library series drew scant notice (they were never reviewed even in the *DHLR*) and elicited next-to-nothing in the way of critical appraisal of the editing methods involved. Only a couple of these editions (including *Women in Love*) were ever made available in America, apparently due to copyright restrictions, and Penguin otherwise continued through 1993 offering to American readers only those unedited "corrupt old texts" that Black condemned.

One particularly controversial aspect of the Cambridge Edition is the audacious claim that "it is indissolubly linked with the copyright of the main works themselves" (Black, "At last" 11). Lawrence having died in 1930, his books were due to emerge from the protection of copyright (life plus fifty years) in England by the early 1980s; in America, they were to enter the public domain at varying times based on the date of original copyright plus seventy-five years for all his works copyrighted before 1978. Thereafter, presumably, anyone who wished could print Lawrence's works without paying the Estate or the heirs. But Pollinger revealed in 1979 that the Estate and Cambridge University Press would seek a re-newed copyright in the "corrected definitive form" (15) of the *Works*, for another fifty years in the United Kingdom and the United States. When the first *Work* appeared in 1980, its title page announced: "This, the Cambridge Edition of the text of '*Apocalypse and the Writings on Revelation*' now correctly established from the original sources and first published in 1980, [copyright] the Estate of Frieda Lawrence Ravagli 1980." (Law-rence had no descendants, so, ironically, the Estate distributes the reve-nues from this renewed copyright to descendants of Frieda Lawrence's first and third husbands, Ernest Weekley and Angelo Ravagli.)

This direct effort to pull Lawrence's writings back into the orbit of copyright has been challenged by surprisingly few commentators. "Copy-righting the Classics," an unsigned article in *The Economist* of April 1982, pronounced CUP's copyright declaration a "sensational read" and warned if it holds up, it would "[bore] holes in Britain's copyright laws." *The Economist* argued that, if CUP can defend its claim that the relatively minor changes in punctuation and spelling in its edition of *The Lost Girl* consti-tute the basis for a new copyright, it "would mean that biographers, scholars and critics would have to pay the publishers for the right to quote from the text." Thereafter, "[a]bsurdly, publishers could refresh old copyrights by hiring scholars to change the commas, dashes and colons in the classics."

As though anticipating similar challenges, CUP issued a circular in 1982 titled *Copyright, scholarly editions and the Cambridge Lawrence*. Textual scholars, that circular argued, spend years preparing editions of the classics, and publishers invest much money in these editions—it thus seems only fair and reasonable that their joint enterprise should be afforded legal protection (see Holroyd 943). But the circular did not make clear precisely what sort of quantitative rule-of-thumb the Estate or the Press would use in claiming that one of CUP's "correctly established" texts qualifies as a newly created work.

In "Copyrights and Wrongs: D. H. Lawrence" in 1982, Holroyd and Jobson countered the CUP circular's argument by pointing to the dangers of "paying royalties to the living editor of a dead author." The "new" authentic text, they observed, "may be the writer's 'old' rejected narrative. The argument that the scholar retrospectively knows more about the author's 'real' intentions than the author . . . knew himself in his lifetime is in danger of becoming over-sophisticated." Holroyd and Jobson suggested that the CUP Edition should survive on its merits in the open market, not on any special legal claims (943–44).

Cambridge's statement that it has "correctly established" Lawrence's texts from original sources seems to imply that other interpretations would result in an *incorrectly* established text. Noting this, Charles Rossman charged that the claim implies "something newer . . . , more stable and incontestable, than is the case" in CUP's *The Rainbow;* it "exaggerates the deficiencies of earlier editions," he protested, "while echoing the discredited notion of 'definitive edition,' as though there were no other defensible way of presenting Lawrence's words" ("Cambridge *Rainbow*" 184–85).[5] As early as 1981, John Sutherland warned of "a real congestion of Lawrence scholarship" if CUP and the Estate do indeed insist on exclusive access for their editors to the primary *MS* and *TS* sources (see Holroyd 944).[6] In short, if CUP and the Estate successfully press their legal claims, readers may be left facing a choice between those "corrupt old texts" and one self-proclaimed "authoritative" Edition.

In *The Death of Literature* (1990), Alvin Kernan complained that "each of the new Cambridge texts is an eclectic amalgamation of several different versions of the same text, mingling unsystematically and incompletely, on no established principles, some details from early drafts with some later changes, producing a kind of bibliographic monster never imagined by the author . . ." (103). Kernan protested that, despite Cambridge's retreat from its initial bold copyright declaration, there remains "a sophistic claim that *all* of the new text now [belongs to CUP], the parts changed and the parts not changed, while only the old texts could be reprinted without permission." This logic seemed to him "very contorted," but "at least it saved face" (100). The Cambridge Edition "was taking for granted, though pushing to the limits of credibility, the print-based, romantic, copyright supported, bibliographic conception of an absolute and perfect Platonic text," he said, adding sardonically: "It was, like the true cross, the true Lawrence text, whose few actual changes had magically made the entire text so whole, harmonious and radiant as to establish copyright for another fifty years" (102–3).

Only a handful of reviewers of the first twenty-one *Works* issued by CUP paid even minimal attention to the crucial matter of copyright. Occasionally a writer would echo Karen McLeod Hewitt's views in a 1984 review, that "[t]hough the edition is splendidly produced, in the case of *The Trespasser* the copyright claim has no real justification" (583). Ronald G. Walker and R. P. Draper likewise raised eyebrows over CUP's effort to recapture the copyright of *Women in Love,* each arguing that the differences between the old Penguin text and CUP's edition seem "often trivial . . . rather than fundamental changes of content and attitude" (Draper 338).

Predictably, many early commentaries on *The Letters and Works* focused on the irony of Lawrence's having his often incandescent writings and vitalistic philosophy cribbed and confined by scholarly apparatus. In "Lawrence and the Scholars," for example, J. C. F. Littlewood condemned CUP for having "virtually eliminated [Lawrence's] genius" through "bad scholarship" (181–82) in the first two volumes of *Letters.* He supplied no convincing evidence of this "bad" work, and seemed less disturbed with the way Lawrence was being edited than with the fact that he *was* being edited. CUP's scholarship, he snarled, gets in the way of the reader's perceiving the "general truth" of Lawrence's writing, and thus Littlewood preferred the "clean, unacademised text" of the 1932 edition of Lawrence's letters.

Less dogmatically than Littlewood, Daniel Schwarz expressed feelings voiced by others when he worried, while reviewing *Apocalypse,* that the CUP scholarship might somehow "[obscure] the seminal role [Lawrence] played as a revolutionary spokesman for feeling, passion, sexuality, and imagination," that in admitting him as a classic author, we might "lose our sense of him as a bull in the china shop of literary culture" (685). The fear was that Lawrence was somehow being domesticated.

But Cambridge had anticipated this response. Before the first book appeared, James T. Boulton, General Editor for *The Letters and Works*, declared: "The charge that annotation dulls the response to the liveliness and spirited creativity of [Lawrence's] letters is a gross overstatement. . . . The political and social context in which he lived no longer exists; the culture he inherited has . . . been immeasurably eroded; the very language he uses, though it may *seem* contemporary with our own, is sometimes markedly, sometimes subtly, different." Tactful editing, Boulton submitted, can give readers a fuller measure of Lawrence's "sensitivity to the world about him, his critical intelligence, [and] his complex personality," leading to consequent greater enjoyment of his *Letters* ("Cambridge" 227). That argument obviously can be extended to the *Works*.

Nearly all reviewers echoed David Bradshaw's 1989 assessment in *TLS*, that work on the first six volumes of CUP *Letters* met "high standards of editorial exactness" (1260). Most reviewers concentrated on the content and beauty of Lawrence's letters or on controversial aspects of his biography, and paid no attention to at least one key issue related to the actual editing work: how well was the volume division of the *Letters* being executed? George Zytaruk, coeditor of *Letters II*, had raised this question before publication began. His 1979 essay "Editing Lawrence's Letters: The Strategy of Volume Division" declared that two of the "most fundamental" challenges of editing the letters are "how many volumes should there be and where should the various volumes begin and end." CUP editors, he reported, were facing crucial decisions: "Should each [volume] be exactly the same size? What periods in Lawrence's life would various volumes try to span? Was it worthwhile to attempt to discover some unconscious artistry in the contents of any given volume?" He admitted that the seven volumes (the eighth will be largely a massive index) will each "have an individual character, determined by our decisions regarding the beginning and the end of each volume" (234–35). In other words, the volume divisions will tell us much about the CUP editors' interpretation of Lawrence's life. And yet, no commentator outside the CUP establishment has made more than a feint toward exploring these "fundamental" issues regarding what Zytaruk called the Edition's "superstructure."

Similarly in regard to Lawrence's *Works*, many key issues related to CUP's editing principles and practices have thus far been passed over lightly in the critical reviewing of the Edition. Because nearly all who have examined the *Works* have been journalists or literary critics, not textual scholars, reviews have typically focused on Lawrence's themes and styles, or on a work's biographical context or political implications, as if the book were perhaps being published for the first time. Or else the reviewer has concentrated on critiquing some literary critical point raised in the editor's Introduction (as, for example, James Cowan did in contesting CUP editor L. D. Clark's conclusions about the final revised ending of *The Plumed Serpent*). This sort of oblique reviewing of major editing projects—where the reviewer seems willing simply to take the scholarly accuracy of the text on faith—is hardly uncommon, as Hershel Parker complained recently. In "The Reviewing of Scholarly Editions," he described the "ideal reviewer" as one who possesses keen "expertise in the life of [the] writer being edited as well as in textual and editorial theory and practice," and who is willing to devote weeks to "dirt[ying] himself in the textual lists" in order to test not only the validity of the scholarly apparatus but of the whole Edition.[7] But few reviewers of the Cambridge Lawrence have bothered thus to "dirty" themselves, and most have remained content to quote from the editors' own delineations of their methods.

Many reviews—especially those of early CUP volumes—seemed simply panegryics to the project. Andor Gomme in reviewing *Letters I,* for instance, hailed the Edition's "auspicious" beginning: the research, he said, shows "obvious thoroughness" so that "the fundamental work will never have to be done again"; editor James Boulton is "patient but also unobtrusive" (262), his "accuracy sets a fine example," his introduction is "well-balanced," his illustrations are "good," his maps "useful"; the book itself is "nice to hold" with pages "well set out and printed"; the job has been "eminently well done" (263). Gomme ended: "It makes one pant for the feast still to come" (266). Others were panting, too. Reviewing *Apocalypse,* Graham Hough proclaimed the text "settled once and for all" (192); and Alastair Niven trumpeted, "[*Apocalypse*] establishes a standard of editing that one cannot imagine being improved upon" (185).

Over the first fifteen or so years of the Cambridge project's existence, the *Works* of Lawrence were accorded considerable attention in most major literary organs in England and America, though in general, periodicals devoted no more space to volumes that raised complicated textual-editorial issues than they did to those that involved comparatively routine textual problems. Until 1987, few reviews discussed any hazards involved in constructing the sort of eclectic texts being issued by CUP, and very few paid more than fleeting attention to the "Textual apparatus." When reviewers did bother to take a closer look at editing methods, their observations tended to settle around two areas: (1) the nature of the *annotations* by CUP editors and the related matter of who a volume's intended "reader" seems to be; and (2) the lack of any kind of *critical context* inside the Edition itself (the absence of either references to previous criticism by non-Cambridge scholars or assessments of the aesthetic qualities of the work being edited or, at least, of particular passages being restored).

Essays by Boulton and Black published early in the project made clear that CUP's policies regarding annotation were dictated by "the needs of a world-wide readership" of ordinary cultivated readers as well as literary scholars and students; that the Edition was also intended for non-native students of English; and that it was being prepared too for readers of the *next* century, when some British colloquialisms and even classical allusions used by Lawrence may seem obscure (Boulton, "Letters" 10). Nonetheless, when *Letters I* and *Apocalypse* appeared, reviewers frequently pounced on editors for their manner of annotating the text. Harry Moore, for instance, wondered who it was that would pick up *Apocalypse*—a complex meditation on the Book of Revelation—and then need to be told who Dante, Mussolini, Charles Lindbergh, Woodrow Wilson, and Abraham Lincoln were. Jeremy Lane, noting "fairly fussy" annotations in *The Lost Girl,* remarked: "Probably there are forceful commercial reasons for this odd conjunction of readerships, but a scholarly edition and a kind of reading primer do not inhabit the same volume altogether comfortably" (707–8). CUP eventually took such criticism to heart. In 1986, Black said CUP had decided "not to gloss any word or annotate any reference which can be easily found in a good desk dictionary or encyclopedia" ("Editing" 206).

Many reviewers faulted Cambridge's introductions for being "explanatory rather than critical" (Hewitt on *Apocalypse*), and for remaining so severely *factual* (attending only to the history of a work's composition, the available documents, and the justifications for the choice of copy-text, which CUP editors called the "base-text"). Editors made no effort to evaluate a work's literary merit or to analyze the aesthetic and interpretative implications of Lawrence's revisions. Defending that policy, L. D. Clark said CUP was wise to restrict introductions to "matters of information" because critical discussion is "soon dated" (Clark reviewing *Aaron's*

Rod 247). Reviewers also frequently griped because CUP introductions recount a work's early critical reception and then "disappointingly [ignore] subsequent criticism" (Draper on *The Trespasser* 18).

The first substantial consideration of CUP editing procedures written by anyone other than a CUP editor appeared in 1984 in *The Library*. Tom Davis's review-essay there compared the editors' working principles in the first six Cambridge volumes with those displayed in two volumes of the ongoing Oxford series of Hardy's novels. While Davis found an "overpowering" editorial presence throughout the Hardy editions (where up to one-third of each page of text is typically occupied by an apparatus), he found the Lawrence texts to be "lightly, almost unobtrusively edited, with the apparatus tucked away at the back of the book" (392). Davis preferred CUP's practices, but nonetheless voiced some objections. For example, he expressed puzzlement over CUP's unusual "backwards route" of emendation: in most stories in *The Prussian Officer* collection, the first edition is selected against a variety of earlier witnesses to the text, but in each case, "where there is variation in punctuation from an authorial manuscript[,] the copy-text is emended back" to the *MS* reading (394–95). Davis faulted the editor for being "uncharacteristically reticent" in the way he "simply asserts in each case that, for instance, 'E1 has been adopted as a base-text, because of the extent of the 1914 revisions,'" without showing the reader what the extent of those revisions were. As Davis noted, "it is a policy of these editions only to record variation that occurred in witnesses subsequent to the copy-text," so the apparatus is "effectively a record of discarded compositorial punctuation, and all of Lawrence's unrevised readings are lost to sight."[8]

A year later, a second review-essay comparing Oxford and Cambridge editions—this time Oxford's *The Tales of Henry James* and three CUP editions of Lawrence's fiction—reached some similar conclusions. Writing in *Archiv* in 1985, Dieter Mehl suggested that, while Oxford's *Tales* seem designed for reference libraries or the specialist's study, CUP editors seem to have "no very clearly definable target reader" in mind (135). Mehl called the CUP *Works* "one of the most impressive" editions of comparable scope ever created (135), but had plenty of suggestions for improvement. His sharpest complaint—one that echoed Davis's—was that CUP's "Textual apparatus" in works such as *The Prussian Officer* volume "either ignored or illustrated rather selectively within the explanatory notes" the "more substantial changes, rejected material, or, indeed, earlier printed versions" of a work (131).

One book Mehl reviewed, *Mr Noon* (1984), was the first literally "new" work added to the canon by the Cambridge project. An unfinished narrative only recently reconstructed by editor Lindeth Vasey from a *MS* lost for fifty years, it generated livelier interest among more reviewers than any previous CUP *Work* issued. Part I of *Mr Noon* had been revised, and published as a short story after Lawrence's death, but the much longer Part II had been abandoned. A CUP publicity release proclaimed the publication of the "long-lost" *MS* of *Mr Noon* a "major literary event," "rivaling in importance the recent discovery of William Faulkner's early poetry, and the publication of the corrected edition of *Ulysses*." As it has often done since 1978, CUP supplemented its promotional efforts by placing a literary critical essay in a prominent British periodical. One week before the publication of *Mr Noon*, the *London Review of Books* featured "D. H. Lawrence and Gilbert Noon" by Michael Black, who called it the "first attempt at a critical essay on the whole novel" (10). Black declared the chapters that describe Noon's first days in the Tyrol with his lover Johanna to be "among the best things in Lawrence" (12).

As an intimate autobiographical account of Lawrence's early days with Frieda, part II sparked immediate interest from reviewers. Most Lawrence specialists naturally were delighted to get hands on the "new" novel, and the book was warmly greeted by such major British literary figures as David Lodge and Anthony Burgess (who declared in the *Observer* that it seemed "something very like a major novel" [qtd. in Jackson 135]). But as so often had happened when Lawrence's books were published during his lifetime, reviewers in British periodicals generally gave *Mr Noon* a far more negative reception than did their counterparts in America. To James Fenton in the London *Times,* for example, the novel seemed "tiresome junk"; to Peter Parker in *London Magazine* it was "a bad novel" abandoned by its creator for good reason (109). Fenton blasted Vasey's "officious overexplaining" of familiar things such as "the Holy Grail" and "Aphrodite" and the "gaps in the explanatory material" that come when she "infuriating[ly]" fails to explain what Lawrence meant by "the alpaca bogey of lust" or the Greeks' "horrid plough metaphor." Lydia Blanchard likewise complained about Vasey's "too-much, not-enough editing" methods that irritated readers (158–59).

Editors of CUP *Works* have shown themselves to be acutely sensitive to such criticism, to what one of them called "ax-grinding reviews" (Herbert 232). Black's 1986 essay "Editing a Constantly-Revising Author: the Cambridge Edition of Lawrence in Historical Context" seemed, in part, to be a direct response to complaints by reviewers such as those who had written about *Mr Noon*. He explained, for example, how CUP's policies regarding their "much criticised" "Explanatory notes" were being changed (so that Fenton and others would have to look up "Aphrodite" on their own).

Black's essay was the most effective apologia for CUP's editorial theories that anyone had written about the Lawrence Edition. Most interestingly, he discussed strong parallels that the CUP Editorial Board perceived between their enterprise and the ideas expressed in Gabler's "Afterword" to the 1984 *Ulysses*, concerning the editing of modern texts. Gabler described how he had examined Joyce's surviving documents of composition and transmission in order to trace the "linear relationship between them," enabling him (in Gabler's words) to "define a continuous manuscript text for *Ulysses*, extending over a sequence of actual documents" (qtd. in Black 199). Thus, Black said, Gabler had recovered an "ideal text" which "the author was by stages moving towards but never actually inscribed whole on one single document" (198). Cambridge thus endorsed Gabler's concept of the "continuous manuscript text" produced by the constantly revising author, and in its own approach sought in the "continuously evolving text" that state where

> [Lawrence] had nearly completed his development of the text, and had not inserted his last thoughts on his proofs, but where publishers and printers had not yet corrupted the text: to take that state as copy-text, and to emend it systematically. Our practice resembles Gabler's historical and theoretical exposition in that we both conceive of a critical text as the attempt to fix, as in a still photograph, a culminating moment in a long process before deterioration sets in. (200)

CUP's "practice" soon began drawing more detailed scrutiny from reviewers. What triggered the newly intense focus on textual-bibliographic issues surrounding the Edition was the 1987 appearance of *Women in Love*, the first of Lawrence's major novels issued in the series. It sparked the first sustained firefight among scholars regarding the *way* Lawrence's *Works* were being edited.

Charles Ross, who had edited *Women in Love* for the Penguin English Library series in 1982, criticized the Cambridge policy of eliminating the creative results of collaboration between Lawrence, Frieda, and publishers. In *Essays in Criticism*, he argued that the text suffers because many "nice touches" and improvements supplied by Frieda (and apparently accepted by Lawrence as they prepared the text for press) are lost in CUP's editing (347). He complained that editors David Farmer, Lindeth Vasey, and John Worthen had disallowed many authorial revisions made in *TSS* or proofs when Lawrence imaginatively played off mistranscriptions or typist errors (and, in Ross's view, often thereby *improved* the work). CUP's *Women in Love,* he protested, "is not the novel that Lawrence struggled for three years to get right, completed, and sent to America . . ." (351). Supporting his Penguin version, he wrote: "An edition of Seltzer emended from the printer's-copy typescript and retaining Frieda's contribution and Lawrence's ingenious responses to error . . . comes much closer to approximating" the ideal text of the novel—one that would, in CUP's words, realize Lawrence's "own expectations"—than what CUP had produced (351, 342). He condemned the way CUP editors create "inconsistency or oddity" (344) in their text by retrieving accidentals from an earlier draft, and the way they restore substantive variants "of dubious authority" from the Secker edition, thus ratifying a textual history "over which Lawrence had much less artistic control" than he had had earlier (348, 351). Such "piecemeal" emendation, he charged, disregards the novel's "internal consistency" (349).

Ross also charged that the CUP editors had committed plagiarism by implying "that no critical editing has previously been undertaken on Lawrence's works," and then "silently incorporat[ing] published scholarship by Eldon Branda, Herbert Davis, and Charles Ross without proper attribution" (343–44). He further protested because "CUP's historical collation does not include substantive differences from" the 1982 edition.

Worthen and Vasey responded in *Essays in Criticism* with a 1989 "Rejoinder," attacking Ross's "malice" and "inconsistent" accusations, and offering a detailed account of what they viewed as his "errors" (178, 176). They denied his charge of plagiarism, saying that the "scholarly articles and books allegedly plagiarised" by CUP editors "were neither used nor usable" (177–78). And they underscored what they considered flaws in the textual argument Ross made regarding *Women in Love* in his review and in earlier writings. He had suggested that the printer's-copy typescript for Seltzer might be adopted as a proper base-text for the novel, but Worthen and Vasey insisted that "*this typescript no longer exists:* all that survives is Lawrence's revised typescript [*TSII*] from which the printer's-copy typescript was *retyped.*" Ross thus errs, they declared, in assuming that *TSII* was the setting-copy, and is naive in thinking that "any artifact typed by another person or set up by a printer can be said to embody its author's unconstrained will" (178). They defended their incorporation of "deliberate and significant changes" Lawrence made in the Secker proofs of *Women in Love,* labeling as illogical Ross's argument that "the Seltzer edition—which Lawrence was unable to revise in proof—is necessarily superior to the 'later' *E1,* for which he did correct proofs" (179). They similarly defended the way they had attempted to eliminate Frieda's influence on the novel "except where we are obliged to accept it," contending that Ross's argument in favor of adopting her emendations was based on his personal preference—"not a sound basis for textual decisions" (182).

Meanwhile, a review-essay centered tightly on the editing theories behind the CUP *Women in Love* and the competing Penguin edition appeared in *Meridian* (October 1988). "Perhaps it's unfair to compare the editions," Annabel Cooper wrote, "since Ross's is not a critical edition" (at least in the sense that it included no apparatus), but she ventured such a comparison, anyway, because "their differences set up a worthwhile debate, and the deficiencies of the Penguin edition illuminate the skill of the Cambridge one" (181). She did give Ross's *Women in Love* credit for having included previously censored passages, for having "made the most dramatic act of restoration," but she faulted him for "inconsistently" attending to substantive errors made in earlier editions, and especially for his allowing "aesthetic judgement" as well as "convenience" to govern his choice of the American edition as his copy-text (181–82).

Worthen devoted a portion of a 1989 essay, "The Restoration of *Women in Love,*" to countering Ross's theories about the relationship and authority of various documents that survive from Lawrence's work on the novel. Worthen charged that Ross, in his history of *The Composition of "The Rainbow" and "Women in Love"* (1979), had not been "able to show what an editor should do" (9) regarding the proper choice of a copy-text for a critical edition of *Women in Love.* Further, he asserted, Ross's 1982 edition emends its base-text "only selectively": "For one thing, it does not emend any of Seltzer's punctuation errors; for another, extraordinarily in an edition claiming to correct 'all major substantive errors in Seltzer,' it emends those substantives both randomly and selectively. . . . I have found substantive errors in it throughout." Adding that Ross fails anywhere to record the source (the corrected typescript, *TSII*) from which his emendations were taken, Worthen concluded: "Such a text, on such a basis, produces an unreliable and untrustworthy edition" (24). At the same time, Worthen made self-congratulatory claims for his own "restored" CUP edition: "[It] presents an authentic text" of *Women in Love,* he submitted, "together with a full account of its compositional history" (8).

The Cambridge-Ross exchange continued in the pages of the *DHLR.* Rallying to the aid of fellow CUP editors, Paul Eggert in "The Reviewing of the Cambridge Edition of *Women in Love*" declared that Worthen and Vasey's "Rejoinder" had exposed the "deficiency" of Ross's views and his "questionable editorial practices" (298). While repeating Worthen and Vasey's arguments about the textual history of *Women in Love,* Eggert expressed his own theories about the versatility of the modern eclectic edition as contrasted to the "historically distinct text" that, Ross had argued, will maintain a "synchronic integrity" (301). Eggert declared that the "textual riches which Lawrence left are certainly not represented by the kind of text Charles Ross would have us read," but he admitted, "nor are they fully represented by the *reading text*" of the CUP edition which inevitably is "chronologically . . . a patchwork quilt: what it offers is a way of reading as a finished product what was in fact an ongoing process" (301).

Ross responded in a 1989 *DHLR* essay that, "If Eggert were to follow the logic of his closing argument, he would agree with me that readers and scholars of Lawrence are best served by discrete, historically 'finished' or (if you will) synchronic texts. In any case, Eggert and I agree tacitly that the list of variants, which will help scholars to reconstruct the compositional process, should prove the most valuable achievement" of CUP's *Women in Love* ("Editorial" 223, 226).[9]

Two other essayists, Eugene Goodheart and Charles Rossman, joined the debate. Goodheart declared that "Worthen and Vasey have much the better" of the "fierce exchange" with Ross. The latter's essential difference from the CUP editors, Goodheart wrote, lay in his view that (in Ross's words) emendation cannot be done "piecemeal, without considering the holistic meaning of a draft or a sequence of revisions." But Goodheart questioned what Ross means by "holism"—Is it "a concept of the whole that existed at the moment of composition or is it the reflection of a process in time that comes to a teleological fulfillment?" Arguing that Ross sets himself up as the arbiter of what the best version of *Women in Love* is, Goodheart warned that such a "readerly exercise of authority" can be "arbitrary and unreliable" (236).

Rossman was less concerned with picking a winner in the debate than he was in expressing his approval that Ross had been willing to challenge

Cambridge's practices; the debate over editorial theory, Rossman asserted, "is necessary and long overdue." He stressed the importance of the "sometimes venomous battles" being waged over the editing of *Ulysses* and of *Women in Love:* "A great deal is at stake here: competing theories of editing; the egos and reputations of the advocates of a given theory; the very language that constitutes two of our century's major literary texts; those same texts regarded, now more than ever, as commercial properties; and millions of dollars in future sales, royalties, and inheritances" ("Metacommentary" 222, 221).

Several other Cambridge Lawrence volumes issued since 1987 have attracted a small number of reviewers willing to grapple directly with important textual issues, and for the first time we begin to see the outlines of a body of more sophisticated critical reviewing focused on the Edition *qua* edition.

As they had with *Women in Love,* Ross and Rossman wrote two of the more intensive commentaries on CUP editorial procedures when *The Rainbow* was published in 1989. Ross complained in *Documentary Editing* that editor Mark Kinkead-Weekes's *Rainbow* had "missed" the "opportunity to restore Lawrence's revolutionary vision of the sexual life" by too cautiously refraining "from restoring more than a few of the many words and passages that Lawrence may have removed or changed in an act of self-censorship under pressure from agent and publisher." Instead, Ross charged, Kinkead-Weekes had decided "to authorize almost all instances of dubious cuts" in the Methuen first English edition rather than giving authority to the *MS* or *TS,* thus ironically displaying a "bias toward the social and sexual values that Lawrence attacked with increasing vehemence" as he revised (40). Ross contended that Lawrence defended the integrity of his *TS* and resented having to censor the proofs. By "deciding not to restore any of the excessive or 'immoral' (Lawrence's word) verbal heightening that Lawrence had likely deleted in proof under pressure" from Methuen, Ross declared, CUP had produced a *Rainbow* text "almost identical in substantives to that already available" (40).

Rossman reached essentially the same conclusion. "Any reader who expects in this edition a radically different text of *The Rainbow* will be disappointed," he wrote in a *DHLR* review-essay. "True, 1,735 changes in the text of a major novel are significant, but matters of punctuation and spelling account for three-fourths of these alterations, and many are at the level of changing 'headmaster's' to 'head-master's'." He added that even

CUP's substantive emendations seem "typically quite minor" ("Cambridge *Rainbow*" 183–84).

The first disinterested criticism of the Cambridge project by a Cambridge editor was L. D. Clark's review of *Aaron's Rod* (1988). He objected to Mara Kalnins's "fundamental" decision to follow only the American (Seltzer) *TS* and not to grant authority to variants in the English (Secker) first edition (set up from a now-lost *TS*). Clark argued that the English edition "contains numerous substantive variations from the American edition which patently do not stem from censorship" by the publisher. Himself a novelist, Clark asserted that many of the substantive variants in *E1* point to "just the sort of revision that most novelists do" as they re-read a *TS:* "sharpening details, finding a more precise or expressive phrase, clarifying a scene." He ventured that "Lawrence's hand is evident beyond any reasonable doubt" in 30 of the 45 substantive variants that Kalnins listed between *A1* and *E1*. "What the argument comes down to," Clark concluded, "is that with less adherence to positive identification and more willingness to exercise an informed judgment from circumstantial evidence, an edition closer to what I see as Lawrence's final intentions would have emerged." He contended that CUP's policy that "unquestionable evidence is to dictate the selection of a copy-text which then possesses overriding authority" too strictly rules out "circumstantial evidence" that might guide an editor in choosing variant readings (248–49).

Reviewing *Aaron's Rod* for the *DHLR,* Hershel Parker claimed to find in Cambridge practice his own reservations about both the Greg/Bowers conception of editing and the socialized conception of Jerome McGann. In *Flawed Texts and Verbal Icons* (1984), Parker had denounced many textual editors of the 1960s and '70s for being excessively influenced by the copytext pragmatics of Greg and Bowers and by New Criticism's tendency to treat any literary text as an autonomous, essentially authorless entity.[10] Thus when he came to reviewing the CUP Edition, with its apparent close attention to the author's life and to the conditions and circumstances of his acts of writing and revision, Parker warmly greeted the editors who sought (in their words) to provide texts Lawrence "would have wished to see printed." Followers of Greg-Bowers, stated Parker, "can only regard this Cambridge policy as heretical," while anyone persuaded by McGann's "notion that the best text is the text that got into print (the authentic social-compact product of author, helpful friends, and a publisher embodying the spirit of the times) will also be aghast at the Cantabrigians, for the editors are not concerned with preserving evidences of the literary tastes and social antennae" of Seltzer in New York or Secker in London.

Others reviewing CUP volumes for the *DHLR* were not likewise willing to bestow such blessings on the Cantabrigians.

The Press's volume division was the focus of Kingsley Widmer's caustic critique of *Reflections on the Death of a Porcupine and Other Essays* (1988). He complained that the essays there do not represent "the choice the author made" when *Reflections* was published in 1925. Without "sensible justification," said Widmer, CUP omitted "The Novel," the essay "many commentators have reasonably viewed as the most important in *Reflections.*"[11] He contended that no very coherent principle of selection of essays is evident in CUP's *Reflections,* and suggested that this may be viewed as part of a more general problem evident in the *Works*—"the arbitrary divisions of the whole enterprise." Wrote Widmer: "In a parochial misapplication of 'historical principles,' we are not given either all the writings of a period or all the writings of a type . . . , but supposed republication of original volumes that sometimes, as with *Reflections,* are no such things. There may, of course, be financial and other crass purposes (maximizing volumes, manipulating copyrights, aggrandizing editors) for the unwieldy and often incoherent combinations of texts" (342).

The limitations of CUP's "Textual apparatus" in *Movements in European History* (1989) drew fire from *DHLR* reviewer Dale Kramer. A modern critical edition, he proposed, should offer a useful historical record of rejected *MS* variants, but *Movements* does not do so fully enough and this "severely limits the edition's value" for scholars. Kramer perceived "confusion within the Lawrence project," noting that after editor Philip Crumpton's introduction dwells at length on revisions made in *Movements* by censors to make it more acceptable to Catholic and Anglican Ireland, his apparatus then falls short of being "flexible enough to accommodate" these revisions (327–28).

Reviewing CUP's *England, My England and Other Stories* (1990) for the *DHLR,* Weldon Thornton expressed deep frustration over "the lack of clarity and explicitness about the justification for the editorial choices" in the edition. He complained that CUP's "puzzlingly unclear" concept of a *base-text* seems "implicitly to involve some attempt to follow the composition/revision process, and in doing so commits the editor to giving a degree of authority to materials so early in this process that they may have little or no relevance to what Lawrence finally 'would have wished to see printed.'" In particular Thornton questioned Bruce Steele's selection of *MS* or periodical versions as the base-text of so many of the stories, arguing that, since Lawrence extensively reworked so many of them prior to book publication, a more authoritative base-text in most cases would have been the 1922 English first edition, which "best reflects the author's intentions most proximate to the act of publication" (322–24).

CUP's eclectic rationale regarding emendation of its base-text also drew a protest in the *DHLR* from Thomas Faulkner. Reviewing *The Boy in the Bush* (1990), he labeled as "inflated" the Edition's claims for the benefits of restoring accidentals from the author's early drafts. To maintain that a holograph *MS* contains Lawrence's "most considered and final preferences in matters of spelling, capitalization, and punctuation is patently absurd," argued Faulkner, because most authors pay little attention to such things while creating a *MS* that they know typists will transcribe and that they fully expect to revise later while reading *TSS* and proofs. Faulkner further charged that Paul Eggert's emendation process in *The Boy in the Bush* is itself arbitrary: "By electing to make certain emendations of accidentals from the typescripts, others from the Secker or Seltzer . . . editions, and still others on his own authority, Eggert in fact becomes exactly the sort of copy editor and house stylist from whose nefarious efforts he seeks to purify the text."

In George Bornstein's *Representing Modernist Texts: Editing as Interpretation* (1991), Eugene Goodheart hailed the CUP project for precisely the same reasons Faulkner disapproved of it. Goodheart's essay, "Censorship and Self-Censorship in the Fiction of D. H. Lawrence," demonstrated strong preference for the way CUP resisted taking a historicist approach to Lawrence's writings: "We diminish the audacious authority of Lawrence's work, its subversive message," he wrote, "if we prematurely absorb it into an author-publisher-audience collaborative" (238). He asserted that the many marks of censorship and self-censorship in Lawrence's texts represent "a formidable obstacle to a historicist approach to editing" such as that advocated by McGann. Lawrence, he said, was an embattled writer with a "transgressive imagination, constantly challenging cultural taboos" (237), and while the censorship threat to his works by publishers and readers may have been Lawrence's enemy, in a sense it was empowering, helping to create his erotic prose style as he sought metaphoric displacements to convey the experience of passion. Goodheart extolled CUP for stripping away the marks of "compromises that Lawrence had to make for his work to see the light of day," and called this effort to give the reader "what the author wished to say" a "truly liberating critical act" (237–39).

Goodheart's examination of the editing done in the first seven Lawrence novels issued by CUP was the most thoughtful assay any scholar had made at a comprehensive assessment of the *Works* published during the 1980s. An ideal textual edition, according to Goodheart, would be one in which the editor "could determine final intentions," "grasp the interactive social process of artistic production, and make cogent literary interpretations and judgments when necessary." Among the CUP novels he surveyed, he believed *The Rainbow* came closest to approximating that ideal. In his view, Kinkead-Weekes had best overcome the difficulties facing anyone who tries to edit the work of (in that editor's words) "a continuously revising and recreating author" whose idea of creativity was essentially one of "process, of continuous and organic change" (Goodheart 232–33). But Goodheart found that, in some CUP volumes, the various contending considerations that have to be adjudicated in the editorial process "do not seem to be properly sorted out and thought through" (231). For example, he complained that Elizabeth Mansfield while editing *The Trespasser* allowed her "choice of final intention" to be enforced by an "aesthetic bias that prefers concise form" (228). Conversely, he argued, the editor of *Aaron's Rod*, Mara Kalnins, failed to make certain needed "aesthetic judgments" and thereby weakened her editorial authority. Similarly, Goodheart faulted L. D. Clark for failing to explain sufficiently the grounds for certain decisions made while editing *The Plumed Serpent*. Clark declared many of his choices to be "clearly authoritative" on the grounds that "the author's later intention obviously supersedes the former"; but Goodheart objected that it is *not* obvious that the later intention should supersede the former. Is the later intention chosen because it is "aesthetically superior" or because it is "the final intention"?

One Cambridge editorial decision guaranteed to draw abounding interest from reviewers was the controversial one that Helen and Carl Baron had to make while editing *Sons and Lovers*. What were they to do? —Should they restore the 2,050 lines (about 10 percent of the *MS*) that Edward Garnett, a reader for the British publisher Duckworth, cut from the novel?—Or should they allow those cuts to stand? Over the years, some prominent scholars had celebrated Garnett's work: Mark Schorer, for instance, said every deletion the "brilliant editor" made "seems to me to have been to the novel's advantage," making it "tighter and more smoothly paced" (9), and Keith Sagar endorsed that opinion in a 1980 article titled "How Edward Garnett made Lawrence's novels fit for public consumption." Sagar himself posited a strong "case against" the possibility that CUP might restore the passages Garnett "very skilfully" cut. (Sagar was then editing *Sons and Lovers* [1981] for the Penguin English Library, and was leaving out the passages Garnett had cut.) Sagar asked: "Are we, as editors, to deny young writers, or any writer, the right to say that they have done what they can, but would welcome informed criticism from a respected friend, and then to accept the suggested cuts? Does not this revision by another hand still constitute part of the author's intention?"

The answer, according the CUP editors, is *no*. When CUP's *Sons and Lovers* appeared in 1992, the cuts had been restored. Helen and Carl Baron decided that Garnett's excisions had simplified Lawrence's depiction of complex family relations; deemphasized his attention to women's rights; censored a few sexual references (e.g., lopping out the description of Clara's breasts as "white, glistening globes" and deleting a scene wherein Paul tries on her stockings); and created a sense of choppiness that damaged the coherence of Lawrence's narrative. Lawrence, the Barons argued, had not *wanted* to accept Garnett's modifications.

The edition carried the stiff price tag of $95, but CUP also made it available as a "popular" hardback (sans scholarly apparatus) that sold for $24.95. Its jacket featured John Singer Sargent's colorful impressionist work, *Paul Helleu Painting and his Wife:* two romantic figures sit in tall grass beside a canoe, with the bearded, Lawrencean-looking male painting a canvas while his female companion leans against him. Emblazoned across the greenish jacket was a red promotional band suggestively declaring this "The unexpurgated text." The hint seemed to be that some sexually titillating passages had been restored, as in the 1959 *Lady Chatterley's Lover*. But reviewers quickly shredded this "unexpurgated" tag—Richard Hoggart in the *New Statesman and Society* growled, "The sexual editing is slight and of not much interest either to the prurient or the student of censorship," and added: "Shame on you, CUP."

As they had with several previous Lawrence volumes, Cambridge supplemented their publication of the novel by arranging for the simultaneous publication of a critical work—written by a CUP Editorial Board member—pointing out the merits of the CUP editorial enterprise. Just as *Sons and Lovers* reached bookstores, CUP published a 110-page critical book by Michael Black, *D. H. Lawrence: Sons and Lovers,* its jacket proclaiming it "the first critical study of *Sons and Lovers* to engage with the new Cambridge edition." Concentrating on the novel's genesis, Black concluded that "by not recognising a structure that was, by the time Lawrence had finished the book, deeply considered, Garnett damaged an actual form without instating an equally considered new one, still less a better one" (38). The CUP edition "supersedes all previous printings," Black declared, and all subsequent critical works must be "indebted" to it (109).

This *Sons and Lovers* predictably received prominent attention in major British periodicals, and was also noticed in an impressive number of provincial British newspapers. In general, the edition was greeted by reviewers on both sides of the Atlantic with favor, if not boundless enthusiasm. Hoggart, for instance, decided that "all in all, the restoration of Lawrence's text is a gain." John Bayley in the *London Review of Books* agreed, though he seemed on the whole innocent of textual issues and thus tentative in saying that CUP and the Barons "probably rightly" decided that Garnett's editing weakened Lawrence's scope and purpose. Bayley acknowledged that "although their restoration does not make the novel feel any weightier or read very differently, it does shift the perspective a little" (13).

Anthony Burgess rejoiced in the *Atlantic Monthly* that at least one editor in the Anglo-American publishing tradition had been put in his place: "The editor, who lacks the creative gift but is compensated with artistic taste, has been overmuch lauded," he complained. "Editors never emend orchestral scores or panoramic paintings; why should the novelist be singled out as the one artist who doesn't understand his art?" Burgess thus exulted that Garnett's "ravagings" had been "canceled out" at last, and hailed CUP's *Sons and Lovers* as "a masterly work of scholarship" (117, 118).

But David Trotter charged in his *TLS* review (11 Sept. 1992) that "the most revealing sentence" in the new *Sons and Lovers* is the copyright notice, and that not enough had been lost through Garnett's cuts "to justify the drastic step of removing the novel from the public domain, where it belongs." The Barons, declared Trotter, offer no solid evidence of Lawrence's wishes regarding the cuts, and wind up having to base editorial choices on "literary criteria." He gave *his* version of the Barons' "weak" case: "Lawrence, the argument goes, felt constrained by traditional notions of literary form; Garnett, the publisher's stooge, upheld these notions; we should prefer the version of the novel which approximates most closely to the writer Lawrence was to become, rather than the writer

Garnett wanted to turn him into." But, Trotter countered: "The problem with this understanding of literary form is that it is unequivocally teleological. It derives from literary-critical assumptions about the development of Modernism, rather than from terms which Lawrence and Garnett might themselves have used and acted upon."

The Barons responded passionately (*TLS*, 18 September 1992) that Trotter "misrepresents us"—"we were concerned to allow to 'come in' the version of the novel which approximates most closely to the writer Lawrence actually *was*," not to the one he "was to become," as Trotter charged. The reviewer's arguments, they said, "do not dissuade us from the view that Lawrence bowed to *commercial* and not artistic necessity." They also protested that they had not made bibliographic decisions based on aesthetic judgments, but had in fact closely attended to "evidence for Lawrence's view" in all matters. They concluded: "We hesitate to take lessons in 'literary criteria' from a reviewer who believes it does not matter how much or what is cut out of a novel as long as 'enough . . . survives for one to get the point.' It's a *novel*. Get the point?"

Cambridge's *Letters and Works* will likely be viewed as one of the major publishing ventures of the last quarter of this century, and will surely be recognized as the most energizing development in Lawrence studies as we head into the next century. For one thing, appendixes of various *Works* are offering readers a treasure of previously unseen Lawrence writings, including fragmentary efforts and full portions of some of his early drafts of works. (And *Mr Noon* included those 196 newly published pages of narrative and *Sons and Lovers* restored that one-tenth of the novel trimmed out by Garnett.)

Also, significantly, Lawrence's works are not only being edited; many of them are in the process of being "*versioned*." As George Bornstein noted in 1991, the strong challenges to traditional views of the "authority" of texts recently have prompted some editorial theorists "to favor concepts of versions or stages over single authoritative texts."[12] He cited, for instance, the critiques that Hans Zeller and Donald Reiman have mounted against the use of "final" authorial intention as a means of establishing an authoritative single-state text. Reiman championed "*versioning*" over "editing" because "it is both more useful and more efficient to provide critics and students with complete texts of two or more different stages of a literary work, each of which can be read as an integral whole, than to chop all but one version into small pieces and then mix and sprinkle these dismembered fragments at the bottoms of pages, or shuffle them at the back of the book as tables of 'variants.'"[13] In other words, Reiman was objecting to just such a "patchwork quilt" as that which Paul Eggert has admitted each CUP *"reading"* text constitutes. Eggert was acknowledging how difficult it is to record a work's successive layers within the scope of a critical edition even *with* the textual apparatus; he wished readers could have "not just the text, but the texts Lawrence wrote" ("Reviewing" 302–3). Such a presentation would seem easy enough for, say, a "text" of a Lawrence poem that had been much-revised. Following Reiman's proposal, the editor would replace the single text of Lawrence's poem with a series of texts. But could this be done with his bulky *novels?*

Remarkably—despite their length and the consequent cost of such an endeavor—his major novels are in fact in the process of being "versioned," of being presented in just such a way as Eggert wished for. For two decades, scholars have had available published versions of the three radically different drafts of Lawrence's *Lady Chatterley's Lover,* and now CUP plans to reissue edited versions of the first two drafts, *The First Lady Chatterley* and *John Thomas and Lady Jane,* in a single volume edited by Dieter Mehl and Christa Jansohn. In addition, Worthen and Vasey are preparing a CUP edition of *The Sisters,* the text of *Women in Love* as it stood at the end of November 1916; and Helen Baron is preparing a CUP edition of *Paul Morel,* an early version of *Sons and Lovers.* Like *The Sisters, Paul Morel* will be published with its own textual apparatus, so that very early stages of composition can also be recorded. Meanwhile, Black Swan Press has published *Quetzalcoatl* (1994), an early draft of *The Plumed Serpent,* edited with an introduction and notes by Louis L. Martz. So readers will soon possess a sizable sampling of what Eggert calls the "textual riches which Lawrence left" ("Reviewing" 302); they will come to know his major novels as both completed textual *object* as well as textual *process.* The result of such "versioning" of his novels (as well as the many stories, essays, and other genres of work being represented in multiple texts in CUP appendixes) will surely make Lawrence's works the most intriguing, accessible laboratory for genetic studies in all of Western literature (with the possible exception of the Cornell Wordsworth).

It is too soon, of course, to predict the likely cumulative impact of the emerging volumes. Lydia Blanchard has assayed a short interim report on how the Edition may affect Lawrence studies. Reviewing *The Rainbow,* she declared that the "philosophy underlying the Cambridge text is close to revolutionary for Lawrence scholarship and criticism" (387). She predicted: "There will be much less criticism that dismisses Lawrence as a didactic writer. The textual apparatus of the Cambridge edition shows a flexible writer, one changing his mind, growing, evolving. There will be much less criticism that takes Lawrence to task for rejecting the intellect. The explanatory notes make clear that Lawrence was a man of learning. . . . Lawrence's place as a Modernist will be reappraised" (389). At the same time, Blanchard ventured that "not everyone will be happy" with the Edition: CUP's editorial choices will result in texts that differ from those Lawrence himself ever saw, and "some textual critics will never be comfortable with that result" (387).

At the Montpellier Conference in 1990, Charles Rossman expressed gratitude to CUP editors for their labors, but added: "Nevertheless, the Cambridge editions should not be accepted on faith. As scholarly efforts predicated on a particular base of information and established according to specific editorial principles, the editions must be regarded as submitted to the body of Lawrence scholars for assessment and judgment" ("Penetrating"). The preceding essays in *Editing D. H. Lawrence: New Versions of a Modern Author* undertake to further that assessment, not only to make the CUP volumes more intelligible to scholars, but also to suggest ways in which textual criticism and editing are advanced by a large project like the Cambridge Lawrence. It remains to be seen, of course, whether "the real D. H. Lawrence" can ever be edited "At last."

NOTES

1. This and all following quotations in my opening paragraph are from Lawrence's preface to Edward D. McDonald's *A Bibliography of D. H. Lawrence.* See *Phoenix: The Posthumous Papers of D. H. Lawrence,* ed. Edward D. McDonald (New York: Penguin, 1980), pp. 232–35.
2. See Mark Kinkead-Weekes, "The Marble and the Statue: The Exploratory Imagination of D. H. Lawrence," in *Imagined Worlds,* ed. Maynard Mack and Ian Gregor (London: Methuen, 1968), pp. 371–418; Charles L. Ross, *The Composition of "The Rainbow" and "Women in Love": A History* (Charlottesville: UP of Virginia, 1979); John Worthen, *D. H. Lawrence and the Idea of the Novel* (Totowa, N.J.: Rowman, 1979); Michael Squires, *The Creation of "Lady Chatterley's Lover"* (Baltimore: Johns Hopkins UP, 1983); and Keith Sagar, *D. H. Lawrence: Life Into Art* (Athens: U of Georgia P, 1985).
3. Mahaffey, "Intentional Error: The Paradox of Editing Joyce's *Ulysses,*" in *Representing Modernist Texts: Editing as Interpretation,* ed. George Bornstein (Ann Arbor: U of Michigan P, 1991), pp. 190, 178.
4. Worthen, "Restoration" 7. See also, e.g., Eggert, "Textual" 61; Squires, "D. H. Lawrence" 13; Black, "At last" 10.

5. Rossman noted that the "real issues" regarding the repossession of copyright of modern authors' works "are at the level of decisions made by publishers and their lawyers—decisions that are antecedent to, crucially enabling for, and perhaps delimiting of, the work of editors." He raised this critical question: how much has "commercialism" enabled the CUP texts and *"determined their nature"*? Specifically he directed that question toward *The Rainbow.* Had its editor selected the *TS* as his copy-text, rather than the *MS,* "he would have lost as many as three-fourths of his total emendations," Rossman wrote. "Would a new text established on such principles be copyrighted? If not, would Cambridge have allowed the choice of *TS* as copy-text?" ("Cambridge *Rainbow*" 186).

6. Paul Eggert noted recently that when CUP negotiated the contract with the Lawrence Estate to publish the Edition, the Press "got what it had to have if the series was to run to completion: unlimited access for its editors to all Lawrence manuscript material and the right to publish without interference, competition, or further negotiation newly established texts of the complete works . . . and all other unpublished material" ("Textual" 75). If it is true that CUP can "publish without . . . competition," then Sutherland's fears may seem justified.

7. Parker, *Editors' Notes* 10.2 (1991): 20–21.

8. According to Eggert, by the mid-1980s CUP editors had changed their policies "in the direction of full textual disclosure," so that their apparatuses would allow fuller access to the developing work, giving all the variant readings within a given state so that readers could construct the sequence of alterations within any one state ("Textual" 73–74).

9. The Ross-Cambridge debate over *Women in Love* continued in *Essays in Criticism* and the *DHLR* beyond what I have outlined here. See Ross, "Rejoinder"; Eggert, "From Paul Eggert"; and Rossman's related "Metacommentary."

10. Parker, *Flawed Texts and Verbal Icons: Literary Authority in American Fiction* (Evanston: Northwestern UP, 1984).

11. Michael Herbert, the editor of CUP's *Reflections,* responded that "The Novel" had been "put with other essays on the novel" in CUP's 1985 edition of *Study of Thomas Hardy and Other Essays* because that had seemed "a logical allocation of texts" (232).

12. Bornstein, "Introduction: Why Editing Matters," in *Representing Modernist Texts: Editing as Interpretation,* ed. George Bornstein (Ann Arbor: U of Michigan P, 1991), p. 6.

13. Quoted in Bornstein's "Introduction," pp. 6–7.

WORKS CITED

[All works not fully documented in my essay and notes are cited in the checklist, "Editing Lawrence: A Selected Bibliography of Works, 1975–93," which follows.]

Editing Lawrence: A Selected Bibliography of Works, 1975–93

Dennis Jackson

The following checklist includes:

- the twenty-eight volumes of *The Cambridge Edition of the Letters and Works of D. H. Lawrence* published through 1993;
- the reviews, essays, and books about the editing of Lawrence's texts that I cite in "'At last, the real Lawrence'?—The Author and the Editors: A Reception History, 1975–93," on pp. 211–38 in this collection;
- other selected reviews and essays (published 1975–93) that devote sustained attention to the topic of editing Lawrence;
- and a few items that represent the vast majority of other reviews of CUP volumes, in the way they focus on Lawrence's art, politics, or biography while offering little to no commentary on the actual editing performance displayed in those volumes.

The checklist is divided into three sections:

I. The Cambridge University Press Edition of the Letters and Works of D. H. Lawrence (volumes published 1979–93)

    A. The Letters

    B. The Works

II. Articles and books on editing Lawrence

III. Reviews of and review-essays on Lawrence editions

Section IA lists separately the seven volumes of Lawrence's *Letters* published by Cambridge through 1993. They are arranged *chronologically* by date of publication.

Section IB likewise lists the twenty-one Lawrence *Works* published by Cambridge through 1993. They are also arranged *chronologically* by date of publication. According to *Books in Print: 1993–94,* several CUP *Works* listed in IB are no longer available.

Entries in sections II and III are arranged *alphabetically by author's last name* or by the title of unsigned items. All reviews are of Cambridge editions of Lawrence unless otherwise noted.

I annotate many entries for reviews and essays, especially when the title does not make clear the subject of a work. The following abbreviations are used in the checklist: "DHL" for D. H. Lawrence; "CUP" for Cambridge University Press; "*DHLR*" for *The D. H. Lawrence Review;* "*TLS*" for *Times Literary Supplement;* "*MS(S)*" for manuscript(s); and "*TS(S)*" for typescript(s).

I. THE CAMBRIDGE UNIVERSITY PRESS EDITION OF THE
LETTERS AND WORKS OF D. H. LAWRENCE (VOLUMES
PUBLISHED 1979–93)

A. The Letters

1979   James T. Boulton, ed. *The Letters of D. H. Lawrence: Volume I: September 1901–May 1913.*

1981   George J. Zytaruk and James T. Boulton, eds. *The Letters of D. H. Lawrence: Volume II: June 1913–October 1916.*

1984   James T. Boulton and Andrew Robertson, eds. *The Letters of D. H. Lawrence: Volume III: October 1916–June 1921.*

1987   Warren Roberts, James T. Boulton, and Elizabeth Mansfield, eds. *The Letters of D. H. Lawrence: Volume IV: June 1921–March 1924.*

1989   James T. Boulton and Lindeth Vasey, eds. *The Letters of D. H. Lawrence: Volume V: March 1924–March 1927.*

1991   James T. Boulton and Margaret H. Boulton, with Gerald M. Lacy, eds. *The Letters of D. H. Lawrence: Volume VI: March 1927–November 1928.*

1993   Keith Sagar and James T. Boulton, eds. *The Letters of D. H. Lawrence: Volume VII: November 1928–February 1930.*

B. The Works

1980   Mara Kalnins, ed. *Apocalypse and the Writings on Revelation.* By D. H. Lawrence.

1981   John Worthen, ed. *The Lost Girl,* By D. H. Lawrence.

1982   Elizabeth Mansfield, ed. *The Trespasser.* By D. H. Lawrence.

1983   Brian Finney, ed. *St. Mawr and Other Stories.* By D. H. Lawrence.

John Worthen, ed. *The Prussian Officer and Other Stories.* By D. H. Lawrence.

Andrew Robertson, ed. *The White Peacock.* By D. H. Lawrence.

1984   Lindeth Vasey, ed. *Mr Noon.* By D. H. Lawrence.

1985   Bruce Steele, ed. *Study of Thomas Hardy and Other Essays.* By D. H. Lawrence.

1987   David Farmer, Lindeth Vasey, and John Worthen, eds. *Women in Love.* By D. H. Lawrence.

John Worthen, ed. *Love Among the Haystacks and Other Stories.* By D. H. Lawrence.

L. D. Clark, ed. *The Plumed Serpent (Quetzalcoatl).* By D. H. Lawrence.

1988   Michael Herbert, ed. *Reflections on the Death of a Porcupine and Other Essays.* By D. H. Lawrence.

Mara Kalnins, ed. *Aaron's Rod.* By D. H. Lawrence.

1989   Mark Kinkead-Weekes, ed. *The Rainbow.* By D. H. Lawrence.

Philip Crumpton, ed. *Movements in European History.* By D. H. Lawrence.

1990   Bruce Steele, ed. *England, My England and Other Stories.* By D. H. Lawrence.

Paul Eggert, ed. *The Boy in the Bush.* By D. H. Lawrence and M. L. Skinner.

1992   Dieter Mehl, ed. *The Fox, The Captain's Doll, The Ladybird.* By D. H. Lawrence.

Helen Baron and Carl Baron, eds. *Sons and Lovers.* By D. H. Lawrence.

Simonetta de Filippis, ed. *Sketches of Etruscan Places.* By D. H. Lawrence.

1993   Michael Squires, ed. *Lady Chatterley's Lover / A Propos of "Lady Chatterley's Lover."* By D. H. Lawrence.

II. ARTICLES AND BOOKS ON EDITING LAWRENCE

Baron, Helen. "Lawrence's *Sons and Lovers* versus Garnett's." *Essays in Criticism* 42 (Oct. 1992): 265–78. [Essay.]

———. "*Sons and Lovers:* The Surviving Manuscripts From Three Drafts Dated by Paper Analysis." *Studies in Bibliography* 38 (1985): 289–328. [Tediously detailed but useful essay showing how, in preparing CUP's *Sons and Lovers,* she relied on DHL's "habits in the use of stationery" to explain "the chronology of composition and interrelations between the surviving portions of drafts in terms of paper-batches."]

Black, Michael. [Announcement ("Laurentiana")]. *DHLR* 8.3 (1975): 375–76. [Letter announcing Cambridge University Press's plans to prepare a "complete edition of the whole canon" of DHL's works.]

————. "At last, the real D. H. Lawrence." *Times Higher Education Supplement* 17 Nov. 1978: 10–11. [Reports on CUP editors' ongoing labors on DHL's *Works,* the first volume of which was still two years away from publication.]

————. "D. H. Lawrence and Gilbert Noon." *London Review of Books* 4–17 Oct. 1984: 10, 12. [Essay meant to "usefully supplement" Lindeth Vasey's "expert introduction to the text" of *Mr Noon.*]

————. *D. H. Lawrence: Sons and Lovers.* Cambridge: Cambridge UP, 1992. [First critical study of the CUP version of the novel, showing how Garnett's editing supposedly "damaged" DHL's original structure.]

————. "Editing a Constantly-Revising Author: the Cambridge Edition of Lawrence in Historical Context." In *D. H. Lawrence: Centenary Essays.* Ed. Mara Kalnins. Bristol, Eng.: Bristol Classical P, 1986. 191–210. [Explains CUP's editorial principles and practices.]

————. "The Works of D. H. Lawrence: The Cambridge Edition." In Partlow and Moore 49–57. [Discusses "corruption" extant in DHL's "very unsatisfactory texts" before CUP Edition was undertaken.]

Boulton, James T. "The Cambridge University Press Edition of D. H. Lawrence's Letters, Part 4." In Partlow and Moore 223–28.

————. "D. H. Lawrence: His Challenge to Our Scholarship." In *D. H. Lawrence: The Centre and the Circles.* Ed. Peter Preston. Nottingham, Eng.: D. H. Lawrence Centre, 1992. 43–55. [Another apologia for CUP scholarship, "(i)n view of . . . the censorious attitude of some reviewers to the alleged solemnity with which Cambridge editors treat every Lawrentian dot and comma. . . ." Boulton concludes: those who devote themselves to the task of "bringing Lawrence's writings to birth and in keeping them alive . . . accept the responsibility for establishing accurate and unbowdlerised texts; for making the meaning and the implications of those texts accessible; and thus for sustaining a creative collaboration with the author to bring his writings into imaginative existence."]

————. "Letters that reveal a life: James Boulton tells of the difficulties encountered editing the Cambridge edition of letters by D. H. Lawrence." *Times Higher Education Supplement* 10 Nov. 1978: 10.

The Cambridge Edition of the Works and Letters of D. H. Lawrence: Prospectus and Notes for Volume Editors. Cambridge: Cambridge UP, 1978 [November 1977].

Cunningham, John. "'There have been times when she has thrown *Apocalypse* at the wall'—John Cunningham meets the Texas researcher who pieced together 80 pages of missing fragments from Lawrence's thesis." *The Guardian* 25 Oct. 1978: 10. [Article about Mara Kalnins's work editing CUP's *Apocalypse.*]

Eggert, Paul. "Document or Process as the Site of Authority: Establishing Chronology of Revision in Competing Typescripts of Lawrence's *The Boy in the Bush.*" *Studies in Bibliography* 44 (1991): 364–76. [Explains methods he used to sort out DHL's mixed-up *TSS,* to distinguish L's "correction copy" from his "transcription copy."]

————. "Ideological Innocence: Editing in Australia." *Meridian* 5 (1986): 175–81. [Refers to his editing of CUP's *The Boy in the Bush.*]

————. "Opening up the text: The case of *Sons and Lovers.*" In *Rethinking Lawrence.* Ed. Keith Brown. Milton Keynes, Eng.: Open UP, 1990. 38–51. [Refers also to CUP's *The Boy in the Bush,* which he edited. Argues that editing can be a means of resuscitating the concept of the "author" by insisting on the "personal agency and chronological dimension involved in the genesis of a text . . . and by designing editions to illustrate them."]

————. "Textual Product or Textual Process: Procedures and Assumptions of Critical Editing." In *Devils and Angels: Textual Editing and Literary Theory*. Ed. Philip Cohen. Charlottesville: UP of Virginia, 1991. 56–77. [Pp. 69–75 characterize editorial principles of CUP's Lawrence Edition. Eggert acknowledges the limitations of such modern eclectic editions—mainly, that their final product "is a synchronic representation of a textual process that was in fact diachronic" (in some cases spanning decades of writing and revision). But he argues that if their textual apparatus properly documents the "process" of composition and revision, such editions can serve critics' and readers' needs.]

Farmer, David. "The Cambridge University Press Edition of *The Letters of D. H. Lawrence*." In Partlow and Moore 239–41.

————. "*Women in Love*: A Textual History and Premise for a Critical Edition." In *Editing British and American Literature, 1880–1920. Papers Given at the Tenth Annual Conference on Editorial Problems, University of Toronto, November 1974*. Ed. Eric W. Domville. New York: Garland, 1976. 77–92.

"General Editors' Preface." *The Works of D. H. Lawrence*. General Editors James T. Boulton and Warren Roberts. Cambridge: Cambridge UP. [Two pages (usually vii–viii) published at the beginning of each CUP volume.]

Goodheart, Eugene. "Censorship and Self-Censorship in the Fiction of D. H. Lawrence." In *Representing Modernist Texts: Editing as Interpretation*. Ed. George Bornstein. Ann Arbor: U of Michigan P, 1991. 223–39. [Appraises editorial work done on the first seven Lawrence novels issued by CUP.]

Hebert, Hugh. "The unkindest cuts." *The Guardian* 19 Sept. 1978: 8. [Story announcing "the coming definitive Cambridge edition."]

Holroyd, Michael, and Sandra Jobson. "Copyrights and wrongs: D. H. Lawrence." *TLS* 3 Sept. 1982: 943–44.

Kernan, Alvin. *The Death of Literature*. New Haven: Yale UP, 1990. [Focuses on copyright and related editing issues in regard to CUP's Edition of DHL's *Works*. See pp. 98–106.]

Lacy, Gerald M. "The Case for an Edition of the Letters of D. H. Lawrence." In Partlow and Moore 229–33.

Littlewood, J. C. F. "Lawrence and the Scholars." *Essays in Criticism* 33.3 (July 1983): 175–86. [Claims harm is being done to DHL's vital writings by having them cast into scholarly editions, as in *Volume I–II* of CUP's *Letters*.]

Moore, Harry T. [Letter ("Laurentiana")]. *DHLR* 6.2 (1973): 231–32. [Urges scholars "to establish Lawrence editions" that are not "corrupt."]

Partlow, Robert B., Jr., and Harry T. Moore, eds. *D. H. Lawrence: The Man Who Lived*. Carbondale and Edwardsville: Southern Illinois UP, 1980. ["Papers Delivered at the D. H. Lawrence Conference at Southern Illinois University, Carbondale, April 1979." Includes seven essays, all cited elsewhere here, which deal directly with CUP's *Letters and Works*.]

Pollinger, Gerald. "The Lawrence Estate." In Partlow and Moore 13–23. [In relation to the "exciting forthcoming" CUP Edition, the Literary Executor of the estate of Frieda Lawrence Ravagli presents here "the texts of some of the most important legal documents affecting the Lawrence estate," including DHL's and his wife Frieda's wills and death certificates.]

Roberts, Warren. "Problems in Editing D. H. Lawrence." In Partlow and Moore 58–61. [Discusses problems that face an editor of *Kangaroo* and briefly treats "the more extensive textual difficulties" associated with DHL's poetry.]

Ross, Charles L. *The Composition of "The Rainbow" and "Women in Love": A History.* Charlottesville: UP of Virginia, 1979. [Reconstructs the history of the writing of these two novels, together with illustrations from the *MSS* and critical discussion of the interpretive acts to which a textual history may be put.]

———. "Ethics of Editing." Paper delivered during a session on "Editing Lawrence" at the D. H. Lawrence Conference. Université Paul Valéry, Montpellier, France, June 1990. [Unpublished. 10 pages.]

———. "Introduction" to *Women in Love*. By D. H. Lawrence. Ed. Charles L. Ross. Harmondsworth, Eng.: Penguin Books (Penguin English Library), 1982. 13–48. [Gives history of novel's composition and publication. Pp. 45–48 offer a "Note on the Text."]

Rossman, Charles. "Penetrating the Monumentality of the Cambridge Editions." Paper delivered during a session on "Editing Lawrence" at the "D. H. Lawrence Conference." Université Paul Valéry, Montpellier, France, June 1990. [Unpublished. 8 pages.]

Sagar, Keith. "How Edward Garnett made Lawrence's novels fit for public consumption." *Times Higher Education Supplement* 1 Nov. 1980: 10. [Sagar posits a "case against" CUP editors restoring the cuts Garnett made in *Sons and Lovers*. See also Sagar's argument in his Introduction to *Sons and Lovers*, ed. Keith Sagar (Harmondsworth, Eng.: Penguin, 1981), pp. 24–25; in "The Cambridge Lawrence," *TLS* 8 Oct. 1982, p. 1102; and in *D. H. Lawrence: Life Into Art* (Athens: U of Georgia P, 1985), pp. 94–95.]

Schorer, Mark. Introduction to *Sons and Lovers: A Facsimile of the Manuscript.* Ed. Mark Schorer. Berkeley: U of California P, 1977. 1–9. [Describes the history of the *MS* and hails Garnett's editing.]

Sexton, Mark S. "Lawrence, Garnett, and *Sons and Lovers:* An Exploration of Author-Editor Relationship." *Studies in Bibliography* 43 (1990): 208–22. [Illustrates the "editorial dynamics" between Garnett and DHL.]

Squires, Michael. "D. H. Lawrence—Which Text Did He Prefer?" *Research Virginia Tech* (Winter 1988–89): 13. [Remarks on his editing CUP's *Lady Chatterley's Lover.*]

———. "Editing *Lady Chatterley's Lover*." In Partlow and Moore 62–70.

Templeton, Wayne. "The *Sons and Lovers* Manuscript." *Studies in Bibliography* 37 (1984): 234–43. [Declares that Garnett's skillful deletions "rather than Lawrence's emendations are what turned a pedestrian and at times problematical manuscript into a powerful, concise, and evenly developed novel."]

Vasey, Lindeth, and John Worthen. "*Mr Noon*/Mr Noon." In *Mr Noon*. Special Issue of *DHLR* 20.2 (1988): 179–90. [Supplements, corrects, and amplifies Vasey's original "Explanatory notes" to CUP's *Mr Noon*.]

Worthen, John. "D. H. Lawrence: problems with multiple texts." In *The Theory and Practice of Text-Editing: Essays in Honour of James T. Boulton.* Ed. Ian

Small and Marcus Walsh. Cambridge: Cambridge UP, 1991. 14–34. [Uses examples from *Women in Love* and *Sons and Lovers* to illustrate the difficulty of choosing between textual variants of seemingly equal authority.]

————. "The Restoration of *Women in Love*." In *D. H. Lawrence in the Modern World*. Ed. Peter Preston and Peter Hoare. Houndmills, Basingstoke, Hampshire, Eng.: Macmillan P, 1989. 7–26. [CUP editors chose to minimize consideration of the novel as social production in order to "restore, like the colours in a restored painting," all evidences that DHL was "a deliberate manipulator of the texture of language."]

Zytaruk, George J. "Editing Lawrence's Letters: The Strategy of Volume Division." In Partlow and Moore 234–38.

III. REVIEWS OF AND REVIEW-ESSAYS ON LAWRENCE EDITIONS
[*All reviews listed are of Cambridge editions of Lawrence unless otherwise noted.*]

Baron, Carl, and Helen Baron. "Sons and Lovers." *TLS* 18 Sept. 1992: 15. [Rebuts review of their CUP edition of *Sons and Lovers* in previous week's *TLS*. See entry for Trotter, below.]

Bayley, John. "Like Ink and Milk." *London Review of Books* 10 Sept. 1992. 12–13. [Reviews, with fleeting reference to editorial issues, CUP's *Sons and Lovers*.]

Blanchard, Lydia. [Review-essay on *Mr Noon*]. *DHLR* 17.2 (1984): 153–59.

————. [Review of *The Plumed Serpent*]. *ELT* 32.4 (1989): 518–20. [Scrutinizes the "high quality" work of CUP editor L. D. Clark, but proposes a "few changes" in the critical apparatus.]

————. [Review of *The Rainbow*]. *ELT* 33.3 (1990): 387–91. [Proposes that Mark Kinkead-Weekes's editorial choices are "defended well in the textual apparatus" of *The Rainbow*.]

Bradshaw, David. "The Nice and the Nauseous." *TLS* 17 Nov. 1989: 1260. [Reviews *Letters V*, devoting one sentence to "editorial" standards.]

Burgess, Anthony. "Lawrence Whole." *Atlantic Monthly* October 1992: 116–18. [Reviews CUP's *Sons and Lovers*.]

Carroll, David. [Review of *Aaron's Rod, The Plumed Serpent*, and *Reflections on the Death of a Porcupine and Other Essays*]. *Modern Language Review* 85 (1990): 164–66. [Approves CUP's concept of audience.]

Clark, L. D. [Review of *Aaron's Rod*]. *ELT* 33.2 (1990): 246–49.

Cooper, Annabel. "Lawrence's *Women in Love*." *Meridian* 7.2 (1988): 179–84.

"Copyrighting the Classics." *The Economist* 10 April 1982: 31.

Cowan, James C. [Review of *The Plumed Serpent*]. *DHLR* 21.3 (1989): 340–41.

Cunningham, Valentine. "Enduring to the End: Pain and Bile, Energy and Natural Beauty in Lawrence's Last Letters." *TLS* 23 July 1993: 4–5. [Reviews *Letters: Volume VII*. Offers "[a]ll praise" to CUP for the "stupendously well edited volumes" of DHL's *Letters*.]

Cushman, Keith. [Review of *Mr Noon*]. *Publications of Bibliographical Society of*

America 80 (1986): 265–68. [Congratulates editor Lindeth Vasey for having been "so significantly present at the creation of this new Lawrence novel."]

Davis, Tom. "Textual Criticism: Philosophy and Practice." *The Library* 6 (1984): 386–97. [Reviews CUP editions of *Apocalypse*, *The Trespasser*, *The Lost Girl*, *The Prussian Officer . . . , The White Peacock*, *St. Mawr . . . .*]

Delany, Paul. "Keeping up the fight." *London Review of Books* 13.2 (1991): 22–23. [One of the six books reviewed is CUP's *England, My England and Other Stories*. Delany quarrels with CUP's claim for a new "copyright" of DHL, and suggests that "In our present age of intertextuality there is more interest in opening out connections from Lawrence's texts than in locking them up in an authorised version."]

———. "Letters of the Artist as a Young Man." *New York Times Book Review* 9 Sept. 1979: 3, 44–45. [Appraises editing work done in *Letters I*.]

Draper, R. P. [Review of *Letters II* and *The Trespasser*]. *Times Higher Education Supplement* 6 April 1982: 18.

———. [Review of *Women in Love*]. *DHLR* 20.3 (1988): 337–39.

Eggert, Paul. "From Paul Eggert (Laurentiana)." *DHLR* 22.1 (1990): 125–26.

———. "The Reviewing of the Cambridge Edition of *Women in Love*." *DHLR* 20.3 (1988): 297–303.

Faulkner, Thomas C. [Review-essay on *The Boy in the Bush*]. *DHLR* 23.2–3 (1991): 205–9. [Paul Eggert, the editor of CUP's *The Boy in the Bush*, responded to this review in "Laurentiana," *DHLR* 24.3 (1992): 297–98.]

Fenton, James. "Bing, Bang, Bump Factions." *The Times* (London) 13 Sept. 1984: 13. [On CUP's *Mr Noon*.]

Gomme, Andor. [Review of *Letters I*]. *English* (Autumn 1980): 261–66.

Gross, John. "The Wars of D. H. Lawrence." *New York Review of Books* 27 Sept. 1979: 17–22. [Refers briefly to editing of *Letters I*.]

Hawtree, Christopher. "The Crawling Snail." *Spectator* 15 Sept. 1984: 30–31. [Reviews *Mr Noon*, with minor attention to editing matters.]

Henzy, Karl. [Review-essay on *Letters VII*]. *DHLR* 24.3 (1992): 271–75. [Intensively scrutinizes CUP practices/strategies in editing L's *Letters*.]

Herbert, Michael. "Correspondence from Michael Herbert (Laurentiana)." *DHLR* 21.2 (1989): 232–34. [Responds to a review of his CUP edition of *Reflections on the Death of a Porcupine and Other Essays* (see entry for Widmer, below).]

Hewitt, Karen McLeod. [Review of *Apocalypse and the Writings on Revelation*]. *Review of English Studies* 34 (1983): 360–62. [Raises interesting "questions about what makes *sense* in a complete edition of Lawrence." After noting the presence in the volume of three *MS* fragments "uncancelled by Lawrence when he made his fresh starts" at rewriting, Hewitt asks: "But what *status* do they have? . . . Are all uncancelled fragments to be included (as here) or is this to be left to the discretion of each editor?" She complains about the nature of editor Mara Kalnins's annotations; questions the volume's copyright claim; and notes that CUP's "declared intention to produce texts that [DHL] 'would have wished to see published' must be always open to interpretation."]

———. [Review of *The Trespasser* and *Letters II*.] *Review of English Studies* 35 (1984): 581–83. [Briefly ponders textual issues.]

Hoggart, Richard. "Kindest Cuts." *New Statesman and Society* 4 Sept. 1992: 40. [Attends briefly to the matter of Garnett's cuts and the Barons' editing of *Sons and Lovers.*]

Hough, Graham. "Shapes of things to come." *TLS* 20 Feb. 1981: 192. [Reviews *Apocalypse* . . . and comments on the editing work.]

Hynes, Samuel. "Corresponding Selves." *Sewanee Review* 89 (1981): 125–33. [Compares DHL's *Letters I,* and *The Letters of Virginia Woolf,* praising the CUP edition as "a model of the editor's craft."]

Jackson, Dennis, and Lydia Blanchard. "*Mr Noon*'s Critical Reception, 1984–1988." In *Mr Noon.* Special Issue of *DHLR* 20.2 (1988): 133–52. [Bibliographical essay on the reviews that greeted CUP's *Mr Noon.* This collection also contains essays on *Mr Noon* by Michael Black, Lindeth Vasey and John Worthen, Philip Sicker, Maria Aline Ferreira, Lydia Blanchard, Peter Balbert, and Paul Delany.]

Kenner, Hugh. "Restoring the Steamy Bits, and More." *New York Times Book Review* 29 Nov. 1992: 9–10. [Protests the claim that CUP's *Sons and Lovers* edition is "unexpurgated." Says Cambridge's sales department seems "unsure how expurgating differs from editing." Concludes that CUP's restoration of the cuts made by Garnett alters "small balances," and "in a novel that's all about balances," that is important.]

Kramer, Dale. [Review of *The Fox, The Captain's Doll, The Ladybird*]. *ELT* 36.3 (1993): 387–91. [Praises CUP's effort—in an era when "powerful schools of editing theory have dipped into the wispy provocativeness of current theoretical questioning of the legitimacy of the author's prerogative"—to provide texts that (the Press says) are "as close as can now be determined" to those DHL "would have wished to see printed." But Kramer finds "particularly lamentable" the fact that the CUP Edition prints—in notes, not in the textual apparatus—"only selected readings from the passages within the manuscript that Lawrence had penned and then revised, or rejected in favor of another passage altogether."]

———. [Review of *Movements in European History*]. *DHLR* 22.3 (1990): 326–28. [Analyzes CUP editorial practices.]

Kuczkowski, Richard. "Lawrence enters the Pantheon." *Review* 4 (1982): 159–70. [Reviews *Apocalypse* . . . , with passing references to the editing work.]

Lane, Jeremy. [Review of *The Lost Girl*]. *Modern Language Review* 80 (1985): 706–8.

Lucas, John. "Off on the preach again." *TLS* 17 Sept. 1982: 995–96. [Praises the "exemplary" presentation of the text of *Letters I* and *II* but complains about the "painfully, even ridiculously, fussy" footnotes.]

Mehl, Dieter. "Editing a 'constantly-revising author.'" *Archiv für das Studium der neueren Sprachen und Literaturen* 222 (1985): 128–36. [Discusses editing principles/practices in the CUP editions of *The White Peacock, The Prussian Officer* . . . , and *Mr Noon.* (In English).]

Moore, Harry T. [Review of *Apocalypse and the Writings on Revelation*]. *Modern Language Review* 77 (1982): 433–34.

Newman, Judie. [Review of Penguin English Library edition of *Women in Love*]. *Durham University Journal* 45 (1984): 308. [One of the few reviews written about the Penguin English Library editions of DHL's novels published in the early 1980s. Newman says Charles Ross's 1982 *Women in Love* edition "straddle[s] . . . two types of reader rather awkwardly": "the reader who needs an explanatory note on Sodom or Cain is unlikely to benefit equally" from Ross's scholarly introduction. Otherwise, says Newman, this is an "excellent edition" by a "well qualified" editor.]

Niven, Alastair. [Review of *Apocalypse and the Writings on Revelation*]. *British Book News* March 1981: 185. [Enthusiastically greets the CUP Edition.]

Parker, Hershel. [Review of *Aaron's Rod*]. *DHLR* 20.3 (1988): 339–41.

Parker, Peter. [Review of *Mr Noon*]. *London Magazine* n.s. 24 (Oct. 1984): 107–10. ["It is an indictment of the whole scholarship industry that the editor of *Mr Noon*, juggling six texts, can produce pages of critical apparatus and a substantial Introduction, whilst entirely dodging the issue of whether the book under consideration is any good as a piece of literature."]

Pollnitz, Christopher. [Review of *The Boy in the Bush*]. *Review of English Studies* 44 (1993): 281–83. [Praises Eggert's negotiation of *The Boy*'s complex textual history. Pollnitz notes an interesting "editorial crux" that involved the omission of certain revisions on the grounds that (in Eggert's words) "they were made . . . under moral pressure" (when Mollie Skinner, shocked by what DHL had done with her narrative, requested that he make changes). Pollnitz concludes: "I do not dispute Eggert's judgment. . . . The revisions introduce inconsistencies in characterization: they could be challenged as tinkerings that have not reentered the original conception of *The Boy*. But the apparently Alexandrian solution of authorial last intentions has come on a strange Gordian knot here, in separating the 'moral' Lawrence who revised the proofs from the man who created them. . . . Strange editorial procedures might arise indeed, if textual possibilities offered by removing from *Sons and Lovers* all those passages influenced by the 'moral pressure' that Jessie Chambers and Frieda Weekley exerted on Lawrence during that novel's composition."]

Preston, Peter. [Review of *Letters I, Mr Noon*, and *Study of Thomas Hardy and Other Essays*]. *Notes and Queries* Sept. 1987: 423–26. [Typical review of the CUP Edition: after three pages of critical scrutiny of DHL's biography or artistry as revealed in these books, the reviewer tacks on one paragraph about editing issues. He notes only two minor "slips" in three volumes "edited to a high standard."]

———. [Review of *Women in Love*]. *Notes and Queries* June 1989: 262–63. [Focuses briefly on the "marvellously sane," "utterly convincing," "right," "clearsighted," and "intelligently annotated" work by CUP editors.]

Ross, Charles L. "The Cambridge Lawrence." *Essays in Criticism* 38.4 (1988): 342–51. [This review-essay on CUP's *Women in Love* launched the first sustained open debate among scholars regarding the major textual editing issues involved in the CUP Lawrence project. See reply by John Worthen and Lindeth Vasey, "Rejoinder: The Cambridge *Women in Love*," *Essays in Criticism* 39.2 (1989): 176–84; see also Ross's response in "Rejoinder: The Cambridge *Women in Love* Again," *Essays in Criticism* 40.1 (1990): 95–97. In addition, see the following related exchange of views in the *DHLR*: Paul Eggert, "The Reviewing of the Cambridge Edition of *Women in Love*," 20.3 (1988): 297–303; Charles L. Ross, "Editorial Principles in the Penguin and Cambridge Editions of *Women in Love*: A Reply to Paul Eggert," 21.2 (1989): 223–26; Charles Rossman, "A Metacommentary on the Rhetoric of Reviewing the Reviewers: Paul Eggert on the New Editions of *Ulysses* and *Women in Love*," 21.2 (1989): 219–22; and "From Paul Eggert (Laurentiana)," 22.1 (1990): 125–26.]

———. "Civilization and Its Discontents in the Editing of Lawrence." *Documentary Editing* June 1990: 40–44. [Review-essay on CUP's *The Rainbow*].

———. "Editorial Principles in the Penguin and Cambridge Editions of *Women in Love:* A Reply to Paul Eggert." *DHLR* 21.2 (1989): 223–26.

———. "Rejoinder: The Cambridge *Women in Love* Again." *Essays in Criticism* 40.1 (1990): 95–97.

Rossman, Charles. "The Cambridge *Rainbow*." *DHLR* 21.2 (1989): 179–86.

———. "A Metacommentary on the Rhetoric of Reviewing the Reviewers: Paul Eggert on the New Editions of *Ulysses* and *Women in Love*." *DHLR* 21.2 (1989): 219–22.

Schwarz, Daniel R. [Review of *Apocalypse and the Writings on Revelation*]. *Modern Fiction Studies* 27.4 (Winter 1981–82): 682–85. [Focuses briefly on editing methods.]

Thornton, Weldon. [Review-essay on *England, My England and Other Stories*]. *DHLR* 22.3 (1990): 321–25.

Trotter, David. "Pedgilling away." *TLS* 11 Sept. 1992: 20. [Sharp-tongued review of CUP's *Sons and Lovers*.]

Walker, Ronald G. "Lawrence's *Women in Love*." *ELT* 32.2 (1989): 256–59.

Widmer, Kingsley. [Review of *Reflections on the Death of a Porcupine and Other Essays*]. *DHLR* 20.3 (1988): 342–43.

Worthen, John, and Lindeth Vasey. "Rejoinder: The Cambridge *Women in Love*." *Essays in Criticism* 39.2 (1989): 176–84.

Contributors

Helen Baron is the coeditor, with Carl Baron, of Cambridge University Press's edition of *Sons and Lovers*. Her edition of Lawrence's second draft of the novel, titled *Paul Morel*, is to be published by CUP.

Michael Black is a Fellow of Clare Hall Cambridge and until 1987 was University Publisher at Cambridge University Press. He is the author of *The Literature of Fidelity*; *Poetic Drama as Mirror of the Will*; *D. H. Lawrence: The Early Fiction*; *D. H. Lawrence: The Early Philosophical Works*; and *D. H. Lawrence: Sons and Lovers*.

William E. Cain, Professor of English at Wellesley College, is the author of *The Crisis in Criticism* and *F. O. Matthiessen and the Politics of Criticism*.

L. D. Clark is the editor of CUP's *The Plumed Serpent*. His books include *The Minoan Distance: The Symbolism of Travel in D. H. Lawrence*; *Dark Night of the Body: D. H. Lawrence's "The Plumed Serpent"*; four novels; and a collection of stories. He is Professor Emeritus of English at the University of Arizona.

Paul Delany is the author of *D. H. Lawrence's Nightmare: The Writer and his Circle in the Years of the Great War* and *Neo-Pagans: Rupert Brooke and the Ordeal of Love*, and the coeditor of *Hypermedia and Literary Studies* and *The Digital Word: Text-Based Computing in the Humanities*. He teaches at Simon Fraser University.

Paul Eggert is the editor of CUP's *The Boy in the Bush* and of their forthcoming edition of *Twilight in Italy*. He edited *Editing in Australia* and serves on the Editorial Committee of the Colonial Texts Series of nineteenth-century Australian fiction being published by New South

251

Wales University Press. He is a Senior Lecturer at the University College, Air Force Defence Academy in Canberra, Australia.

Dennis Jackson edited *The D. H. Lawrence Review* from 1984 to 1994 and coedited *D. H. Lawrence's "Lady"*; *Critical Essays on D. H. Lawrence*; and *D. H. Lawrence's Literary Inheritors*. He is Professor of English at the University of Delaware.

Christopher Pollnitz is collaborating with Carole Ferrier on the CUP variorum edition of Lawrence's *Poems*. He is a Lecturer in English at the University of Newcastle, Australia.

Charles L. Ross is the author of *The Composition of "The Rainbow" and "Women in Love"* and of *"Women in Love": A Novel of Mythic Realism*, and has edited a critical edition of *Women in Love* for the Penguin English Library series in 1982. He teaches English at the University of Hartford.

Michael Squires is the editor of CUP's *Lady Chatterley's Lover*, and his books include *The Pastoral Novel: Studies in George Eliot, Thomas Hardy, and D. H. Lawrence* and *The Creation of "Lady Chatterley's Lover."* He edited *D. H. Lawrence's Manuscripts* and coedited *D. H. Lawrence's "Lady"* and *The Imagination of D. H. Lawrence*. He is Chair of English at Virginia Polytechnic Institute and State University.

John Worthen is Professor of D. H. Lawrence Studies at the University of Nottingham. His books include *D. H. Lawrence: The Early Years, 1885– 1912; D. H. Lawrence and the Idea of the Novel*; and *D. H. Lawrence: A Literary Life*. Worthen's editions of Lawrence's works include *The Rainbow* for Viking/Penguin, and *The Lost Girl, The Prussian Officer and Other Stories, Women in Love* (with David Farmer and Lindeth Vasey), and *Love Among the Haystacks and Other Stories* for Cambridge. He is general editor for the new Penguin paperback series of Lawrence's *Works* based on the CUP texts.

Index